The Enchanted CHRISTMAS Activity Book

ARCTURUS

ARCTURUS

This edition published in 2024 by Arcturus Publishing Limited
26/27 Bickels Yard, 151–153 Bermondsey Street,
London SE1 3HA

Author: Ivy Finnegan
Cover Illustration: Kathryn Selbert
Interior Illustrations: Dan Crisp, Kate Daubney, Lizzy Doyle, Camilla Garofano,
Megan Higgins, Sam Loman, Jo Moon, Ed Myer, Andy Passchier, Angelika
Scudamore, Kathryn Selbert, and Claire Stamper
Editor: Nate Rae
Designers: Sarah Fountain and Lucy Doncaster

ISBN: 978-1-3988-4373-8
CH011479NT
Supplier 29, Date 0524, PI 00006466

Printed in China

Santa's Reindeer

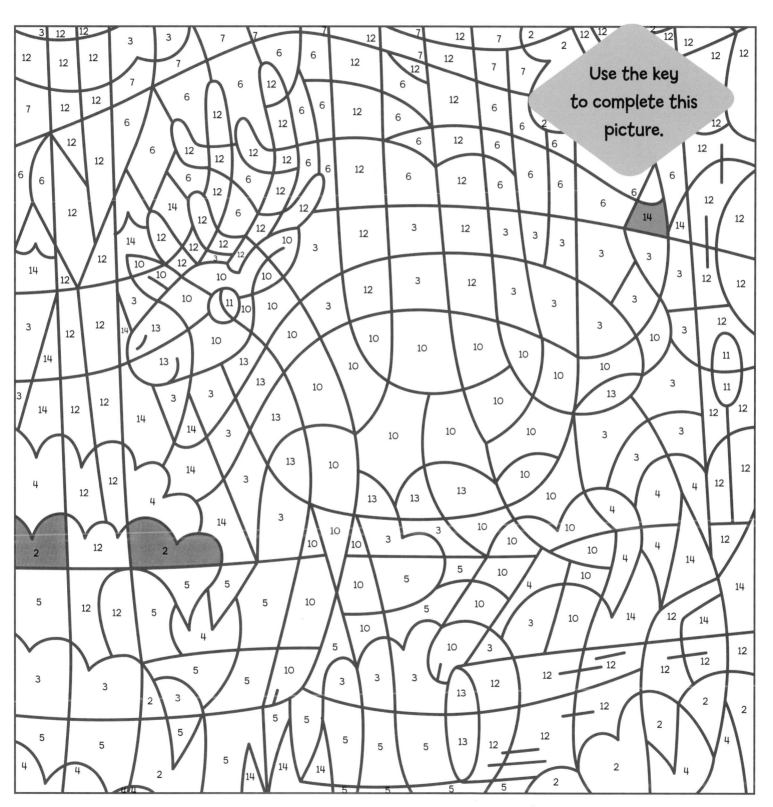

Use the key to complete this picture.

3

Winter Wonderland

Christmas is coming! Join the dots to complete this North Pole picture.

Dasher is Santa's chief reindeer.

Papa Elf looks after all the children's Christmas lists.

Penguin Puzzle

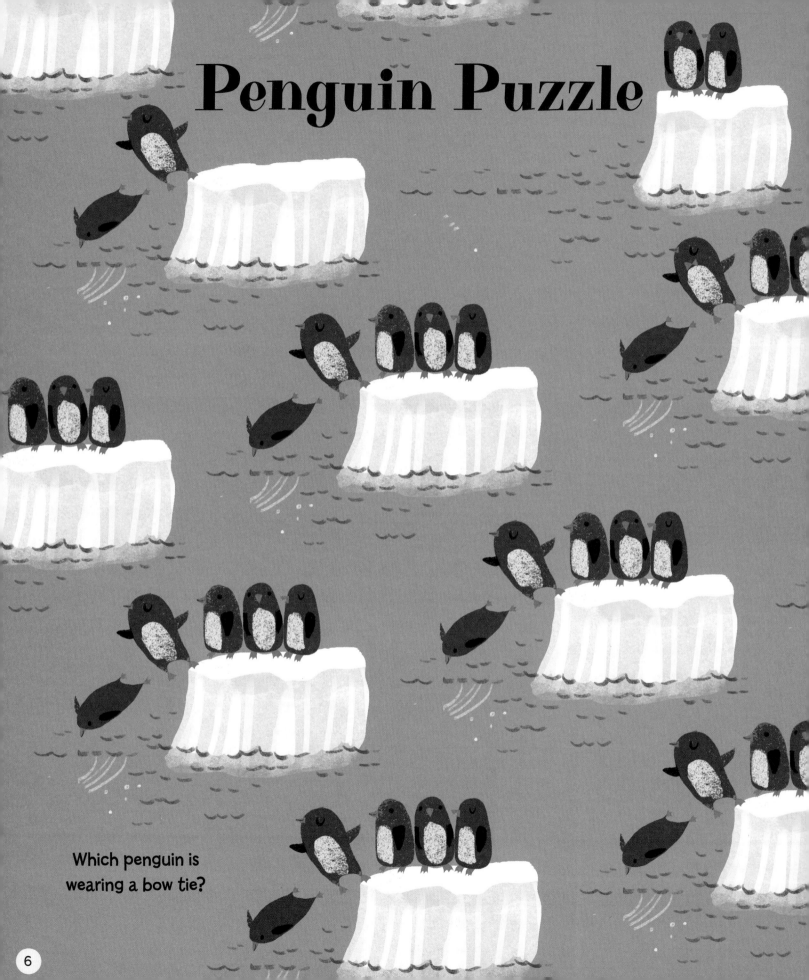

Which penguin is wearing a bow tie?

Odd Deer Out

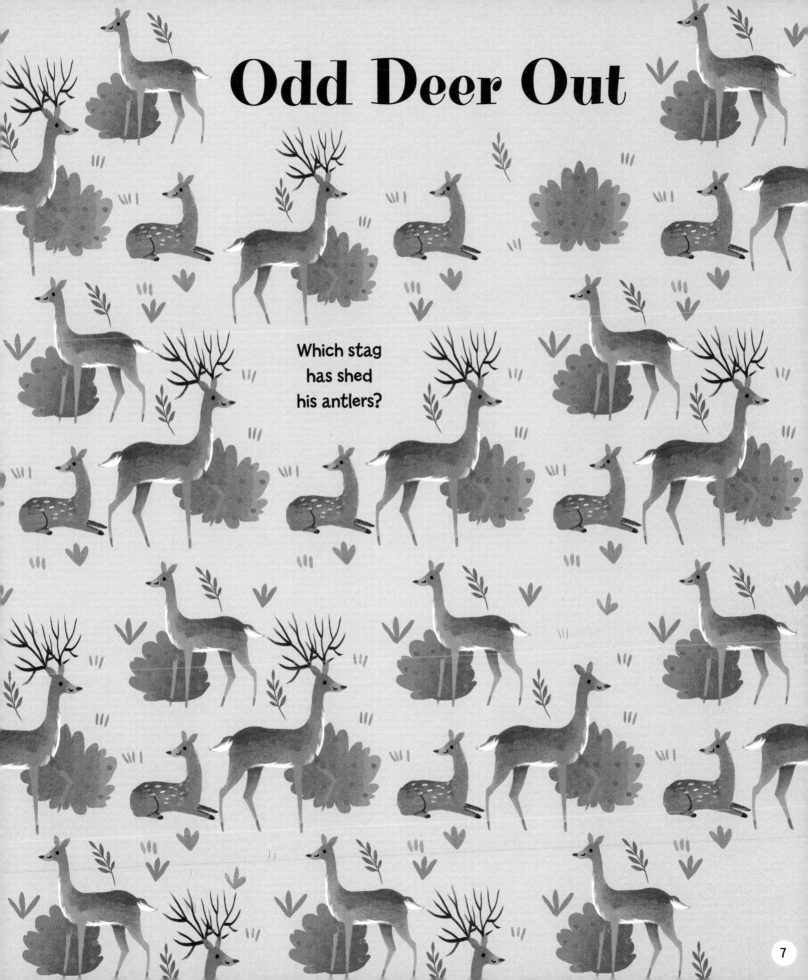

Which stag has shed his antlers?

Snow Cat

Use brown, black, and white paints to create this spotted lynx.

You will need:
Paints
Your hand
Cotton swabs
Your fingertips
Pen

1

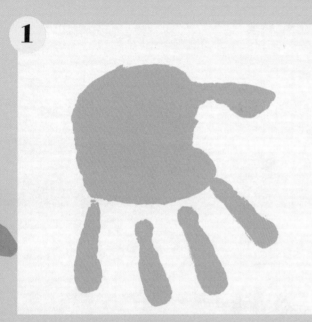

Make a handprint.

2

Use a cotton swab dipped in black paint to add the spots.

3

4

Use smudged fingerprints for the ears, nose, and tail, then finish with pen.

These cubs are waiting for their parent to turn up. Add a big lynx to this snowy scene.

Winter Maze

Can you guide the boy through this maze to the ski lift? Trace a line from each problem to its solution.

33

100

10×4

Start

40

10

10×10

10×9

50

19

90

75

10×5

Top Tip!
Multiples of ten end in 0.

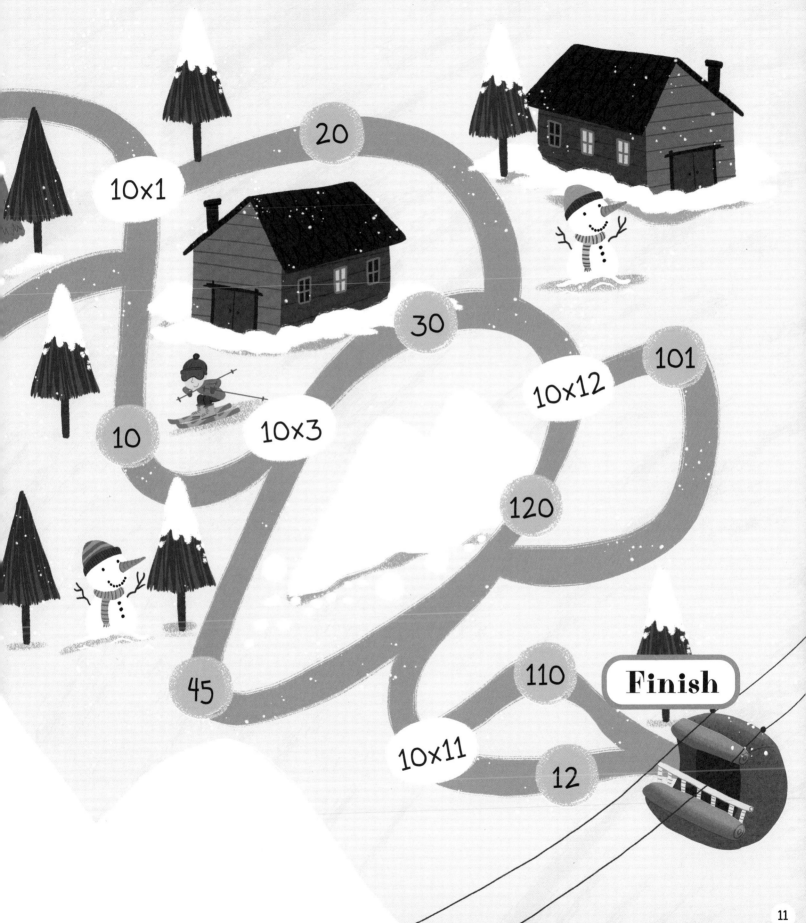

20

10x1

101

10x12

30

10

10x3

120

45

110

Finish

10x11

12

11

Sparkling Elf

Jingle the elf is looking a bit plain. Add some Christmas magic to this picture!

1

Draw Me

Follow the steps to create the frostiest of snowmen.

2

3

4

Origami Polar Bear

Follow these steps to create your very own origami polar bear.

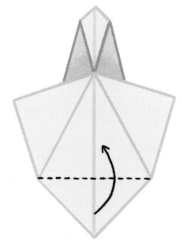

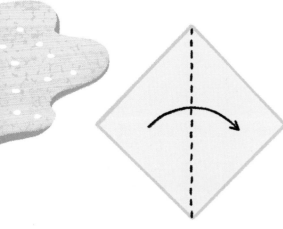

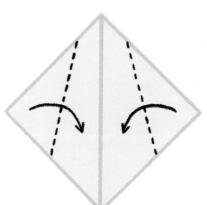

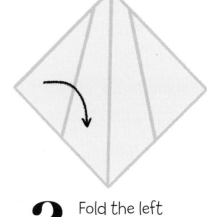

1 Take a sheet of origami paper and place it white side up, with a corner facing you. Fold it in half from left to right, then unfold.

2 Fold both sides in to the central crease, then unfold.

3 Fold the left side back in.

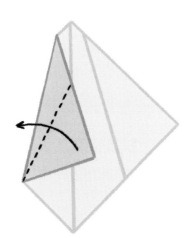

4 Make a small fold on the left side.

5 The paper should look like this. Repeat steps 3 and 4 on the right side.

6 Fold the bottom point up.

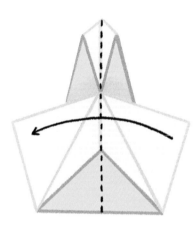

7 Fold the paper in half from right to left.

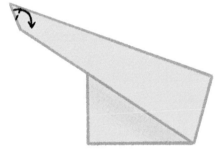

8 The paper should look like this. Rotate the paper 90° to the left, so it looks like the paper in step 9.

9 Make a fold near the left point, then fold it back again. Then fold it back on itself so the inside of the paper is facing out.

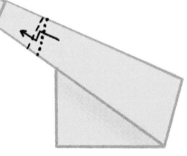

11 Repeat step 10, slightly to the right.

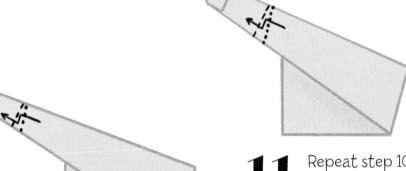

10 Make two little folds close together, to look like a step.

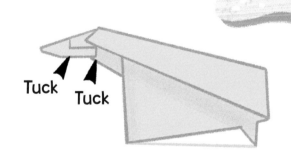

Tuck Tuck

12 Tuck the folds you made in step 10 inside the fold from step 11.

Continues on the next page.

15

13 The paper should look like this. Open up the fold you made in step 7 so that the paper is lying flat.

14 Make a step fold on the right side.

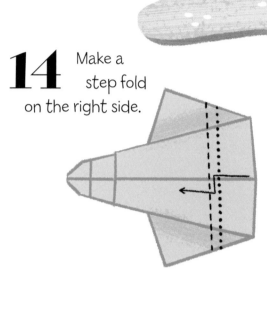

15 Fold in half, as shown here.

16 Make a small fold on the right side.

17 Fold the fold from step 16 back the other way.

18 Tuck the fold in.

Tuck

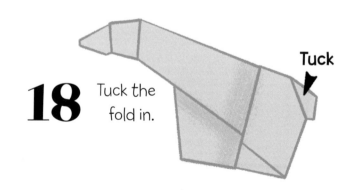

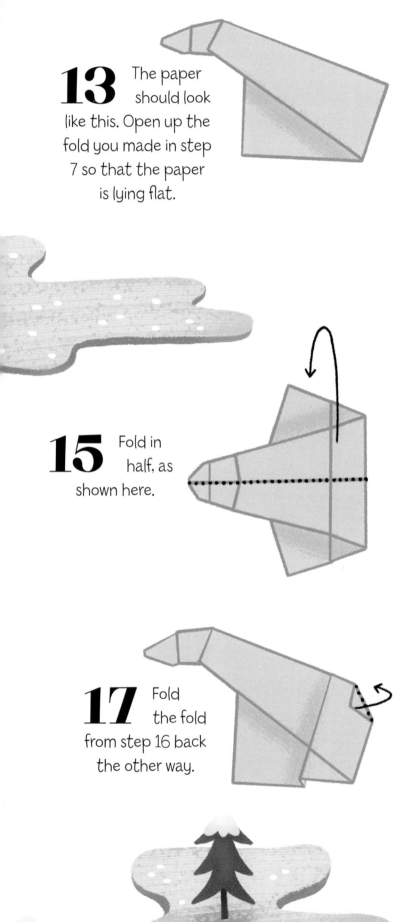

19 Make a fold in the top layer of paper and tuck it in. This is the first front leg.

20 Make a small fold to form a foot.

21 The paper should look like this. Repeat steps 19 and 20 on the other side to make the other leg and foot.

22 Draw on eyes and a nose. You've just finished an origami model of the largest land carnivore.

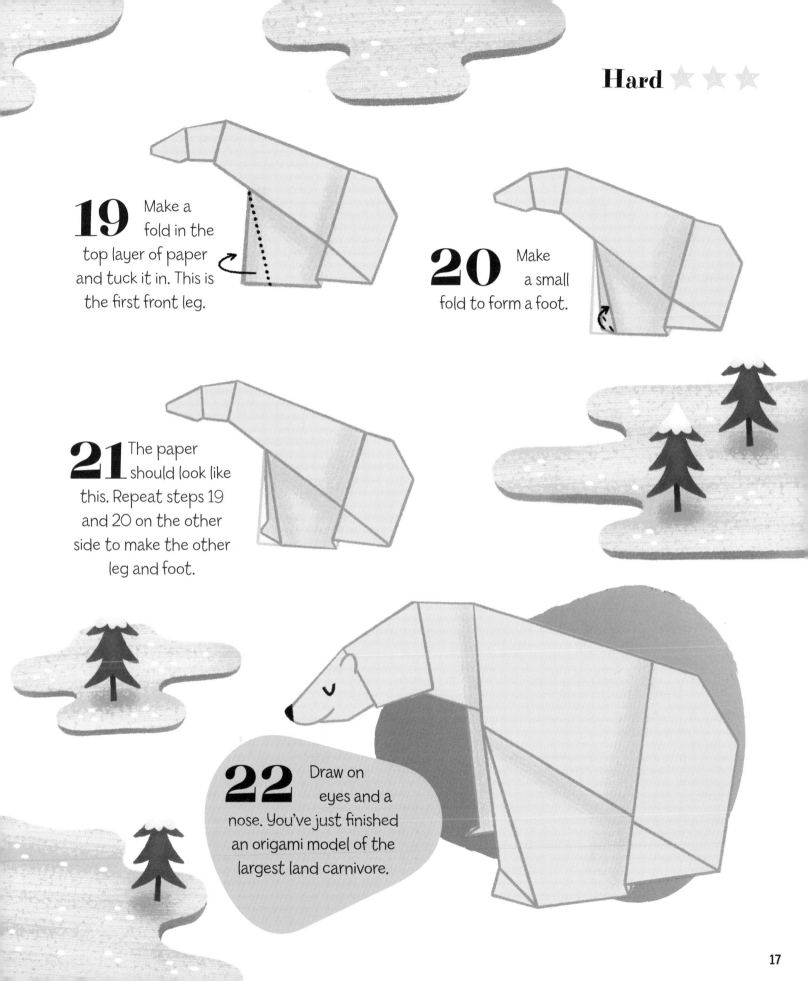

Christmas Village

Join the dots to reveal these happy Christmas carol singers.

What are these people looking at?

Paint a Deer

Paint the body, head, and legs in shades of brown. Then use a little lung power to breathe life into this woodland creature.

You will need:
Paints
Paintbrush
Drinking straw
Pen

1

Start by painting the shape of the deer.

2

3

4

5

Blow paint through a straw to create the antlers.

6

Finish by adding the eyes, nose, mouth, and hooves using pen.

Add some more deer friends to this forest scene.

Snowflake Spotter

What a flurry of pretty snowflakes! Can you spot the one that does not have an exact match?

22

Penguin Parade

Which goofy bird is wearing goggles?

Find three feathers on the page.

Which pair of penguins is holding hands?

Can you see Percival in his bow tie?

Plucky Penguins

Use the key to complete these pictures.

Paul the Polar Bear

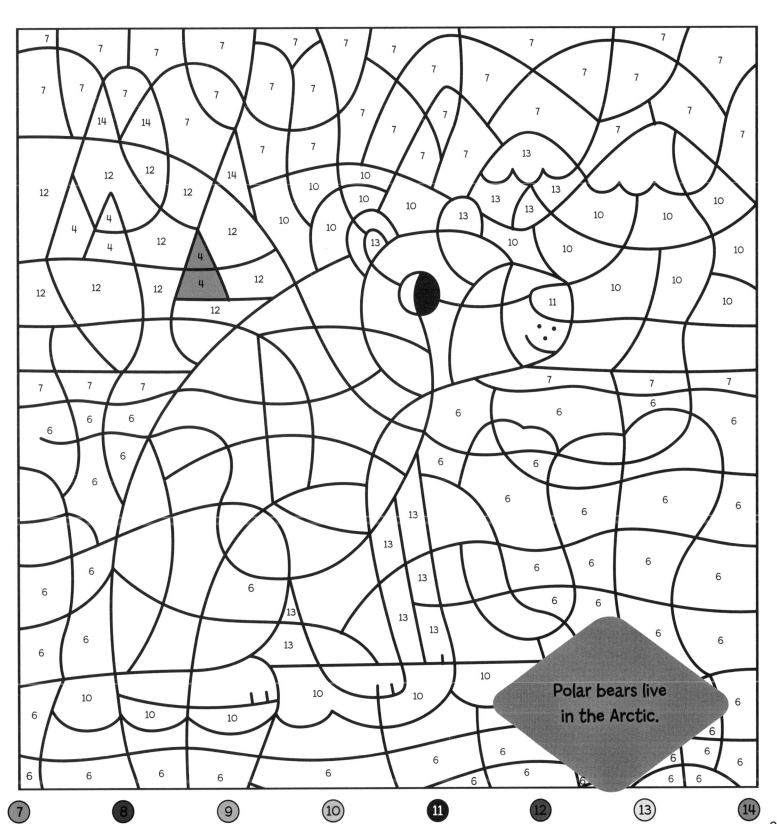

Polar bears live in the Arctic.

7   8   9   10   11   12   13   14

Find 9

Muskoxen

Muskoxen form a circle around their young to protect them from wolves.

Find 8

Arctic hares

The pale, winter fur of the Arctic hare helps it to hide in the snow.

Find 8

Wolves

This ancestor of the pet dog hunts in a pack.

How many Arctic creatures can you find in this chilly scene?

Find 8

Arctic foxes

In summer, Arctic foxes swap their thick, white coats for thinner, darker ones.

Find 9

Reindeer

Reindeer may travel thousands of miles each year in search of food.

Find 3

Snowy owls

With no trees here, owls make nests in hollows on the ground.

Find 11

Snow geese

The snow goose flies south to Mexico in the coldest months.

Find 6

Lemmings

Lemmings dig tunnels under the snow. Some lemmings have light brown fur.

Find 4

Polar bears

These huge predators stalk seals and walruses from the shore and sea ice.

Find 3

Walruses

Walrus tusks on males can grow as long as human arms.

Fun in the Snow

These pets love playing in the snow.
Join the dots to complete the picture.

Dogs like
to chase
snowballs.

Who brings
cats presents?
Santa Paws!

Christmas Memories

Santa is looking through his photo album. Can you spot which picture is the odd one out?

A

B

C

D

E

Ornament Surprise

Can you fit these baubles into the grid?
Each bauble should appear once in every row and column.

Toy Shelf

These toys are waiting to be played with.

Can you spot ten differences between the two pages?

Delivery Day

The delivery van needs help delivering the parcels in time for Christmas. Solve the calculations and follow the correct answers to guide the truck to the house with the green door.

15

3×6

10

27

3×5

12

18

6

3×9

10×3

5

6

2×3

Start

30

11×3

33

9

12

3×4

3×3

15

30

10

7×3

20

13

3×1

21

1

16

3

8×3

24

Finish

35

Snowy Day Fun

Spin white chalk around side-on to create
a snowman. Then dress him up!

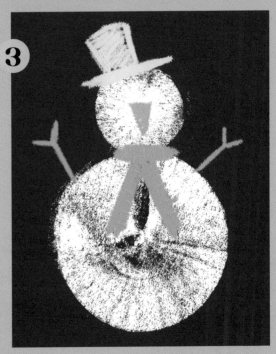

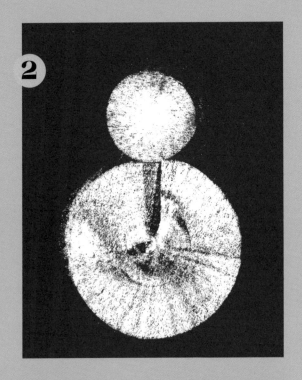

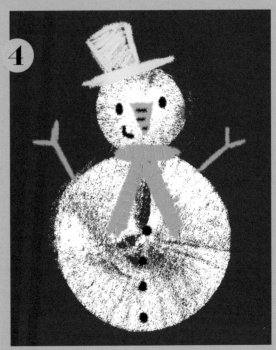

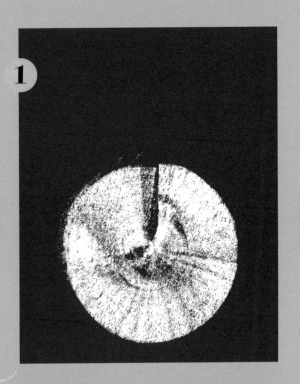

Build a snowman, or use your white chalk
end-on to add more snowballs!

Penguin Playtime

Here in the Antarctic, penguins live and play on the ice.

Can you spot ten differences between the two pages?

Magical Moose

Bring these Christmassy critters to life.

40

Penguin Family

Use the key below.

Origami Star

This origami model looks tricky, but it's really easy once you get the hang of it. You'll need six pieces of paper to create one star.

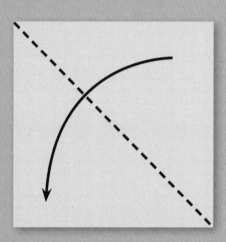

1 Start with one piece of origami paper, white side up. Fold it in half, as shown. Unfold.

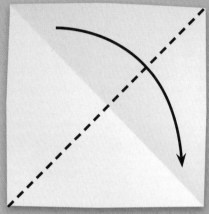

2 Fold the paper in half the other way, then unfold.

3 Fold the paper as shown, from left to right. Unfold.

4 Do the same again, from top to bottom, then unfold.

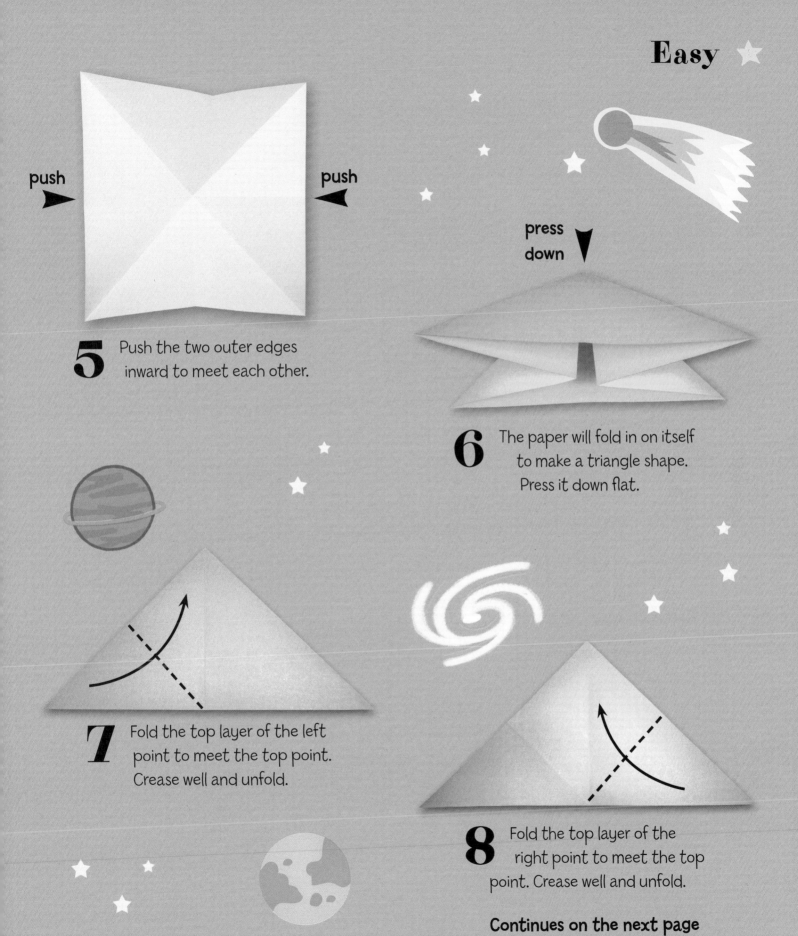

push ▶   ◀ **push**

5 Push the two outer edges inward to meet each other.

press down ▼

6 The paper will fold in on itself to make a triangle shape. Press it down flat.

7 Fold the top layer of the left point to meet the top point. Crease well and unfold.

8 Fold the top layer of the right point to meet the top point. Crease well and unfold.

Continues on the next page

9 Turn over the paper. Repeat steps 7 and 8.

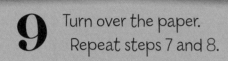

10 Create five more triangle shapes, by repeating steps 1 to 9. Once you have six in total, you can start creating your star.

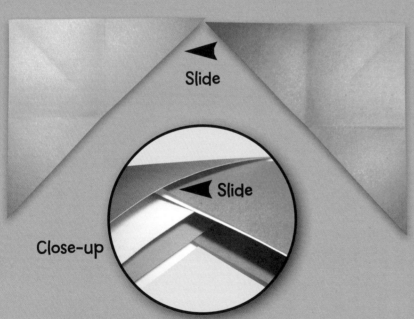

Slide

Slide

Close-up

11 Start with two triangles. Slide the left points of the right triangle into the top pockets of the other triangle, as shown. Slide the points in as far as they will go.

Pull out

12 Your paper should now look like this. Pull the middle crease toward you to open up the top. Pinch the two top corners to shape your star.

13 Your paper should now look like this.

Slide

14 Repeat steps 11 and 12 with the remaining sections, adding them one at a time.

15 Finish your star by slotting the last section into the first section and repeating step 12. Your star is now complete!

Draw Some Prickly Holly

You will need:
Paints
Bottle cap
Paintbrush
Your fingertips

Follow these steps to make a spiky holly leaf and berries.

1

Paint half the rim of a bottle cap, and use it to make the points of the holly leaf.

2

3

Keep adding bottle-cap prints until the leaf is complete.

4

5

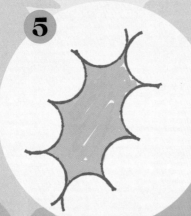

6

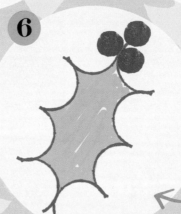

Paint the inside of the leaf green, then finish it off with red fingerprint berries.

This bright red bird is eyeing up the holly berries. Add some more leaves and berries for it to feed on.

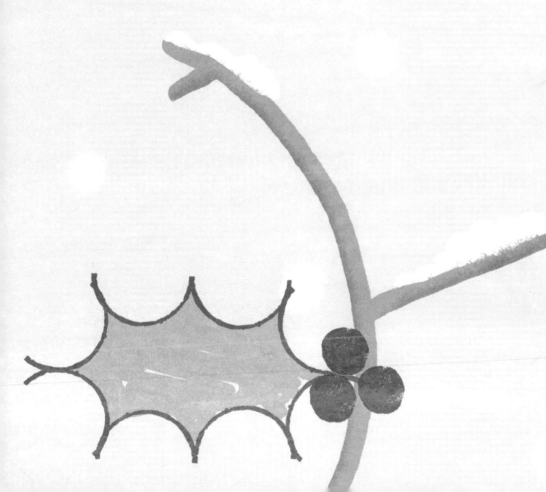

Gingerbread Puzzle

Snowbell the Christmas unicorn has been baking for the Christmas party. These gingerbread cookies all have matching pairs except for one. Can you see which one it is?

Christmas Baking

Snowbell has been baking cupcakes for Christmas Day.
Brighten up this scene with your pens and pencils.

In the Forest

Join the dots to discover this woodland Christmas scene.

Rabbit has a gift for Squirrel.

54
55
53
46
47
56
41
45
52
48
40
42 44
51 50 57
49
58
39
43
38
59
37
60
61 72
73
36
70 71 74
35
63 62 69
64 75
66 67
81 65 68 79 78 76
80
4
8 77
10 7 1
11 5 3 2
6
12
9
33
13
32
30 23
29 15
14
28 31 17
16 18
19
25 24 22
27 26 21 20

50

Squirrel has a gift for Rabbit.

51

Paint a Winter Grouse

Start by making the body and head with a purple handprint, then add green leaf prints for the bird's belly.

You will need:
Paints
Your hand
Leaves
Your fingertips
Pen

1

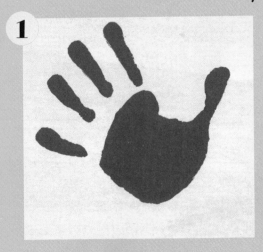

2

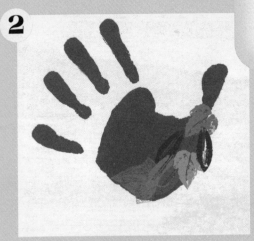

3

Use leaf prints for the black tail feathers.

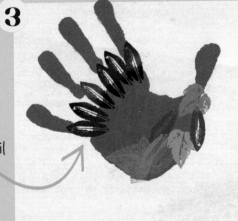

4

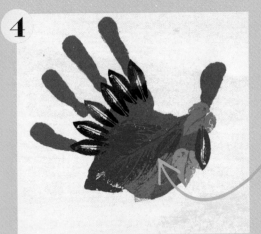

Make a red wing using a leaf print.

5

Add a red fingerprint for the eye.

6

Finish with pen details.

52

Add more grouse looking for berries in the snow.

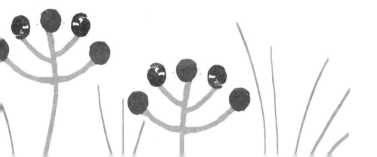

Decorate an Ice Rink

Make loops, zigzags, and wavy lines, first with one crayon, then two to match the skaters' two feet.

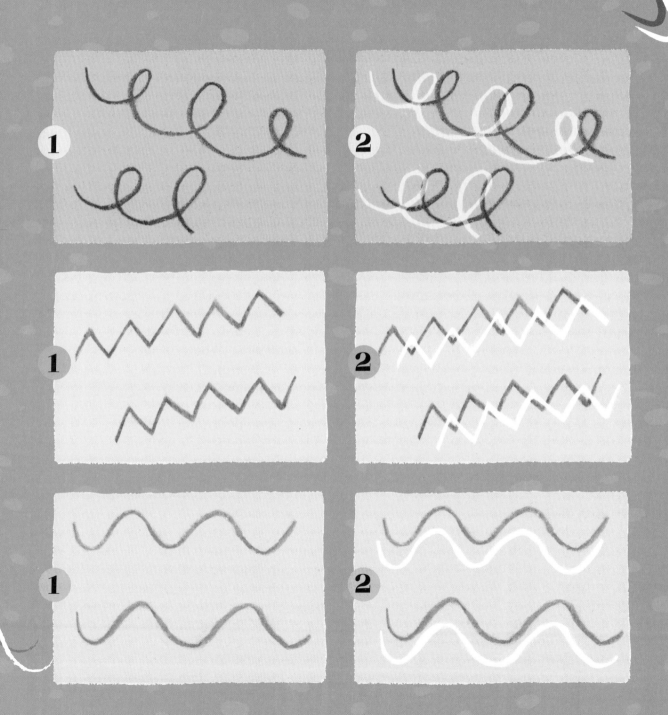

Help these skaters to make cool trails
and patterns on the ice!

Treat Time!

Which sweet treats would you choose?

Can you spot ten differences between the two pages?

The Nutcracker

Brighten up these pictures!

Shining Stars

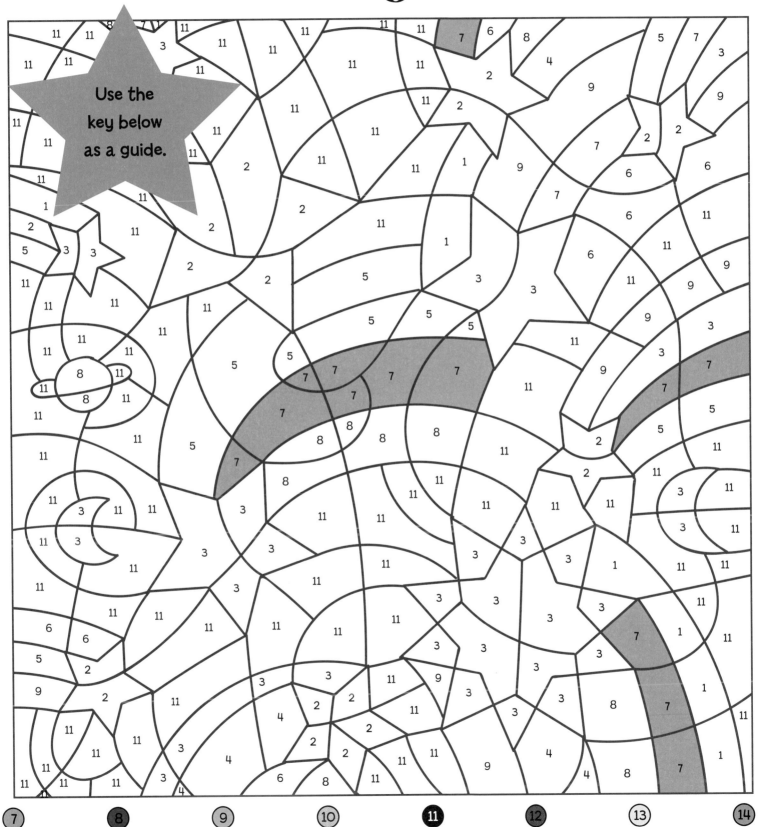

Use the key below as a guide.

Spot the Snowman

Which snowman can't smell anything?

Special Snowflakes

Which
snowflake is
different?

Feeding Time

Complete the dot-to-dots to find out which animals are feeding in this snowy scene.

Mice like to eat nuts.

All the birds enjoy nibbling on seeds.

Looking Good!

These snowmen are looking a little underdressed. Follow the lines to see which snowman each item of clothing belongs to.

Santa Slip-Up

Santa has dropped some parcels. Guide him through the maze to pick them up again.

Start

Finish

Make a Chalk Penguin

Start with two circle shapes for the head and body.
Then add the details.

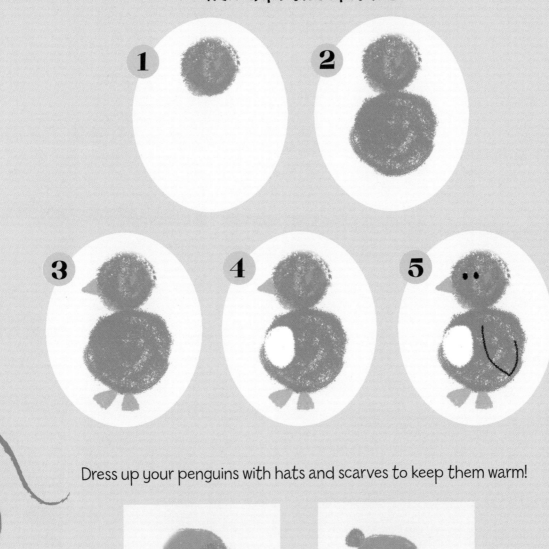

Dress up your penguins with hats and scarves to keep them warm!

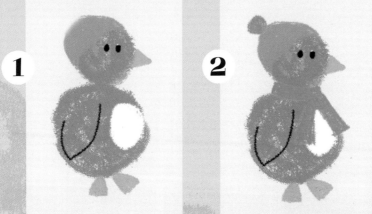

Give these two penguins some friends
to play with in the snow! Then use the side
of the chalk to add ice to the lake.

Hidden Reindeer

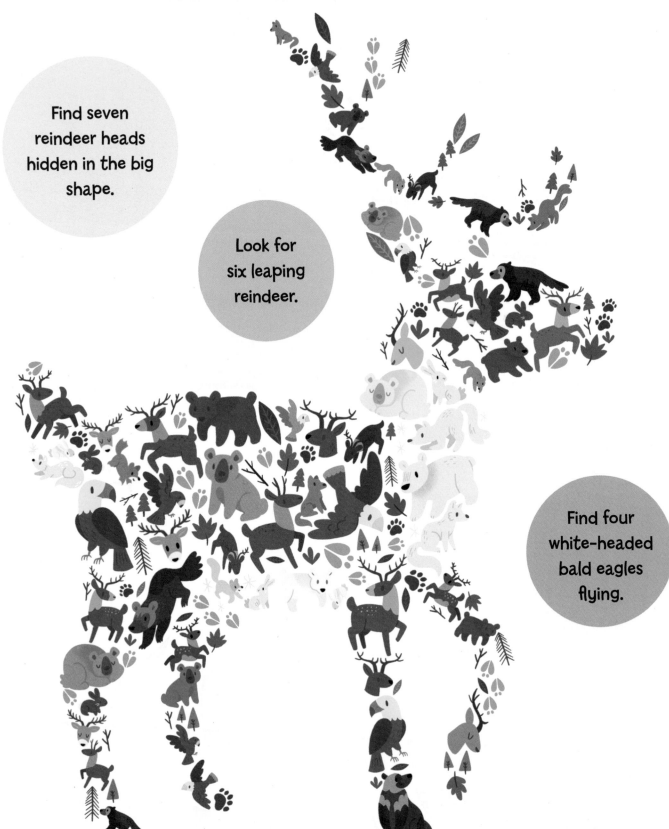

Find seven reindeer heads hidden in the big shape.

Look for six leaping reindeer.

Find four white-headed bald eagles flying.

Ice Rink Search

Find three blue bobble hats.

Which skater has yellow ear muffs?

How many skaters are wearing red mittens?

Frosty Fun

These Christmas fairies are busy
making snowmen.

A

Can you spot eight differences between these two icy scenes?

B

Paint a Pine Marten

This slinky mammal can be made using just a few simple steps.

1

Use bottle-cap prints to make the body and head.

2

3

Add a sweeping tail with a toothbrush print, and then add the final details with pen.

4

Add a marten returning home to its burrow in a tree.

A Very Special Night

Join the dots and find out what the children
can see in the sky on Christmas night.

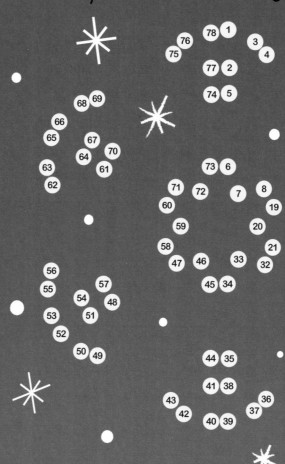

And what else is in the sky?

No two snowflakes are alike.

75

Snowman Search

The elves are making snowmen! Look at the list and cross off each item as you find it.

5 x snowballs
1 x broom
2 x dogs
1 x sled
4 x ear muffs

Sleigh Ride

Make Santa's sleigh look extra special, ready for Christmas Eve.

Reindeers Rule!

Follow the steps to draw your very own reindeer.

Create a Crayon Snowman

Begin with a simple oval. Lay the picture over a textured surface, then fill in the white with the side of the crayon. Add details with the crayon tips.

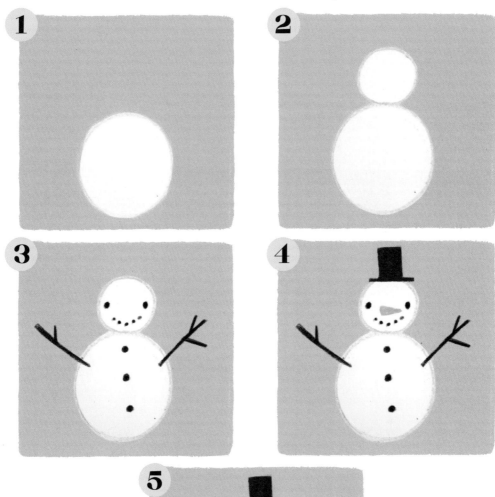

Brrrr! Draw a snowman—and make sure
you give him a warm hat and scarf!

Woodland Deer

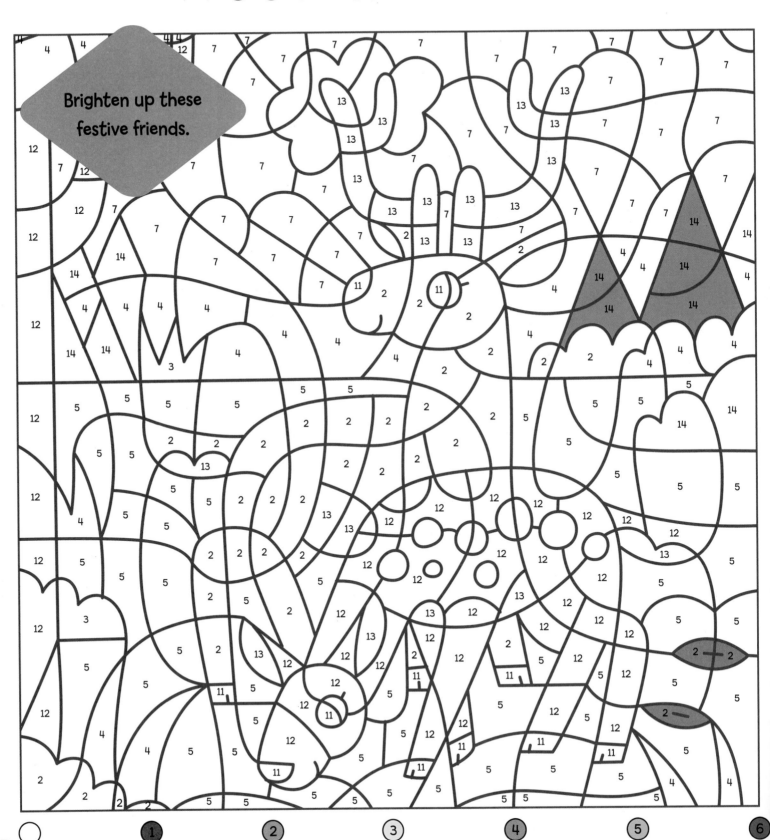

Brighten up these festive friends.

Wintry Walrus

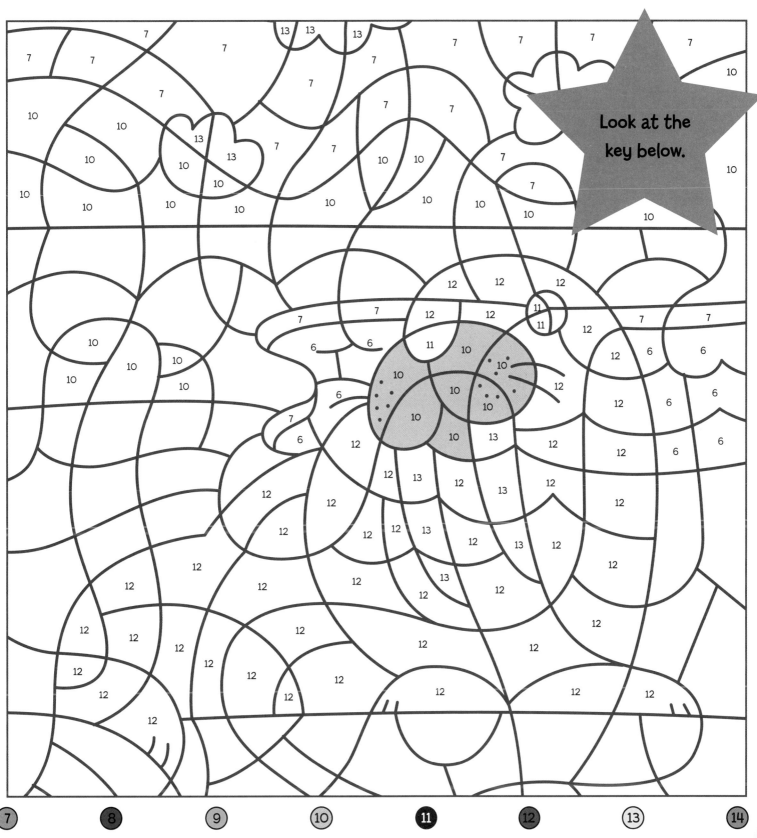

Look at the key below.

Origami Arctic Hare

This hare has thick fur to protect it from the cold. Brrr!

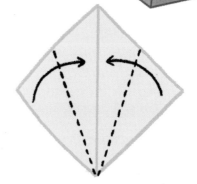

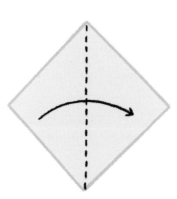

1 Place your origami paper white side up with a corner facing you. Fold it in half from left to right, then unfold.

2 Fold the left and right points to the central crease.

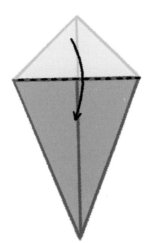

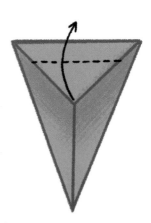

3 Fold the top point down.

4 Fold the top point so that it just reaches over the top of the paper.

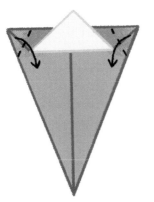

5 Make two small folds on the left and right sides.

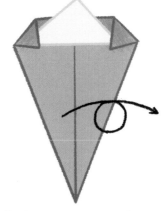

6 The paper should look like this. Turn it over from left to right.

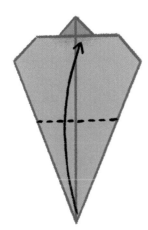

7 Fold the bottom point up to the top edge.

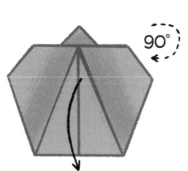

90°

8 Unfold, and turn the paper 90° to the right.

Continues on the next page.

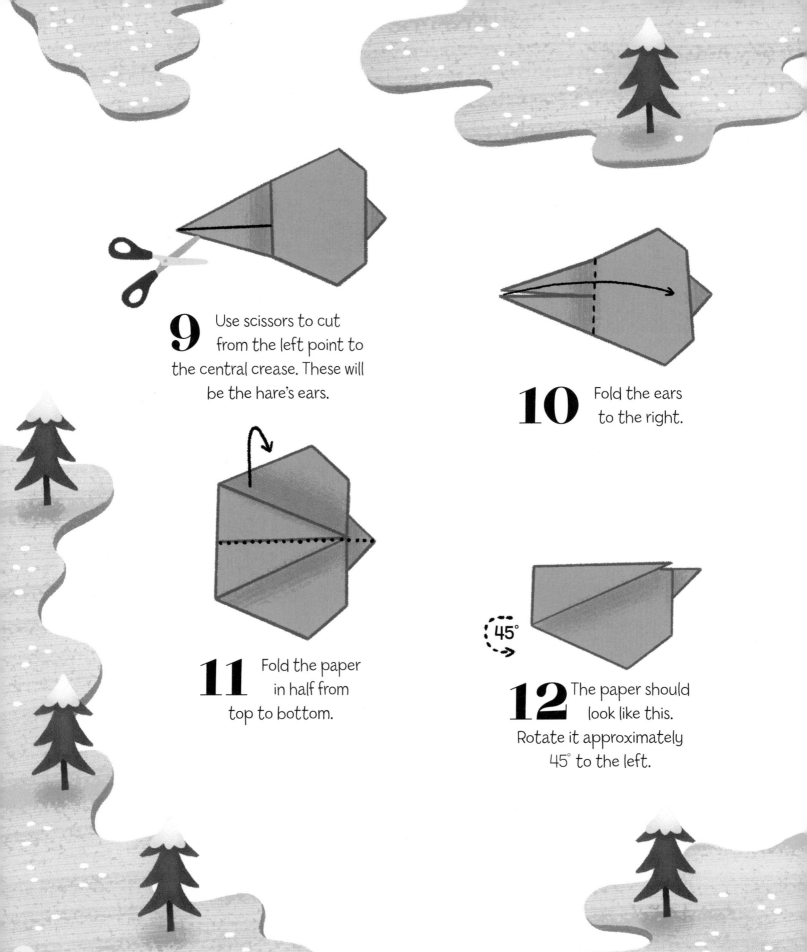

9 Use scissors to cut from the left point to the central crease. These will be the hare's ears.

10 Fold the ears to the right.

11 Fold the paper in half from top to bottom.

12 The paper should look like this. Rotate it approximately 45° to the left.

45°

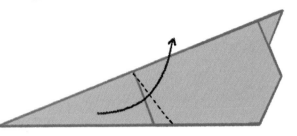

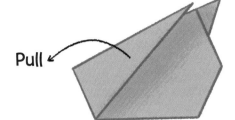

Pull

13 Pull the top point all the way over to the left.

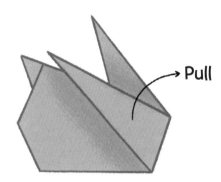

14 Make a fold at a slight angle to form the first ear.

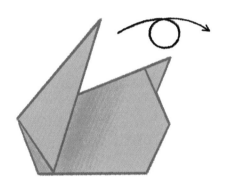

15 The paper should look like this. Turn it over from left to right.

Pull

16 Repeat steps 13 and 14 on this side.

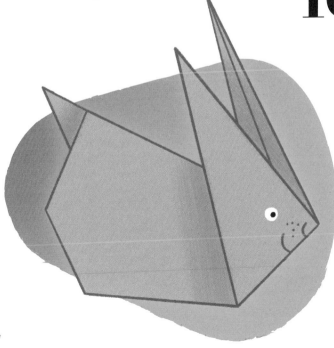

17 Add a face, and the Arctic hare is ready. Does it look like it's listening for danger?

All Wrapped Up

Decorate this gift with patterns and bows.
What could be inside?

Simply Tree-mendous!

The elves have one last tree to decorate. Can you help them by filling it in?

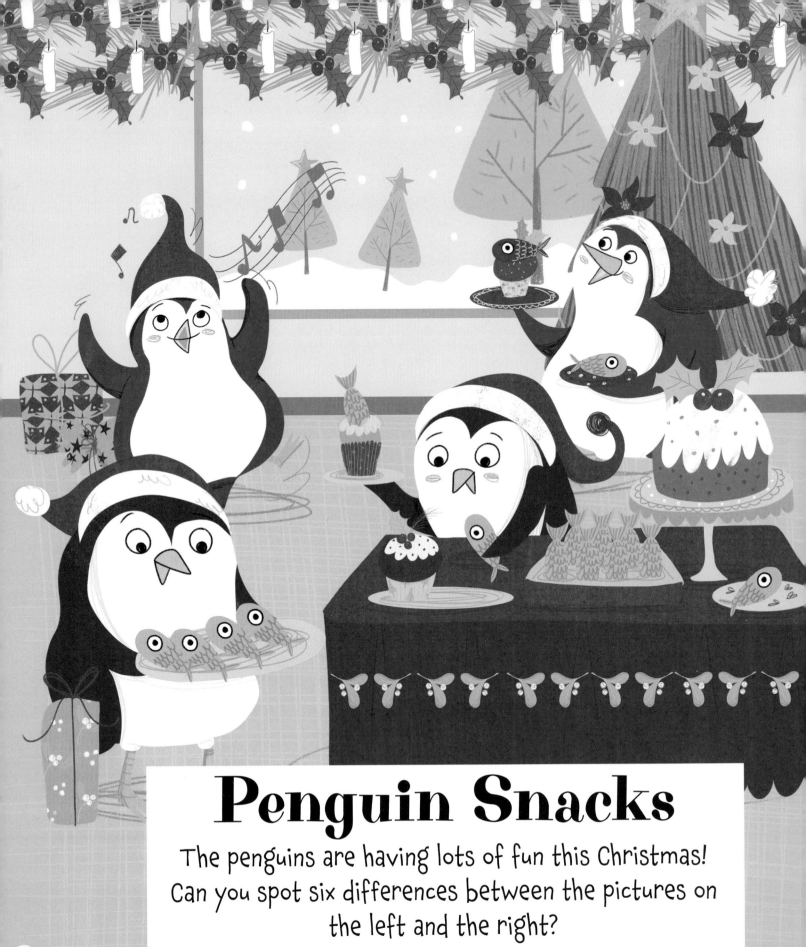

Penguin Snacks

The penguins are having lots of fun this Christmas!
Can you spot six differences between the pictures on
the left and the right?

Answers

Page 3 Santa's Reindeer

Pages 4–5 Winter Wonderland

Page 6 Penguin Puzzle

Page 7 Odd Deer Out

Pages 10–11 Winter Maze

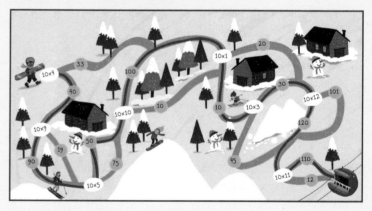

Pages 18–19 Christmas Village

Page 22 Snowflake Spotter

Page 23 Penguin Parade

Page 24 Plucky Penguins

Page 25 Paul the Polar Bear

Pages 26-27 Frozen Fields

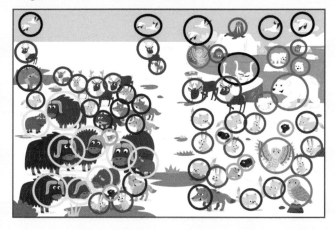

Pages 28-29 Fun in the Snow

Page 30 Christmas Memories

Page 31 Ornament Suprise

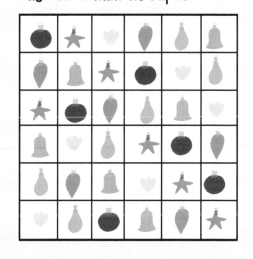

Pages 32-33 Toy Shelf

Pages 34-35 Delivery Day

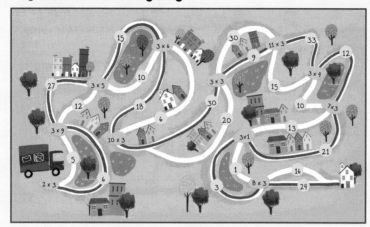

Pages 38-39 Penguin Playtime

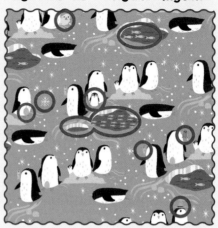

Page 40 Magical Moose

Page 41 Penguin Family

Page 48 Gingerbread Puzzle

Pages 50-51 In the Forest

Pages 56-57 Treat Time!

Page 58 The Nutcracker

Page 59 Shining Stars

Page 60 Spot the Snowman

Page 61 Special Snowflakes

Pages 62-63 Feeding Time

Page 64 Looking Good!

Page 65 Santa Slip-Up

Page 68 Hidden Reindeer

Page 69 Ice Rink Search

3 people are wearing
red mittens.

Pages 70-71 Frosty Fun

Pages 74-75 A Very Special Night

Pages 76-77 Snowman Search

Page 82 Woodland Deer

Page 83 Wintry Walrus

Pages 90-91 Penguin Snacks

Becoming a Translator

A Wiley Brand

Becoming a Translator

by Regina Galasso, PhD

A Wiley Brand

Becoming a Translator For Dummies®

Published by: **John Wiley & Sons, Inc.**, 111 River Street, Hoboken, NJ 07030-5774, www.wiley.com

For general information on our other products and services, please contact our Customer Care Department within the U.S. at 877-762-2974, outside the U.S. at 317-572-3993, or fax 317-572-4002. For technical support, please visit https://hub.wiley.com/community/support/dummies.

Wiley publishes in a variety of print and electronic formats and by print-on-demand. Some material included with standard print versions of this book may not be included in e-books or in print-on-demand. If this book refers to media such as a CD or DVD that is not included in the version you purchased, you may download this material at http://booksupport.wiley.com. For more information about Wiley products, visit www.wiley.com.

Library of Congress Control Number: 2024941685

SBN: 978-1-394-23202-4 (pbk); ISBN 978-1-394-23204-8 (ebk); ISBN 978-1-394-23203-1 (ebk)

10079036_070924

Contents at a Glance

Table of Contents

Introduction

As an educator, author, translator, and language access leader, I often find myself sharing what it takes to become an effective, efficient, and responsible translator because I run into too many people of all backgrounds and experiences who think that because a person speaks more than one language, they can translate anything and everything under any circumstances and at any time of day. Many of these people also think that by just changing the language button or flipping the language switch on a machine translation application or website, they'll receive an effective translation that they can readily share with the world.

Many of these people have the best intentions. They want to provide written documents in more languages so that more people can understand their content. However, they've most likely never had the ample opportunity to hear translators speak about their work, to learn what a responsible translation process looks like, and to build their translation literacy. It's not really their fault. It's just that there aren't too many places to find this information and to hear about these experiences. And because language, for most, comes across as being easy to produce, it doesn't occur to most people that moving what's said in one language into another would be challenging. Many people think that moving something from one to the other should be just as simple as the initial production of language.

At the same time, at least in the context of the United States, there's little knowledge about the benefits of studying languages, literatures, and cultures. Most k-12 schools don't offer languages other than English until an advanced grade. Universities are eliminating language requirements and doing away with language professors and programs. Ironically, universities and beyond are expressing a commitment to diversity, equity, inclusion, accessibility, and belonging efforts. That can't happen if the language needs and linguistic diversity of local communities and the world are overlooked.

In this context then, people aren't aware of the range of advantages that their language skills can have for them as they build and transform their careers. They might have an idea that they can be a language teacher, an interpreter, or a translator, but they might not know that they can be project managers at a translation agency or even establish and grow their own language companies that provide language services to the world. It's seldomly talked about at the general level that the language industry is one of the wealthiest and fastest growing in the world.

The lack of promotion of this information doesn't incentivize the learning and continued learning of languages or even confidence in the fact that speaking multiple languages has value. What's more, it helps to make the larger language companies even larger and limits the opportunities for new ventures.

Another part of the picture is that as people continue to be displaced by natural and human-provoked disasters, language access needs are growing and becoming more formalized through certain legalities and commitments by organizations of several types. Therefore, the provision of translation services is growing. Additionally, other more voluntary or strategic efforts of globalization call for translation and localization.

The rise of artificial intelligence (AI) also contributes to this picture. On the one hand, some AI can make translation seem as though it's easy, fast, and cheap. You usually get a translation produced by AI when you click on the Translate button or your browser automatically offers you a translation without your asking for it. There's a lot to know about AI and language production. To start, you need to keep two things in mind. First, these translations aren't reliable and should be checked by a qualified translator before being distributed. This is especially true if it's a high-stakes situation. Next, AI-generated translations don't have the same quality for every language. Because some Spanish translations that AI generates might not be that bad (although a qualified translator always needs to check them), this doesn't mean all translations are of the same quality for all languages. AI is better at some language pairs than it is others. And without getting too into the weeds, users of AI-generated translations need to be aware of the biases contained in these translations. Thus, some of the work that humans have worked hard to accomplish can be reversed in AI-generated translations. Overall, AI has the potential to get some poor language use into circulation. Although this is harmful for all languages, it's especially harmful to those that don't have as widespread circulation as others or that don't have as many resources, including qualified translators.

A final thing I'd like to bring awareness to as you read this book is the disappearance of languages. The world is made up of a little over 7,000 human languages. Not all of them are written, and more than half may disappear over the next century. As Victor D. O. Santos shares in his book *What Makes Us Human*, "when one of them disappears, a culture may also disappear. A unique way to view and understand the world." Translators can help prevent languages from disappearing. When people move around the world, they bring their languages with them. If their new location is committed to giving them access to information in their preferred language, until they no longer need it — because they've sufficiently learned the main language of the receiving culture — that effort keeps languages in circulation. Not only that, the translations make the languages visible, which is key for representation, inclusion, and awareness efforts.

I provide all this context to make it clear that translation is about so much more than just words and that the work of a translator, regardless of how many tools are at their disposal, is in need and must be done in a responsible manner to provide equitable opportunities and to prevent languages from disappearing, among other things.

I don't tell you how to translate in this book. Yet, I do spell out a process for translation. Rather, the focus is on the becoming: how to get there, and the potential wrapped up in the required skills. This book is more about the mindset than the how-to. If you rush to the how-to without establishing the mindset, the path to becoming a translator will be rocky and the results will be unstable. Mindset is the foundation to becoming a translator. Then you can add tools, areas of specialization, services, marketing efforts, clients, and more. And I do touch on all those things. What I share in this book will get you to the starting line of being a translator.

With that perspective in mind, this book is for many different audiences. It is for those who want to become translators and for those who love a person who wants to become a translator. It's for those who want to support translators in their workplace and beyond and for those who want to encourage someone already within their organization to become a translator. It can also be for those people who are interested in learning more about how human translators work.

About This Book

If you're curious about becoming a translator, you're a bilingual person who's regularly asked to translate in the workplace, or you're interested in learning more about translators, you've come to the right book.

Many of the examples in this book are from the Spanish-speaking world. That's because I speak Spanish and have carried out most of my professional life until now in the United States where Spanish is widely spoken and translated into. If you work with languages other than Spanish, don't dismiss the examples. I encourage you to think about the translation problem in the example and ask yourself if you might envision a similar problem in your language pair or pairs. As you grow as a translator, you'll find that you need to work with translators of language pairs other than your own to find translation solutions. Translators don't limit themselves to colleagues who work within the same languages. Translation itself is like a language.

This book offers something for different audiences. Check out the table of contents and start wherever you'd like. However, if you're a beginner, it's recommended that you make your way through the book from start to finish. Regardless of how you're reading this book, mark the pages you think you'll need to come back to in the future. Some of the information you might not need when you read it, but you can refer back to it later when you do.

Part 1 covers what translation is all about. If you can't think about translation and what it is all about, it's more difficult to translate. That said, I want you as a reader to get a foundation in defining translation, noting where it already exists in your daily life, breaking away from the common misconceptions about translation, and learning a few key translation terms. Part 1 then gets into recognizing the importance of human translators and the translations they produce, covering both the access to information that translators provide in addition to the more macrolevel contributions that translators and translations make for everyone. The intention is to make you aware that, as a translator, you spend a notable amount of time and energy advocating for the work and pushing for greater translation education for all. Then Part 1 covers the available paths to becoming a professional translator.

Part 2 picks up at the point of your decision to become a translator. It first discusses building your translator skill set and notes how you can apply your skills as a translator to other fields. Then it turns to where you can find translator education, including university and non-university programming, and covers specializations, certifications, certificates, and the importance of professional development.

After articulating what translators contribute to our world and how, and the credentials that translators often need and how to get them, the book, in Part 3, delves into the process of creating translations. It includes chapters on the process, machine translation, awareness and acceptance of the changes that translation introduces in the process, and the ethics of translation.

Part 4 gets into making translation your career or business. It explores doing the work on your own as an independent translator, having direct clients, working for an employer, and looking for work. It also takes you into the professional services you can curate as a translator, the tools you need to do the work, ways to break into the profession, and avenues for being paid and recognized.

The book ends with the Part of Tens. Here, you'll find tips for getting started as a translator; ten influential translators, organizations, and supporters of translation; and ten sources for learning more about translation.

I hope you'll find this content useful both today and years from now, when you're a translator or work with a successful team of translators and can appreciate the foundations that this book helped you establish.

Foolish Assumptions

Translators have many things to say and many opinions. After all, translators are constantly asked to make decisions and to defend those decisions via the words they choose for each translation they make. Thus, translators don't always agree with each other on the same topic. What's more, translator decisions often depend on when, how, and where you were when you decided to become a translator, and your language pair or pairs.

Some experienced translators might say this book should have been organized in another way. Some readers might want more coverage about a certain aspect. Both of those are valid observations.

What I share in this book comes from my academic and professional experience as a translator, educator, author, and language access leader. I've been through several institutions and worked with many translators and other language professionals as well as with a variety of clients. I've also been a keen observer of how languages interact with each other (or don't) by spending time in places where multiple languages are in circulation. Could I have presented this content in other way? Of course. My experience in translating, educating, working with organizations, and listening have taught me that the how-to needs to be accompanied by some reflection on what translation is and does and why it's necessary regardless of the number of languages one speaks.

Just as there's no perfect translation, there's no perfect book about it. Translation is a work in progress and a reminder that humans have the capacity to reflect and adapt.

Translation teaches society to question everything. It's a necessity and an avenue for personal growth and engagement with the world.

If you're curious about learning more about what it takes to become a translator because you yourself want to become one or because you work with translators, I hope you'll learn from reading this book.

Icons Used in This Book

Throughout this book, the following icons appear in the left margins to alert you to special information.

REMEMBER

This symbol marks an important truth that's worth repeating. Noting these ideas can help you make progress with your strategic plan.

TIP

The information next to the Tip icon always includes a helpful hint to keep your strategic plan moving forward as smoothly as possible.

WARNING

Any information next to this icon is something you want to be wary about. Watch your step when you see a Warning icon. The info can include mistakes others have made that you can learn from or moments in which you have to weigh the cost of doing one thing over another.

Beyond the Book

In addition to the information and guidance you'll find in the pages of this book, you can access the *Becoming a Translator For Dummies* Cheat Sheet online. Just go to www.dummies.com and enter "Becoming a Translator For Dummies Cheat Sheet" in the search box.

The Cheat Sheet includes even more information to help you get started as a successful translator. If you have any questions, please reach out to me via LinkedIn.

Where to Go from Here

Jump right into the book! If you've heard about translators and are interested in becoming a translator yourself, start at the beginning of the book and keep on going. The beginning is also a good place to start if you want to learn more about the translators you work with. If you're already being asked to translate at your workplace but you have little or no training, try starting with Part 3.

Go to the Part of Tens at any time. You'll find many goodies there that you can start reading or listening to while you're reading this book.

And if you're wondering where to go when you're done with this book or even as you're reading it, I've snuck in this extra list of nine (not to compete with the Part of Tens):

>> Listen to and read your working languages.

>> Start translating any interesting text you see around you. Pick short passages. Even if you don't arrive at a translation you're satisfied with, contemplating what it means to translate certain phrases or texts does offer a bit of practice.

>> Follow some translators, Translation Studies professors, or other language professionals on social media. You can detect from their number of followers, credentials, and quality of the posts if they're worth your screen time.

>> Get into a translation class, if possible, at your local college or online.

>> Advance your education after reading this book if you think it would be helpful on your road to becoming a translator.

>> Note the ways that learning about translation has changed the way you look at written language.

>> Check out *How to Succeed as a Freelance Translator* by Corinne McKay if you're ready to set yourself up as a freelance translator.

>> Read *Small Business for Dummies* for more on setting up your own operation.

>> Update job duties, descriptions, and compensation as necessary if you ask your employees to translate as part of their work or you plan to hire translators.

1
Understanding What Translation Is All About

» Identifying translation in everyday interactions

» Clearing up common misconceptions

» Familiarizing yourself with key terms and concepts

Chapter **1**

Turning Your Attention to Translation

Translation enables communication in a multilingual world. If you want to read something that was written in an unfamiliar language, it has to be translated into a language you understand. Translation has been in practice for more than 2,000 years, and it's pervasive today in everything from books and product manuals to movies and advertising. Yet, few people understand what it is and what it takes to create a successful translation. It's not as simple as looking up words in a bilingual dictionary or pasting text into a translation app.

In this chapter, I explain what translation is and isn't and what it entails. I cover definitions of translation and their limitations, correct widespread misconceptions about translation, and introduce some of the basic terminology to get you started on your journey to becoming a translator.

Defining Translation

When you think about what translation is, you may surmise that it involves converting a text written in one language into another language. You may think it encompasses both spoken and written language. You may imagine a person working on a computer at a desk surrounded by bilingual dictionaries. You may think of the people who work in booths at United Nations meetings and conferences. You may picture a situation in which a person is standing between two people who speak different languages and helping them communicate. You might even think about an app or a website you've used at some time to translate a word or phrase. Broadly conceived, translation can be all those things and more. In general, translation encompasses any means of converting verbal expression from one language to another.

The English word *translation* comes from the Latin *translatio*, which means to carry across or to bring across. For English speakers, *translation* deals with written materials, whereas *interpretation* is the process of translating speech from one language to another. However, people often confuse the two words and use the word *translator* to refer to both translators and interpreters. The people who work in the booths at the United Nations and help two individuals who don't speak a common language are interpreters. Translators are those who work with the written word.

REMEMBER

As you set out on your path to becoming a professional translator, maintain the distinction between the two terms. Refer to yourself as a translator if you translate written documents and as an interpreter if you focus on oral communication. Gently correct future clients and colleagues when, in the English-speaking context, they refer to translation as interpretation and interpreters as translators. While you, as the professional, may know what service and task those people have in mind, others may not. Knowing and advocating to call the services by their correct terms can avoid unnecessary confusion and service delays.

REMEMBER

Being a translator involves working in multilingual contexts. Keep in mind, however, that although many languages distinguish between translating and interpreting, some don't. As a professional, you'll need to rely on the context to determine which service is needed and to communicate clearly to everyone involved whether the situation calls for a translator or an interpreter.

Exploring traditional definitions

Translators read a text in one language and then write it in another language. The text that they write in the new language is called a *translation*. The word *translation* can be used to talk about three distinctly different things:

>> **A process:** The series of steps taken to convert a message written in one language into another language. The process involves reading, analysis, translation, revision, and editing. It often calls for research and may involve formatting, graphics, and other forms of communication.

>> **A product:** The end result of the translation process, which might be a book, brochure, legal document, movie script, or something else. You can think of the original text as the input and the translation as the output. For example, the Colombian-born, Nobel-Prize-winning author Gabriel García Márquez (1927-2014) wrote several novels in Spanish that were later translated into English and other languages.

>> **A phenomenon:** Translation can refer to a phenomenon — something that can be observed and studied. In the study of translation, you can examine the social and cultural factors that influence translators' choices, for example.

Practically speaking, as a translator, you're going to be most consciously involved with the first two items: process and product. You're going to be doing translation and creating translations. However, subconsciously, you'll also be actively involved in the phenomenon of translation — you'll be using knowledge outside the dictionary definitions of words to determine how to phrase expressions. You may even study the phenomenon to increase your awareness of what translation involves and to improve your skills.

Translation can also be broken down into various types to shed light on different approaches to it. Part of your job as a translator will involve educating people about what you do. The more information and clarity you have about what translators do and how they do it, the better you can explain what you do to future clients and others.

Roman Jakobson (1896–1982), a Russian-born linguist and literary theorist who eventually became a professor at Harvard University, identified three types of translation:

>> **Intralingual translation:** Commonly referred to as *rewording*, *intralingual translation* involves rephrasing an expression in the same language; for example, you translate "I'm famished" to "I'm starving." Yes, technically speaking, anyone who's ever cracked open a thesaurus to find a more precise word or different way to express a thought has done translation. Anyone who's ever said "in other words" before rephrasing what was previously said, has also done translation.

>> **Interlingual translation:** *Interlingual translation* involves converting text written in one language into another language; for example, in English, you think, "I'm hungry," and then you write a note telling your Spanish friend, "Tengo hambre." This is also referred to as "translation proper" and usually what most people are thinking about when they hear the word "translation."

>> **Intersemiotic translation:** *Intersemiotic translation* involves converting a verbal expression into a nonverbal expression, and vice versa; for example, it might be turning a poem into music or a performance, or drawing the definition of a word.

REMEMBER

This discussion may strike you as a touch too theoretical, but it can help you explain what you do to other people who don't have a background or training in translation. Monolinguals who are asked to reword something can get a sense of the decision-making process you go through as an English-to-Portuguese translator, for example, by engaging in intralingual translation. Keep these terms in your back pocket to help people better understand how translation works and the decision-making process that guides the work of translators.

Expanding the definition

A simple definition of *translation* is reading a text in one language and then rendering it in another language. As you become a translator, you'll become more and more aware of how limited that definition can be and how it affects the way you talk about your work. You won't want to bore someone with all the details of what translators do, although they're fascinating, so that basic definition is a good starting point. But keep in mind that the limited definition can lead to misunderstandings regarding what you do and what people expect of you. Working with an expanded, more nuanced definition of translation can help prevent misunderstandings and manage client and professional partner expectations. Here are some takes on translation that can help you expand your definition of it:

>> **Translation is a critical part of communications in a multilingual world and especially in multilingual communities.** Translation must be considered at the onset of planning for any communication within a multilingual community. Treating translation as an afterthought compromises the translation's quality and delivery time.

>> **Translation extends beyond words.** Translators need technical skills to work with that efficiently and effectively help create quality translations. This ranges from knowing how to manage files to using translation memory tolls to ensure consistency among the use of terms.

>> **Translation is education.** The recipients of a translation receive a text with information and ideas that they otherwise wouldn't have access to had the translation not been done. For example, the translation process and products can increase familiarity of the languages and cultures in a given community so that community leaders have deeper insight into the unique needs of the different populations that make up the community. Translations also educate the individuals who do the work.

>> **Translation requires advocacy.** Because those not in the field may not fully understand what translation entails, translators often find themselves advocating for appropriate timelines, planning, and resources, including compensation. Translators might also find themselves advocating for equality among different language groups in a given community.

>> **Translations are originals.** Translations are often thought of as inferior to the original because the author of the original had to be clever enough to come up with the idea and have the creativity and skill to express it in words. People often assume that the original required far more work, creativity, and skill than the translation. However, every translation is an original. It has never existed before, and it has taken considerable knowledge, creativity, and skill to produce. The effort and expertise that a translator brings to a project is different from but not inferior to those of the author. Some translations, often including ones which have been highly localized, are even preferable to the original for multilingual audiences. For example, many people who are bilingual in Latin American Spanish and English consider the movie *Shrek* (2001), directed by Andrew Anderson and Vicky Jenson, to be more enjoyable in Spanish because of the quality of the translation.

As you grow as a translator, think of what you might add to the list that further defines translation and reflects translation's value.

Seeing Translation All Around You

Translation is ubiquitous. All you have to do is pick up the phone, flip through a magazine, surf the web, turn on the TV, or browse the community bulletin board at your local grocery store to see translation in action. As the world becomes more global and our communities become more multicultural and multilingual, translation becomes an even greater necessity. After all, whenever people who speak different languages need to communicate or rely on the same resources in their everyday lives, there is a need for translation. This exchange enriches all our lives.

As demand for translation grows, so do the opportunities for trained translators who are able to efficiently and effectively be part of the translation process. Since this need grows along with the development of other translation tools, translators will continue to translate, revise, work in human and machine-translation hybrid situations, and perhaps be called upon for more consultation work.

In this section I highlight several areas where you can observe translation in action.

On the smartphone

You don't have to go very far to encounter translation. Sometimes all you need to do is pick up the phone. From automated customer service contact centers to AI-driven text messaging apps, you can't avoid bumping into translation services. Here are a few examples:

>> **Automated customer support centers:** Whenever you call a customer support line, one of the first prompts you get is to press the number key for the language you want to use. Maybe you press 1 for English or 2 for Spanish. Maybe you're given other options. You're then presented options in the language you chose. All these systems rely on input from translators.

>> **Operating system (OS):** Whether you have an iPhone or an Android, you can specify the language you want to use. Apple's iOS can be localized to more than 100 languages and regions, and the iOS itself has been translated into more than 40 languages.

>> **Smartphone apps:** Many smartphone apps these days are available in multiple languages. You access settings for the app and specify your preferred language. From that point on, the entire interface is presented in your preferred language.

>> **Text messaging:** With most text messaging apps, you can specify your preferred language, and the app will function in that language. For example, as you type, the autocomplete feature will try to predict the word you're typing in the specified language. Some text messaging apps may try to detect the language that they sense you're typing (or speaking, if you're using talk-to-text).

As you may have noticed, technology has a lot of catching up to do when it comes to living a multilingual life. For example, if you communicate with someone in multiple languages, texting can be a nightmare. How frustrating is it when you try to type a text message in a language other than English and your phone resists and keeps pushing what you type into English! Even worse is when your phone tries to help you by detecting the language it thinks you're using and guesses wrong, creating a mashup of languages best described as gibberish.

TIP

Changing the language setting on your phone on a regular basis is one way to practice using all your languages. For instance, if you've always had your phone in English, try switching it to Spanish.

On the internet

On the internet, some sites are available in multiple languages, and some aren't. Among the sites that are accessible in multiple languages, the quality of the translation can vary considerably. In fact, people who manage sites take different approaches to providing multilingual access. Some of these approaches are done by professionals and others are not. Here are some of the most common approaches:

>> **Professional translation:** Some website administrators hire professional translators to adapt their site to accommodate differences in languages and countries, including differences in currencies. In fact, large global operations may have entirely separate websites for different countries, with a distinct address for each site. For example, in the United States, shoppers go to Amazon.com, but in Spain, they shop at Amazon.es. In addition, in the navigation bar at the top of the page, shoppers can choose to navigate the site in Spain in Spanish or in Portuguese.

>> **Partial translation:** Some sites provide multilingual access to only relevant areas or content. In some cases, the website administrator hires a professional to summarize the website's content and then translate that summary into other languages. For examples, help parts of a website are usually a big one for translation.

>> **Crowdsourced translation:** Some sites crowdsource their translation. This means that they have volunteers translate their content. The quality of the translations can be questionable.

>> **Automated translation:** Some sites employ the use of Google Translate, or another machine translation tool, to automatically translate the site's content and menu options. Visitors to the site can click an icon to translate the site into the language of their choice. If you're on a site that uses Google Translate, you're reading a machine translation. You can usually tell because some of the wording can be awkward and unnatural, and depending on the language, not make any sense at all.

If you access social media content in multiple languages, you may have noticed that Facebook, Instagram, and other social media platforms seem to determine your preferred language for you. You pull up a post written by a contact of yours in German, and the platform automatically translates it into English because that's the language you typically use. So even though you're capable of communicating in multiple languages, the app pushes your multilingual life into a monolingual one. These translations aren't done in the moment by human translators; rather, they're done by machine translation. After using the app, you may be prompted to provide feedback to make the machine translations better.

The next time you're on a social media app and read a post with language that sounds a bit off, check to see if it's a translation. You'll know if it's a translation if you see "See original" usually located somewhere in the post. You might think that a user has a poor use of language when really it's just a poor translation that you're reading.

On television and in films

Thanks to the growing popularity of video streaming around the world, people have access to movies and series produced in distant countries — everywhere from Mexico to Norway to China and beyond. In many cases, you can still enjoy this video content even if you don't know the language thanks to translators who create the subtitles or translate the screenplay so the shows can be dubbed. Sometimes the dubbing is so well done that you can barely tell that the actors are speaking in a different language from the one you're hearing.

When you're watching a film, enable both subtitles and dubbing and look for differences between the two. What an actor says and what appears in the subtitle are often different. When done with high standards, the dubbing needs to make adjustments so the words line up better with the movement of the actors' lips. Subtitles also have parameters such as word economy. The industry standard is a maximum of 35-40 characters per line, two lines maximum, between one and six seconds per subtitle. Some of the first things to go when cutting down subtitles to make them fit will be a character's name, for example. Often the people that translate for dubbing aren't the same people that do subtitles.

Here are some important points about dubbing and subtitling that may come in handy as you pursue a career in translation:

>> **Pros and cons of dubbing:** The primary benefit of dubbing is to increase engagement. It makes movies and series more accessible to a broader audience, which means they're more profitable for the studios and creators. For some viewers, it also makes movies more enjoyable if they don't like having to read subtitles. Despite these benefits, dubbing isn't always the solution. It's expensive because the entire soundtrack needs to be replaced, which requires a recording studio and a whole new cast of actors to deliver the lines. Critics of dubbing also claim that dubbed films lack authenticity due to subtle changes in meaning, tone, and cultural nuances. Language pride and politics also come into play — in some regions, audiences don't want to or are discouraged from hearing anything other than their own language. Dubbing also allows for censoring, which was done by fascist regimes in Germany, Italy,

and Spain. Fortunately, times have changed. Italy now hosts the annual Gran Premio Internazionale del Doppiagio, which is a ceremony for excellence in dubbing.

>> **Challenges of subtitles:** Some languages with smaller markets choose to subtitle their content. This has been the case in the Scandinavian countries where English proficiency is high. Subtitling is usually a cheaper and faster option than dubbing, but it's no less challenging. It's not merely a translated transcription of what's being said. Subtitles need to be concise, accurate, and readable. They need to comply with strict time and space requirements. They need to fit within a limited area on the screen so that they don't distract from the action, and they need to be succinct enough to be read in the limited amount of time the actors are delivering their lines. Translators also need to produce a time code to indicate at what point in the action each line appears and how long it needs to remain onscreen. Subtitling requires technical and linguistic knowledge along with specialized software.

REMEMBER

A *transcription* is a written, word-for-word record of what someone said orally in the same language. A *translated transcription* is a translation of that transcription. A film's translated transcription isn't the same as its subtitles.

WARNING

Don't confuse closed captioning with subtitles. Closed captioning is in the same language as the original video production or a translation of the original video production. Subtitles are translated from the original language into a different language. Closed captioning, even if it is a translation of what is being said, is not to be confused with subtitling.

The instructions you read

Many products — everything from games and home appliances to automobiles and yard equipment — come with manuals or instruction sheets. Often, they're provided in multiple languages. Sometimes you turn to the English and it sounds great. That's probably because the instructions were first done in English or, if they weren't, the translator did an excellent job. When the instructions are poorly written in English, it could be because the company didn't use a skilled translator. They might have used a person who spoke some English, but not a qualified translator. If you're faced with instructions that have you scratching your head, try reading one of the other languages as a viable workaround.

Some companies are foregoing the process of trying to provide instructions in multiple languages for different audiences. Instead, they're opting to communicate entirely with images. If you've ever put together a piece of furniture from IKEA, you probably followed the instructions, which are a series of drawings. IKEA has more than 450 stores in over 60 markets around the world. Their website is available in many languages, including Basque, Catalan, and Galician. However, providing instructions in all those languages wouldn't be very cost efficient, so IKEA cleverly decided to use what can be considered a universal language: illustrations. Instead of *telling* customers how to assemble their furniture, they *show* them how. Customers don't even need to be able to read in any language; they can just follow the pictures. Yes, sometimes the pictures can be difficult to decipher, but they typically provide all the instruction you need to get the job done, and they're fun to look at.

Translated books

Some of the books you have at home might be translations. You can certainly find some at your local library and bookstore. Without translated books, thanks to the work of translators, there would only be books written by authors in the languages you know. If that language is English, you'd only have access to books by authors who write in English. That may not be a huge issue unless the leading author on a topic that interests you writes only in French or Swahili. In certain countries, having access to only those books written in the local language can pose an even bigger problem. As Mette Holm, Danish translator of the Japanese writer Haruki Murakami, points out, if all you had to read were books written in Danish that weren't translations into Danish, within your lifetime, you would run out of books to read. Is this accurate? It depends on how fast you read and what kind of books you want to read. But what it does tell us is that our reading list and our world would be impossibly limited.

The market for translated books certainly has room to grow, especially in the United States. Currently, it struggles for several reasons, including the following:

>> **Publishers in some countries market a relatively low percentage of translated books.** In countries like France, close to 20 percent of all books on the market are translations. In Spain, the number is closer to 30 percent. In the English-speaking world, it's about 3 percent. This imbalance can be attributed to a number of factors. When translation doesn't happen it's a missed opportunity for authors who write in languages other than English to expand their reach and for people who read books in English to expand their minds.

>> **Many publishers in the English-speaking world have the perception that monolingual people who read books in English aren't interested in reading a translated book.** This perception has been in circulation for some time, but the situation is like the chicken and the egg scenario; if publishers think that demand for translated books is low, they won't publish them, but if readers don't have access to translated books, they don't have any idea what they're missing. Book publishers can learn a great deal from video streaming services. When viewers have access to entertaining foreign films and series with quality subtitles and dubbing, they stream that content and often discover that some of the most innovative and entertaining content is coming out of lesser-known regions and cultures.

>> **Translators aren't named.** Because the translator's name is omitted from the cover, people often read translated books without ever realizing that they're reading a translation. By omitting the translator's name, publishers are failing to advertise and promote translated books, and recognize the efforts, art, and skill of translators. As a result, they're missing an opportunity to grow the market for these titles.

>> **Finding translated books in bookstores is a challenge.** Most bookstores in the United States don't have a translated book section or any way to draw more attention to translated books. As a result, little is done to attract shoppers to translations.

Pay more attention to the books in your hands. Are any of them translations? If not, make a concerted effort to read a translated book. Find an author who writes in a language you don't understand and see if a translation of one of their books is available. In doing so, you'll be supporting fellow translators! If you know someone who lives abroad, ask them about popular authors who live in that region and see if you can find a translation of one of their books.

Figure 1-1 illustrates the many ways reading translations benefits everyone.

Encouraging news! The Booker Prize Foundation shows that younger readers are interested in translated fiction. In the United Kingdom, for example, book buyers under the age of 35 account for almost half of the purchases of translated fiction.

Library Book Card

Check Out Translation!

Benefits of Reading Translated Books

DATE	ISSUED TO
01	Travel without boarding a plane.
02	Learn about different cultures for free through your local library.
03	Connect with authors who don't speak your language.
04	Discover books that readers who know other languages are reading.
05	Meet characters who experience similar things as you in different ways.
06	Expand your view of the world.
07	Read two art works in one: the author's ideas and the translator's creatively selected words.
08	Help writers become known outside their languages.
09	MAKE PUBLISHERS UNDERSTAND THAT READERS WANT DIVERSE BOOKS.
10	Support the people who make all of this possible: Translators!

Designed by Adelyn Hoyt, Concept by Regina Galasso. Content created by Adelyn Hoyt, Carolina Valenain, Grace Juma, Isabel Ford, Lauricny Da Costa Vilela, Olivia Dimarzo, Samuel Suárez Murias, Stella Rubaleaba, and Tomás Estrada Hevia as part of the UMass Amherst course Spanish 514: Practicing Literary Translation (Spring 2024).

SPANISH & PORTUGUESE Catalan Studies · University of Massachusetts Amherst · UMassAmherst Translation Center · Forbes Library

FIGURE 1-1:
How translation broadens horizons!

Busting Common Translation Misconceptions

People get funny notions in their heads about a lot of things in this world. We still have people walking around who are convinced that Earth is flat, that humans have never landed on the moon, that we use only 10 percent of our brains, and that if you shave hair it grows back thicker.

The world of translation has its own myths as well. In this section, I challenge some of the more common myths and share what you really need to know about translation.

Translation isn't fast, cheap, and easy

Thanks to Google Translate and other free machine translators, translation comes across as being fast, cheap, and easy, but it's none of those. Translation requires knowledge, creativity, and skills, which take tremendous time and effort to acquire. Translation takes time. You can't translate a 30-page document from English to Arabic in a couple hours; depending on the word count, complexity of the document, and many other factors, a translation of that magnitude could take more than a week. Machines and other tools can make the process more efficient, but human translators need to be involved to ensure the quality of the translation and that it was done in a responsible and ethical fashion.

You don't need to know several languages

When you start to tell people that you're a translator, some may ask you right away how many languages you know. To be an excellent translator you need to know a lot about language in general, but you only need to know two languages — the one you're translating *from* and the one you're translating *into*.

REMEMBER

Some people think that the language you need to know better is the one you're translating from because you need to fully understand what you're reading before you can translate it. However, you need to be stronger in the language you're translating *into*. Why? Here are several reasons:

>> When reading the source document, you need to understand everything about it. To achieve that understanding you can consult dictionaries, other texts and resources, and people. You have to do your research. When you're a translator, what usually counts most is the translation or the document you produce so your writing skills in the language of the translation need to be top notch. Reading and understanding are generally easier than writing.

>> To create a translation, you need to understand the cultural context, idioms, and expressions of the target language to write in a way in the translation that makes sense to the target audience and resonates with them.

>> Having a strong command of the target language enables you to create translations that will be effective to your readers.

>> In your stronger language, you have a more robust vocabulary to draw from. When reading something in another language, if you encounter an unfamiliar word, you can look it up.

>> You don't need to catch typos or errors in grammar or spelling in the document you're translating from, but you do need to catch and correct these errors in the translated document you're producing. Keep in mind that it's an effective practice to have another person, who is a qualified editor, review your translation for typos and grammatical errors. Many times you'll know your translation so well, that you won't be able to see the little things.

Being bilingual isn't enough

People often assume that just because someone's bilingual (they know two languages), they can translate. This belief isn't entirely accurate. In fact, in certain situations, translating can be stressful on bilinguals when they don't have the knowledge, training, and experience that go into translation skills. In addition to knowing the source and target languages, translators need skills that include the following:

>> Cultural awareness of both cultures

>> Research skills so that you can find an effective way to make the translation

>> Grammar and writing skills

>> A robust vocabulary — sometimes a highly specialized vocabulary, as is needed in medical, legal, or any other area of specialization

>> Computer skills

>> Attention to detail

>> Time management skills such as planning and scheduling

>> Knowledge of the profession

>> Interpersonal skills to work with colleagues or clients effectively

Translators aren't automatically interpreters

Translators work with written texts. Interpreters translate spoken language from one language to another. Translation and interpreting each requires its own skill set. Being a translator doesn't automatically qualify you to be an interpreter, or vice versa. However, knowing the differences between what translators do and what interpreters do is important because, as a professional, you may be mistaken for an interpreter. You'll have to educate your clients on the differences between the two.

In the previous section I presented the skill set of a translator. An interpreter requires a different skill set that includes the following:

>> Excellent language skills in both the source and the target languages

>> Cultural awareness of both cultures

>> Strong listening skills

>> Oral fluency, or the ability to speak clearly and confidently

>> Decision-making skills

>> Focused concentration

>> Ability to pick up on and understand nonverbal communication in the context of the two cultures

>> Good short-term memory

Translators aren't just walking dictionaries

When you tell people you're a translator they might ask you to translate a single word on the spot. This is not a fair ask of translators because they need to know the context to produce an accurate translation. For instance, if someone asks you to translate the Spanish word *ROSA* without giving you any contextual information, you could translate it as *rose* (the flower), *rose* (the color), *pink* (the color), or *Rose* (the woman's name). And if you found out *ROSA* was a woman's name, you'd probably recommend not translating it because proper nouns usually aren't translated. The range of possible meanings of a single word can be eye-opening to non-translators.

In short, translating words out of context is not what translators do. So testing their translations skills based on throwing random words at them is not fair game. Translators want to know where the words are appearing, why they're being used, and what other words surround them. As a translator, you'll need to educate people that translators translate context instead of words, although words is the material they work with.

Translators can't translate anything and everything

Just because you know a language doesn't mean you're equipped to translate anything and everything written in that language. For example, if you're a German-English translator who specializes in the cosmetic and skin-care industry, you understand very well what's written in German and know how to identify reliable sources if you need to research something. You know the specialized words in English so that you can translate the documents adequately for the English-speaking audience. However, being a translator in the cosmetics and skin-care industry doesn't automatically make you the best choice for translating an Individualized Education Program document for the local school district's Special Education Department. You'd need more of a background in education — more specifically, special education.

Translation transcends loss and impossibility

Have you heard the phrase *lost in translation*? It's an overused phrase implying that whenever something is translated from one language to another, the meaning or clarity is diminished. It seems to be the go-to phrase for news and media headlines to tag events involving multiple languages. Loss does happen in translation. Translation changes everything. You can't convey the full meaning, tone, and cultural nuances of an expression written in one language in another language. Yes, something gets lost, but often something is gained as well. For one, information, ideas, and a text that were not previously accessible to speakers of a given language are made accessible thanks to translation.

Some people say that translation is impossible. This is something we could talk about for hours, but what I want to point out is that these very words, "translation is impossible," don't help non-translators embrace the translation process, one that is needed so that people get information to the access they need and so that our minds can grow. To counter the idea of translation being impossible, I offer the following two insights:

>> Translation is possible because it's been done successfully and continues to enable people to understand one another through texts written in different languages.

>> Language is an imprecise communication medium. Even two people speaking the same language, living in the same home, or working in the same office can have misunderstandings based on the words they use to express what they're thinking. Until humans start communicating telepathically, language will serve as both a bridge and a barrier to communication.

REMEMBER

Maintain a positive attitude about translation. Don't think so much in terms of the limitations but more in terms of possibilities and opportunities. Translation is the key to communication and understanding in a multilingual world.

Imagine a house built with MAGNA-TILES. Now, you're given Legos and told to replicate that MAGNA-TILE house (see Figure 1-2). That's what translating is like. Think of each Lego or tile as a word. In one language, you're working with Legos. In the other language, you're working with tiles. The houses can't possibly be identical, but they can be similar, serve the same basic function, and have some things in common. Thanks to Barcelona-based writer and translator Javier Calvo for introducing the building block metaphor into the world of translation.

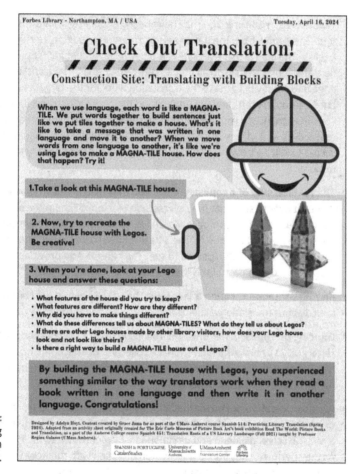

FIGURE 1-2: The building block translation metaphor.

INDIRECT TALK ABOUT TRANSLATION: TRANSLATION METAPHORS AND MORE

Understanding what translation is and what it involves can be difficult until you've studied it and done translations. To describe it in ways that the untrained mind can understand, people have created some descriptive metaphors over the years. Here are a few that may help you conceptualize translation more clearly in your mind:

- **Traduttore, traditore:** You may have heard people say that translators are traitors. This comes from the Italian saying *traduttore, traditore*, or *translator, traitor* in English. The idea is that translation is a betrayal. As change happens in translation, no translation can fully do all that its source text does. The translator uses knowledge and creativity to make the translation work for the target language and audience. Although I can certainly understand the concept of translation as betrayal, I prefer to think of it more as a valuable service, product, and creative and intellectual activity — it makes something accessible to people who would otherwise lack access to it. It's a betrayal if it's done poorly or used intentionally to mislead or misinform.

- **The reverse side of a tapestry:** Have you ever held a tapestry? Have you ever flipped it over to see what the reverse side of it looks like? In the second part of the literary classic *Don Quijote de la Mancha* is a metaphor about translation being like the reverse side of a tapestry. The side intended to be viewed shows the image of what the creator wanted people to see. The reverse side provides a different perspective that is part of the same work.

- **Kissing someone through a lace veil:** The Israeli poet Chaim Nachman Bialik talked about translation as being like kissing a bride through her veil.

- **Dancing on ropes:** In her book *Dancing on Ropes: Translators and the Balance of History* (2021), Anna Aslanyan shares a collection of anecdotes from the world of translation. She presents translators and interpreters as the go-betweens and highlights their key roles in history.

- **An interpretative performance:** When an artist performs in front of an audience or camera or in a recording studio, they're usually following something in writing — a musical score, dialogue and direction in a play or movie script, the lyrics of a song. As they perform, they infuse that written direction with their own interpretation of it, their own background, their unique personality, their training. No two artists deliver an identical performance of the same work. In the same way, two translators could work on the same text and produce different translations. Neither is better than the other, just different.

- **The bridge:** This go-to metaphor for describing translation compares it to a bridge that connects two languages, two cultures, two people.

- **The purest form of writing:** Jason Grunebaum, a writer and Hindi translator, presents translation as the purest form of writing. He says that "no other mode of writing is as exclusively focused on language as translation."

Although these metaphors and indirect talk about translation are helpful to convey a general idea of what translation is and what it's like, more concrete descriptions are necessary for its practical application and for educating people. Only through education can people begin to understand, appreciate, and respect what the translation process entails and the important purpose it serves.

Deciphering Key Translation Terminology

As a translator or future translator, you appreciate the meanings of words. Communicating in any language requires that everyone in the loop have a shared understanding of what the words they're using mean. When you're becoming a translator, you need to know the meanings of a few key terms, such as *source* and *target*, *equivalence*, *localization*, and *translation industry*. In this section I define these terms.

Source

The text you translate is called the *source text*. The language of that text is called the *source language*. If you're translating documents for a school district, you may receive a request to translate a parent handbook from English to Spanish. In this case, the English version of the parent handbook would be the source text, and the source language would be English.

In your process of becoming a translator, you're soon going to realize that translators don't only think critically about the words they translate and the words they select for their translations; they think critically about all words, everywhere! *Source* can be uneasy for translators because it often gives the impression to nontranslators that the translators find all they need to know to create their translation in the source text. The source text doesn't contain everything necessary for the translator to produce a quality translation. Many times, translators need to consult texts and other resources beyond the source text to produce an accurate translation. So the use of *source* may diminish the extent of the work that translators need to do.

Target

The *target language* is the language you're translating into. If you receive a parent handbook from a school district to translate from English into Spanish, the target language is Spanish and your translation will be the target text. Who is your target audience? The Spanish-speaking parents of the school district who will read your translation. You're translating with them in mind as the readers who need to understand the manual.

As you can imagine, although *target* may work as jargon and to communicate with clients and fellow translators, it doesn't sit well with all translators. *Target* implies a selected spot that's the aim of attack or the one well-defined objective. Having a single objective, a bull's-eye, implies that only one translation can hit the mark. In translation, two translators aren't likely to translate a text the same way, and neither translation is the absolute right one; they may be equally good. *Target* doesn't convey the variety that can be produced in translation.

Translators can decide how to translate a word based on its denotation and connotation. A word's *denotation* is its literal meaning. You can think of it as its dictionary definition. A word's *connotation* refers to the feelings and attitudes that the word suggests. The late Gregory Rabassa (1922–2016) translated Latin American literature into English. He translated Gabriel García Márquez's *One Hundred Years of Solitude*. García Márquez was known to say that Rabassa's English translation was better than his Spanish original. Rabassa tried to avoid the jargon of *target* because he was an infantryman, and a target was something you'd aim at with the intention to kill it.

Regardless of the negative connotations that the words *source* and *target* convey, you'll probably encounter them and use them in your training and work experience. Just keep in mind the limitations that these words place on what translation actually is and be prepared to expand your description when necessary and when people are open-minded enough to expand their understanding.

Equivalence

Equivalence, throughout history, has been a word that has been related to the definition of translation. Many definitions of translations express a desire for the target text to be equivalent to the source text. Equivalence as related to translation is heard to define. As a beginning translator, think of it as a concept that is built on the idea that the target text should accurately convey the meaning, style, and intent of a source text. Because languages and their contexts are different, there is no such thing as perfect equivalence. You might hear about different types of equivalence. To achieve whatever type of equivalence it is, a translator aims to make the target text match the source text as closely as possible in form, function, and the impact it has on the reader, despite it being in an entirely different language. Keep in mind, though, that translation isn't a matching game. It is more of a decision-making process.

User manuals and policy documents tend to stay very close to the source text because those source texts are also written in a formulaic way. Texts that are more creative, such as novels, poems, and plays, tend to seek a balance between the meaning of the source text and how to get that meaning across to the target audience by taking some deeper deviations. For example, if you're translating an advertisement, your goal may be to convey the same meaning while triggering a similar emotional response in the viewer. Accomplishing that feat may require bigger changes than you might expect as a beginning translator to a degree that enables you to employ different stylistic techniques to evoke the desired emotion. When this happens, you might hear the term "transcreation."

Most translations go for the communicative approach.

You can view translation as being on a spectrum ranging from literal translation to open and free. At the literal end, you might encounter translations that are done for very specialized readers that are for whatever reason looking for a word-for-word translations. At the free end you encounter translations of more creative works. Most translations fall somewhere in the middle in the *communicative* range.

Keep in mind that a translated document doesn't need to be entirely literal or entirely free. Most translated documents contain a bit of all the types.

Localization

Localization is the process of adapting content, products, or services from one language or culture to another in a way that makes them more appropriate for a specific population. In the context of translations, it's mostly applicable to adapting a translation to a population that speaks a *dialect* (a variation of a standard language), such as Spanish for a Spanish-speaking Puerto Rican audience, French for a French-speaking Haitian audience, or English for an English-speaking audience in Britain. Localization usually includes more than translating a text. It can include considerations of visual content and layout. Translation is just one step in a process to prepare print materials for a given audience. Localization usually involves a team of experts that include translators, consultants, and project managers.

TIP

To look up the differences in the regional usage of specific words, terms, and expressions, check out Diatopix at `olst.ling.umontreal.ca/diatopix`. For example, you can enter **tennis shoes** and **sneakers** and see where these words are used. The tool works for English, French, Portuguese, and Spanish.

Here are a couple other sites where you can gain insight into localization:

>> The MacMillan Dictionary quiz on British and American English at www.onestopenglish.com/kahoot-quizzes/macmillan-dictionary-quizzes-british-or-american-english/1000756.article.

>> *Babbel Magazine's* Argentina Spanish quiz at www.babbel.com/en/magazine/quiz-argentine-spanish.

Translation industry

The *translation industry,* also known as the language industry or the language services industry, refers to the sector of the economy that makes products and provides services for facilitating and enhancing multilingual communication. These services include translation, interpretation, subtitling, dubbing, localization, terminology, editing, technical writing, testing, teaching, and more. It is one of the fastest growing and wealthiest industries in the world. In 2022, its value was estimated to be nearly $67.2 billion.

TIP

On your way to becoming a translator, keep your eye on the translation industry. Check out slator.com, a source of analysis and research for the global translation, localization, and language technology industry. Slator.com hosts SlatorCon, an executive conference; publishes *SlatorPod,* the weekly language industry podcast; and owns LocJobs.com, the language industry talent hub.

IN THIS CHAPTER

» **Recognizing that translators provide access to written content**

» **Appreciating the access that translators give us to others' ideas**

» **Embracing translation as part of diversity, equity, inclusion, and belonging efforts**

» **Understanding the legalities behind the provision of translations in the United States**

» **Promoting translations for stronger communities**

Chapter **2**

Recognizing the Importance of Translators and Their Translations

M any people would agree that translators and translations are important, but they might not be able to readily articulate why that's the case. As a translator, you're going to have to have your reasons lined up and ready to share when you talk about what you do and why you do it.

Translators help people get essential information they need in a language they can fully understand. In doing so, translators also share ideas and knowledge across languages so that these languages survive and thrive. Without translation, each of us would be trapped in the languages we could each read.

When translations are provided it's often because of a legality. At other times, they're provided because it's the right thing to do. Translations are educational and valuable. What's more, just their presence can be meaningful in many ways.

Keeping in mind how translations affect the world and why they matter will help you on your journey to becoming a translator.

In this chapter, I'm going to help you really get behind by providing a foundation on the importance of translation and translators. I'll talk about what translators and translation do for society and how. These are not only aspects of translation that you as a translator need to understand, but that everyone else who works and is part of a multilingual community should understand as well.

Expanding Access to Information and Ideas

In the English-speaking world, translations are often provided because someone doesn't yet have a required language skill. Translations are a necessity for knowing what's going on and what to do or to be independent. Translation is this and more. Translation is also about sharing ideas. In this fast-paced world, translation is often overlooked as an act that allows people to learn about ideas and share knowledge across languages. Ask yourself: what would the world be like without translation?

What's more, because translations are usually made with a specific audience in mind or because they're offered because someone doesn't yet speak a language, the widespread benefits of translation are overlooked. Translations can be for everyone, and in multilingual communities, everyone has the responsibility to care for translation. Understanding this global value of translation will help you as you develop the skills, knowledge, and creativity to become a translator.

Spreading the ideas of people who write in other languages

In many parts of the world and especially in the English-speaking world, translation is often seen as something useful. Translations are made because people who can't yet speak a particular language — often English — need them. Translation is often seen as something to help people who don't yet have the language skill that is necessary to live in a certain place at a certain time. It's all these things. But what often gets overlooked in seeing translation as a necessity that makes essential information available is the multiple dimensions of translation. One of those multiple dimensions is thinking about what translators — especially translators of longer texts that share ideas — contribute to the circulation of ideas.

Translators read a text in one language and then write it in another one, expressing what was said and how it was said, but in a language that's different from the language of the text they read. Why does it matter that people in this world dedicate their working — and often part of their personal — lives to doing this?

There are myriad reasons, and all are important. As you become a translator you should make your own list of reasons. They'll keep you inspired on a low-energy day and help you articulate what it is you do professionally to people who aren't translators or aren't informed about how translation works. But you should plant two key seeds while establishing your garden of translation.

1. Writing is thinking and sharing knowledge and ideas. If you could only read the books written by the people who write in the languages you can read, you would only have access to the knowledge and ideas of people who wrote in those languages. This would mean that you'd never know what people with whom you didn't share a language write about.

   If you didn't read French, for instance, you'd never know how a French-speaking person thought and wrote about the French Revolution. If you didn't read Spanish, you'd never know how a 19th-century Cuban described New York City. If you didn't know Portuguese, you wouldn't know how people from Brazil thought about pedagogy. You'd never get to read the short stories of Haruki Murakami if you didn't read Japanese. If you didn't read English, you'd never get to read the United States of America's Declaration of Independence or Dr. Martin Luther King Jr's "I Have a Dream" speech.

2. If you read English, Spanish, Portuguese, or Chinese, some of the most popular languages in the world, you might think this wouldn't really be a problem because there are a lot of different people with a lot of different views and backgrounds who write in any one of these languages. You'd have a lot to read — enough to last you a lifetime — but you'd still be trapped in your language, and the ideas expressed in that language would still be determined by that language.

   Now think about the people who don't speak one of the popular languages. Danish is an example. If you only spoke Danish (about six million people in the world speak Danish), and you couldn't read any other languages, and if you didn't have translations from other languages into Danish, you might run out of literature to read during your lifetime. The Danish translator Metter Holm, known for her translations of the writing of Japanese writer Haruki Murakami, expresses this well in the film *Dreaming Murakami* by Anjaan Nitesh (2017). Check out *Dreaming Murakami* to get an idea about how literary translators work.

   Any language that doesn't have other languages translated into it might eventually die. It wouldn't get new ideas coming into the language, and the language would keep doing the same things over and over again. It wouldn't develop.

   Figure 2-1 shows commonly spoken languages in the world.

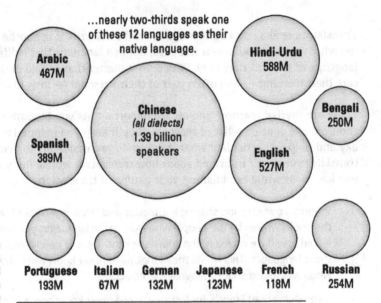

...nearly two-thirds speak one of these 12 languages as their native language.

Arabic 467M

Hindi-Urdu 588M

Chinese *(all dialects)* 1.39 billion speakers

Bengali 250M

Spanish 389M

English 527M

Portuguese 193M

Italian 67M

German 132M

Japanese 123M

French 118M

Russian 254M

FIGURE 2-1: Nearly two-thirds of the world population speaks one of these 12 languages.

Sources: Ulrich Ammon, University of Düsseldorf, Population Reference Bureau
Note: Totals for languages include bilingual speakers.

Providing language access

Translation gives people access to information in a language they can fully understand. In some sectors, such as education and public service, the term *language access* has in some ways replaced the use of the term *translation*. In the US context, when an organization says it provides "language access services" to its clients and community, it's referring to translation, interpreting, and other related language services.

Often language access is provided to fulfill a demonstrated need. These services are offered because an organization knows members of the community who need the information in another language, which is usually a language other than English. They know this because of census information, community connections, or specific requests for the services. Language access is often seen as something an organization must do and as something that's helpful to the non-English-speaking communities.

Offering access to language

Language access is also seen as access to language. Have you ever gone into an office and seen brochures in several languages on display? You might not need those translations or even read those other languages, but their presence does at least show you multiple languages. You might ask yourself, "Which language is that?" or say to yourself, "Oh, that's how you say _____ in Spanish." So even though you're not in need of the services, you get access to other languages because the services are available for someone else.

If you come from a bilingual household or already know multiple languages, you might take such instances for granted. However, if you come from a monolingual English-speaking household, exposure or access to these languages can be inspirational and transformational. As a result, the provision of language access has benefits for society beyond communicating information. It's educational and inspirational for others.

AT-RISK LANGUAGES

There are about 7,000 languages spoken in the world today. UNESCO's Alliance for Linguistic Diversity estimates that about half of the world's spoken languages will disappear by the end of the century. When a language is a lost so is a unique way of expression. In the United States, for example, endangered languages are located along the west coast and on reservations of indigenous people. Globally, the most languages will be lost in the Amazon rain forest, sub-Saharan Africa, Oceania, Australia, and Southeast Asia. For a greater appreciation of how language shapes our lives, check out Victor D. O. Santos picture book *What Makes Us Human* (2024), a celebration of how language connects people around the world. The following figure shows some of the world's at-risk languages.

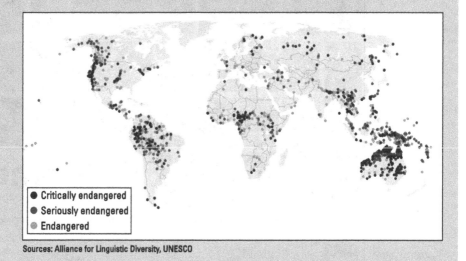

Sources: Alliance for Linguistic Diversity, UNESCO

Don't underestimate the impact of a multilingual welcome sign. Check out an example that I developed through the Translation Center at the University of Massachusetts Amherst (see Figure 2-2).

Supporting Equity, Inclusion, and Belonging

Beyond providing translations because of the need for it, the availability of language access services support equity, inclusion, and belonging efforts in multiple ways. This might be obvious to you because you're interested in language, you know that languages matter, and you're reading this book.

You may or may not be surprised, though, to find out many organizations have advanced equity, inclusion, and belonging efforts but haven't yet given much attention to language as part of those efforts. This can be the case for many possible reasons. As time goes on, language will make its way into these efforts, which will mean more work for translators and other language specialists. Read on for how translations and the work of translators contribute to these efforts.

Leveling the playing field

Translations give all the members of a community access to the same information. Think of a US school community, for example. In that school community, many parents speak English, and some who don't yet speak English need to receive communications in a language other than English. If the school is there to serve everyone in the community but shares communications only in English, the school is only reaching the English-speaking families. Providing translations into all the languages of the community offers an equitable experience for all involved. Everyone is receiving the information, not just the English-speaking families.

The same scenario could be applied to a city's mayoral office communications as well as its museums. Basically, information in one language only provides information to the people who speak that language even though the community might be made up by people who speak a variety of languages.

Another important aspect to think about in terms of equity as related to translation is that all language versions of a document should be released at the same time. In other words, the non-English-language documents shouldn't be released weeks after the English version goes out. Equity means that all people have access to the same information at the same time.

Similarly, the translations need to be quality. It's not always enough to just communicate the message. If a non-English speaker receives a poor translation, they may understand the message, but they will feel like an afterthought because they will pick up on the fact that there was not much effort put into the translation, and that the author figured it was "good enough."

Take a look at the sign on the Neighborhood Free Book Box in Figure 2-3. What do you notice about the English? What do you notice about the Spanish? Does the Spanish-speaking audience have access to the same information as the English-language readers? Is the key information available in both languages? How can you make this sign better?

FIGURE 2-3:
Neighborhood
Free Book Box.

Giving everyone a seat at the table

When information is made available to everyone in a given community, people have a greater sense of belonging because it allows for participation for everyone in all processes, services, and programs.

As an organization actively begins to translate and provide content and communications in multiple languages, the culture of that organization shifts to create a more inclusive approach to initiatives.

Celebrating diversity

When all the community's languages are included, it demonstrates an effort to further acknowledge and celebrate the diversity of a given community.

Celebrating diversity doesn't only have to be about naming where people are from in English or showing a variety of people in print material. It's also about knowing their languages and how those look and sound.

Languages that use the Latin alphabet share a sign with languages written in another script. Many places I've seen in the northeastern United States post these banner welcome signs only in English. Making and printing them in multiple languages is an excellent way to provide access to language. Can you identify places in your community that would benefit from this type of signage?

Preserving and Protecting Legal Rights

In the United States, translation and other language access services are often provided because of some legal framework that requires organizations to do so. This framework can be linked to federal, state, or local mandates.

For example, school districts are required to provide language access services as part of the following mandates:

Equal Education Opportunities Act of 1964

Language Opportunity for Our Kids Act (LOOK Act)

Individuals with Disabilities Education Act (IDEA)

Parental engagement requirements under Title I and III funding

Although, as a translator, you'll encounter several clients that want their material translated just because, it's helpful to keep in mind that legalities can surround the need to translate.

Supporting civil rights

The right to translation and its related services can be interpreted as part of Title VI of the Civil Rights Act of 1964, which prohibits discrimination based on race, color, or national origin by recipients of federal funds. Federal law requires that all providers of federally funded services take steps to ensure language access.

Another significant moment was in 2000, with President Clinton's Executive Order 13166: Improving Access to Services for Persons with Limited English Proficiency. The order specifies that any federal, state, or local agency receiving federal funding must provide everyone "meaningful access" to the programs it supports.

Several pieces of this legal framework work to ensure that people who don't yet speak English have meaningful access to public services. A number of states and local governments have adopted their own laws, ordinances, policies, and plans in an effort to comply with federal regulations. You don't need to know all of these to translate, but they're helpful to be aware of, especially as you develop as a translator.

Promoting language rights and justice

As mentioned earlier, *language access* is a term that has come to substitute *translation* in the broad sense in certain areas. There are two other key terms to be familiar with as you set off on the path to a career dedicated to language.

Language rights is a fascinating topic. It can describe obligations on state authorities to use certain languages in several contexts or not to interfere with an individual's choice to use their language with other people who speak their language. Language rights prohibit discrimination based on language and promote respect toward an individual's linguistic choice. They also preserve the world's linguistic diversity.

Language justice, according to the Community Language Cooperative (https://communitylanguagecoop.com/language-justice/), "is a key practice used in social justice movements in order to create shared power, practice inclusion and dismantle traditional systems of oppression that have traditionally disenfranchised non-English speakers." Through the language justice lens, translation is one of the tools that opens communication and empowers more voices.

Leveraging the Symbolic Value of Language

On your way to becoming a translator, you'll discover that some organizations only want to translate if there's a specific request for translation into a particular language or they know of an identified need for the translation in the community. Both are reasons for providing translations. Translations, though, can be provided proactively, without a specific request, in an effort to promote diversity, equity, inclusion, accessibility, and belonging efforts.

In other words, translation can be provided to show that an organization is interested and open to trying new ways and to reaching out to more people.

The words mean something

You might find that some clients and partners are hesitant to translate because a need for it hasn't been designated or because they're just not sure they have the budget or capacity to keep up with translations of everything. However, as mentioned earlier, proactively going multilingual has benefits. Overall, it signals, especially in places in the English-speaking world, that others are welcome.

Try sharing anecdotes about how this works so that clients or the organizations you work for understand what this looks like. Here's one to start with:

A library in a small city in a rural part of the northeast United States put a multilingual welcome sign outside the front door to the library. Students who were studying at the local college were speaking in another language outside the library and looking at the sign. When a person going into the library asked them which of those languages on the sign was theirs, they responded that none of them were, but they knew they were welcome when they saw the sign.

Translating some material isn't usually seen as a negative move. It's usually seen as an extended hand and an invitation to engage.

If your coworkers, potential clients, and community members aren't swayed by anecdotes or the belief that it opens doors to a wider audience (which should be enough in an ideal world), from an economic standpoint, there are options, too. For those languages where you can prove by the numbers that there is a significant audience, you can invest more in translation efforts. For those languages where there isn't as much data, you can machine translate, leverage translation memories, and do machine translation with post-editing. Machine translation (if done right) can make diversifying languages much more affordable.

Breaking away from all or nothing

As you become a translator and start talking to clients and even friends and family about your work, some might ask you how you decide what to translate. When you're interacting with clients, they might be concerned that they can't yet afford to translate everything or can't translate everything into every language. These are valid concerns.

The translation of everything into all languages at once isn't a likely scenario. The provision of translations and what an organization translates and when are all part of an ongoing process. Translation is about communications, and those develop and transform over time.

As a translator, you can help clients and organizations understand that getting started in some way is the first step, and they can grow from there. It's also helpful to encourage your clients or organizations to be transparent about what they're translating and what their plans are. Sometimes a short message communicating that an organization is committed to offering content in translation and would like feedback from its audience can make a significant impact.

Educating the General Public about Translation

Talk of translation has often been reserved for people who know many languages, for translators, or for the people who need translations. The general public hasn't yet embraced conversations about translation unless, of course, it's when a bad translation was delivered or something humorous happened as a result of translation. This is unfortunate.

As you become a translator, you can support and promote your future profession by educating the layperson on what translation is, how it's done responsibly, and how everyone benefits from translations in circulation. Expanding the conversation about translation to other audiences has the potential to result in more frequently requested and stronger translations.

Going beyond providers and recipients

Before you decided to learn more about becoming a translator, how did you find out about translation? What were the conversations like surrounding translation?

In general, in the United States, conversations about translation have been reserved for the people who provide the service. Bilingual people usually learn about translation as something that can lead to a rewarding profession. Or they're introduced to translation accidentally just because they're bilingual. And then once they learn that translation requires a skill set, they might start to build the skills in that set through courses, workshops, mentorships, and other opportunities.

You might say that talk of translation is for translators. And it is! Translators love to talk about what they do, their doubts, the choices they make, the research they had to do to make a translation, and more.

In addition to translation being the talk of translators, another focus of translation has been on the recipients of translation. Translation has been seen as being for the people who need translations with no widespread acknowledgement of the benefits for others. There's a general sense that if you don't need translations or you're not making them, this really isn't your business.

But now that everyone can see translation icons and options on their screens and more legalities are connected to the provision of language access services, including translation, it's everyone's business to become literate about what translation is, when it needs to be provided, who can provide it, and how they can provide it. Otherwise, lawsuits can emerge as well as the circulation of poorly used and uninteresting language.

It's also part of civic engagement to have people look out for someone who needs translation. For example, in a school setting, you're not only helping a family but also the school itself if you can connect a parent and a school about translation services just as you would let them know about any other needed support groups that exist.

Planning for translation

As you become a translator, you'll notice that the more people know about translation and what it takes to get the job done right, the more they'll plan for it. Planning for translation will make your job as a translator easier for several reasons:

>> Fewer requests will come with an ASAP due date, allowing you to plan better and for your clients to plan better.

>> Because translation will be part of what organizations do and not an afterthought, expectations will be clearer.

For instance, if you know that an organization has planned to translate all its public-facing print material into your target language, you can build word lists and glossaries for them, adjust your translation strategies, and, if necessary, help them adjust their content for translation and a multilingual community.

>> If clients are planning for translation, they'll be able to budget better for translation. That will help them know how many translations to commission in one year. It will also help you know how much work and money is coming from a particular organization and that you can commit to them. Further, it could help your client save money, while translating more. This might be the case if, in the planning, you realize the client keeps translating the same document year after year but with minimal changes.

Perhaps you'll decide not to charge them your full rate, but only what it costs to make the changes. This will free up funding for more translations.

Chapter **3**

Becoming a Professional Translator

t's exciting to think about the words "I want to be a . . . ." They're full of wonder and hope. How will you get to be what you want to be? Which path will you take to get there, and what will you need once you set off on that path?

This chapter helps you sort out the basics of becoming a translator, what you'll need to be one, and all the other things you'll be able to do as a professional.

Choosing Your Path to Becoming a Translator

Once you start sharing with people that you're a translator, they'll probably ask, "How did you become one?" Although each translator has their own unique story and will tell it in their own way, two paths usually lead people to becoming translators. On the first path, people fall into the role because of their circumstances.

On the second path, they know that translating is what they want to do and create a plan to do it. Are you already on one of these paths? How does your story about becoming a translator begin? Will it start with this book?

Accidental paths

If you speak more than one language, you've probably found yourself in one of these situations.

You've been asked how to say something in one of those languages or how to translate a certain word. You probably have lots of questions if you're asked to translate a single word. That's because translators, to make an effective translation, translate context and not individual words, although words are the material translators work with. So translating a single word (which is a silly task) without being able to explain your translation, can make a translator uneasy.

Maybe you were traveling, and you had to translate a restaurant menu for your fellow travelers. Food items can be tricky to translate because they're so tied to culture. A menu in Catalan might say *galtes de porc*. They're pig cheeks. That's no big deal in Catalan, but English speakers usually prefer not to be reminded which part of the animal they're eating. *Fork-tender pork* might be more appealing to a general English-speaking audience, though foodies might be able to stomach the directness of *pork cheeks*.

Maybe you've even been asked to translate some document or form for a family member. Although it might not contain long sentences or poetic language, the document or form can be challenging because of the technical terms it includes or another culture's way of organizing and asking for information. On top of that, you have the pressure of the document being a form, which can be somewhat of an official collection of information.

It's not unusual for people to call on an individual's bilingual skills to help navigate the multilingual world. It's also not usual for these asks to happen on a larger scale. In the workplace, especially in the United States, bilinguals or people who haven't even yet reached professional bilingual status are called upon to translate all sorts of documents, from fliers and letters to signs and handbooks. This is a big task if you're untrained, and it's not a responsible way to produce translations in a professional setting.

In the best-case scenario, individuals asked to casually carry out the role of the translator eventually receive the education and preparation they need to responsibly do the job, and get properly compensated for it. These people go on to become professional translators. A path like this or a similar one is what might be considered an accidental path. It's a path that took you somewhere you didn't expect to go.

LITERARY TRANSLATOR, EDITH GROSSMAN

Edith Grossman was an American translator who was born in 1936 and died in 2023. She wrote a book called *Why Translation Matters*, which was published by Yale University Press in 2010. I hope you'll read on your way to becoming a translator. In the opening pages she shares a bit about her journey to becoming a literary translator. Even if you don't want to become a literary translator, you'll still find her story curious and inspiring.

"When I was young — a high school student — it was not my intention to become a translator. I knew I wanted to learn languages and had a vague idea about being an interpreter. (I wasn't quite sure what the difference between the two professions was, but interpreting sounded more exciting; it suggested travel, exotic places, important events, world-shaking conferences at the United Nations.) As an undergraduate at the University of Pennsylvania, I changed direction and decided my ambition was to be a literary critic and scholar, even though, operating under the mistaken assumption that apparently simple poetry was simple to translate, I do recall submitting a few poems by Juan Ramón Jiménez and, if I remember correctly, Gustavo Adolfo Bécquer, to the campus literary magazine. I embarked on an academic career, served my time in several graduate schools, and moved from a focus on medieval and baroque to peninsular verse, first the Galicia-Portuguese love lyrics and then the sonnets of Francisco de Quevedo, to contemporary Latin American poetry, a change brought about by my first reading of works by Pablo Neruda, and soon after that César Vallejo. (I came on this stunning poetry fairly late in my student career: I have no memory or reading any Latin American literature written after the Mexican Revolution until I made the cross-country trek to Berkeley.) Neruda's *Residencia en la tierra* in particular was a revelation that altered radically the professional direction I followed and actually changed the tenor of my life. It elucidated for me, as if for the first time, the possibilities of poetry in a contemporary environment. Above all, it underscored the central position of Latin America in the literature of the world, its impact made possible and even more telling by means of translation.

I began teaching while I was a graduate student, and then continued giving classes full-time when I moved back east and enrolled in New York University. During most of this time I was thinking more about my dissertation than about translation. But one day Ronald Christ, a friend who edited the magazine *Review*, the publication of the organization once called the Center for Inter-American Relations and now known as the Americas Society, asked me to translate a story by the Argentine Macedonio Fernández, a writer of the generation just before Borges. I said I was a critic, not a translator, and he said that might be true, but he thought I could do a good job with the piece. I agreed to translate it, more out of curiosity about its wildly eccentric author and the process of translation than for any other reason. I discovered to my surprise that I not only enjoyed the work more than I had imagined but could do it at home, an arrangement that seemed very attractive then, and still does.

(continued)

(continued)

My translation of Macedonio's "The Surgery of Psychic Removal" was published in *Review* in 1973. From that time on, I moonlighted as a translator of poetry and fiction in a fairly regular way while I sunlighted as a college instructor until 1990, when I left teaching to devote myself full-time to translation. I have been a visiting professor several times since then, and when I am not teaching I miss being in a classroom and talking to students, but my main concentration and professional focus have been on translation. And I have been very fortunate: I have liked, and often loved, practically every piece of writing I have brought over into English, and after all these years I still find the work intriguing, mysterious, and endlessly challenging."

Translators in schools

Not only to individuals accidentally become translators, but so do groups of people because of an emerging need or attention to an issue that needs a certain kind of support. In the recent years, schools in the United States have been turning their attention more and more to the fact that parents prefer or need to communicate in a language other than English when it comes to engaging with the school. Spoken-language interpreters are needed in school meetings and translators are needed to translate documents from English into the other languages of the school. School often call upon their bilingual employees to serve as interpreters and translate documents without verifying if those employees are trained interpreters and translators. Many times, they are not. Thus, the school or another supporting organization will begin to offer interpreter and translator training to the employees depending on their language skills. Eventually these employees become trained interpreters and translators, improving their schools' language access efforts, and some will continue to provide language services outside the schools they work in.

Intentional paths

On this path, you decide at some point to be a translator and then plan to go after that goal. What happens on that path will depend on your circumstances, including your location, your available financial and educational resources, and the point in your professional trajectory during which you choose to get on the path to becoming a translator. You can choose to formally study languages and translation throughout all your degree programs. You can specialize in an area as an undergraduate and then go on for a graduate degree that allows you to study translation. You can study other things and then be intentional about finding opportunities to practice translating and get involved with a community of translators. There's not one single way to do it.

Developing your languages

Arabic, English, Chinese, Portuguese, Spanish. Whatever your working languages may be, do all you can to be regularly reading, listening to, and writing in your working languages. Listen to the radio and podcasts. Watch television shows and movies. Read the newspaper, magazines, and books. Eavesdrop on the bus and train. It will be most important to do the listening and writing in your target language because it's the language you need to produce writing in. If you're a high school student, study your languages by taking whatever classes are available at your school or local language school, if your location has one. Sometimes colleges allow high school students into their language courses. And if you're a college student, take language, literature, and culture courses. If you're not a student, keep in touch with your languages any way you can. Enroll in language courses in local language schools and seek other continuing-education opportunities. Set your phone in a foreign language and/or add an additional keyboard. If you have autocorrect on, this can help you improve your spelling, especially in languages like French. Ever since I added a French keyboard to my phone, I noticed that Q takes the place of A. I subsequently noticed more typos in text messages such as "Hqhqhq" and was able to realize that the sender meant to write "Hahaha," but had their French keyboard enabled.

Learning about translation

While you keep in touch with your languages, you'll also have to plan for how you're going to study translation. If your college years are still ahead of you, choose a college that offers some kind of translation programming, or make your own plan that combines the study of language with some courses on translation. If your college years are behind you, look into graduate or certificate programs.

Wherever you find yourself, always remember that you need to develop your language skills in addition to developing your translation skills and knowledge of the field. Following the resources in Part 5 will help you keep in touch with the many aspects of the profession.

Once you realize you're on a path to becoming a translator, one of the first things you can do is look for a mentor. A good mentor might be a professional translator or someone who often works with translators.

Whether it be the accidental or the intentional path, neither has an end. Translators, like other professionals, need to invest in professional development throughout their careers to be successful.

Mastering Two Essential Skills: Reading and Writing

Translators read a text in one language and then write it in another. They can't say it's the same text because it's written in another language, and languages aren't the same. Rather, it's a translation. Translators create the translation by reading the text and fully understanding it. Then they write it in another language. Their ability to do what it takes to fully comprehend the text and re-create it in another language determines the strength of the translation. You'll need to love reading and writing to become a translator.

Developing an intimate knowledge of the source text

As a translator, you need to read the source text and understand it completely. You have to resolve any doubts about the words and content. To do that you need to do research, including talking to other people. There's no set formula or list of places to go to figure out translation problems. Each translation will present its own set of problems. You use your knowledge and creativity to find solutions, which makes translation fun. Remember: you can't effectively translate anything you don't fully understand. Knowledge of the source text is a must!

As a translator, you don't need to comprehend only what's written, or the content. You also need to pay attention to *how* it's written. How is the language crafted so that the message is effective?

>> **What's the register?** *Register* in language refers to the way a speaker uses languages differently in different circumstances. An email to a friend isn't going to be the same as a cover letter for a job application. If the source text uses more of a formal register, as a translator, you need to identify that and figure out how to do that in your translation. If the text is trying to reach an audience of a certain age, you'll want to make sure your translation does the same thing.

>> **What's the tone?** What's the tone or attitude of the text? Is it motivational, informative, or sarcastic? Detect what the tone is, and keep that going in the translation.

>> **Is there repetition?** Does the text repeat certain words or sounds? Is that repetition effective, and will you need to keep it going in the translation?

In addition to caring about how the message is communicated, as a translator you need to care about how it looks. If the layout is done using desktop publishing, do you have the skills to replicate that in some way in the translation? If not, you'll need to point that out to the client or requestor of the translation and plan how to get it done. The client might take care of it, or you could team up with another professional. Keep in mind that if you commit to dealing with layout issues as the translator, and the issues are significant, you need to charge for them.

If you're working with computer-assisted translation tools, known as CAT tools, many of them can also help with formatting, as they can maintain the majority of a document's format from upload of a job to download of the completed file.

One more thing I want you to know about translator's relationship with the source text is that some translators translate from languages they don't yet know. This sounds wild but it does happen. They do this by relying on others to speak to them about the text. They ask others questions about the source text. This is not usual and mostly happens with literary texts. Translation isn't just about knowing two different languages. It's also knowing about translation.

Understanding why directionality matters

The term directionality is used when translators talk about the direction of transfer. As a translator, are you translating away from or into your dominant language? What languages do you know? What language do you feel most comfortable writing in? How confident are you writing in that language? Comfortable and confident don't always mean the same thing. Translating is a good test of how well you write in a language.

When you begin to tell people that you're a translator and that you translate from Portuguese to English, their immediate reaction might be, "Wow, you must know Portuguese really well!" Sure, of course, you'll know Portuguese well. But what they might not realize is how well you need to know English as a Portuguese-to-English translator. Translators usually translate into their stronger language.

You might have heard that you should translate into your mother tongue or your native language. This language is probably the one you grew up speaking at home and then were schooled in that language, and speak and write in that language most of your days.

However, it's not unheard of for translators to translate into languages that aren't their mother tongue or their native or dominant language. This is sometimes called *inverse translation*, *reverse translation*, or *service translation*.

If you grew up as a bilingual or multilingual person, your stronger language is probably the one you heard in school. Remember, translation is about writing, so you need to think about which language is your stronger writing language.

If you've always lived a bilingual life at home and at school, then determining which language you're strongest writing in might not be so straightforward. First of all, congratulations for living bilingually! And don't worry about what that means for how you will determine which language you translate into. With professional preparation, you'll become aware of how to translate responsibly so you'll know your limitations and where and when you need to seek additional support. Professional translators look things up and ask for support.

Also keep in mind that translation has a process and allows you to work with tools. Mastering the process, using tools, collaborating with other professionals, and investing in professional development will help you produce quality translations no matter which direction you're translating to.

Developing the skills to write well

Most people can write, but not everyone can write well. Writing well not only means knowing the conventions of writing in the target language but having a range of vocabulary and knowledge in that language. Although the industry to which translators belong is growing, the competition is tough and no client wants to pay for poorly translated documents filled with typos and grammatical errors. Omitting a single period or spelling a word incorrectly might cost you a job and a client. Most of the time you're not granted a second chance. As a professional translator, take note of the aspects of writing to pay attention to, as spelled out in the next four sections.

Audience and tone

Recognize who the audience is and how they need to be addressed. When addressing the identified audience, are there certain expectations regarding the use of language? If it's a letter from a doctor going out to patients of a medical practice, the language might do one thing to communicate guidelines to the recipients. If it's a persuasive announcement from a local politician during election season, the language and use of the words require a different approach than the doctor's letter. Knowing how to write for different audiences is an important skill for a translator. Knowing how to create the right tone for a certain text through language is also something you'll need to know how to do in writing. You can improve your ability to do these things by reading a variety of texts in your target language. Pay attention not only to what the texts are saying but how the texts use language to communicate the message.

Punctuation and capitalization

The sentences "It's time to eat, Grandma!" and "It's time to eat Grandma!" use the same words but have completely different meanings. A single comma makes all the difference. Solid ideas expressed with the right words can only go so far if you don't know the writing conventions of a language. In addition to punctuation, this also includes the mechanics of writing, like how to use capitals. Not all languages treat the names of days of the week, months, and holidays the same. In English, the first letter of the months of the year are capitalized. In Spanish, they're not. You might see documents — even ones that aren't translations — with the months capitalized. Just because things are written doesn't mean they're correct. This could happen because of interference with the English language. But it's a detail that could cost you a job.

It's important to study the punctuation rules of your source language or languages as well. For example, Spanish is very similar to English with comma and quotation use, but there are some key differences that are important to keep in mind. Once again, it goes back to being an expert in your working languages.

Grammar and spelling

As a translator you'll need to be a solid speller. For example, you can't use *your* when you need to write *you're*. Do you know the difference between *its* and *it's*? How about between *affect* and *effect*? Or *every day* and *everyday*? Knowing what each one means and how to use it is a must for translators. The spell-check feature of a word processing program won't necessarily catch all spelling errors, especially when the spelling is correct but the usage is wrong. It usually takes a human to detect all the errors.

As a translator you also need to manage well other aspects of grammar, such as subject/verb agreement — "The group walks to the park" — and the passive voice versus the active voice. In some languages the passive voice is more acceptable than in others. English tends to prefer the active voice, such as "The committee is planning a party" instead of "A party is being planned by the committee." Once again, use of the passive voice isn't technically wrong grammatically, so an automated program might not flag that the active voice is preferred in English.

Vocabulary and cultural knowledge

Because translators choose the words of their translations, the larger a translator's vocabulary is, the more there will be to choose from without having to look up every single word in the dictionary or the thesaurus. Translators must be able to detect the difference between, for example, *choose*, *select*, and *opt for*. The context will let them know which word is best.

The best translators usually always have a thesaurus open just in case. English tends to repeat words a lot more than in Spanish, for example. Translators usually want to do everything they can to vary language in Spanish in order to avoid repeating words while always staying true to the meaning.

Go the extra mile, butterflies in my stomach, and once in a blue moon are examples of idiomatic expressions that translators need to be aware of as they work. You'll have to be able to detect them in the source text, know what they mean, and then find an idiomatic expression in the target language that does something similar or find other ways to be creative with language. Translators are wordsmiths!

To be an effective translator, you have to meet at least some of the expectations of the readers of your target language. When a translation doesn't do that, it can be distracting for readers, and they'll be paying attention to aspects of language instead of the content.

You can improve your writing by reading. Read as much as you can in your target language, especially the kinds of texts you want to translate. And also leave time to read in your source languages. Remember you're training to be a word expert!

If you know that you have a weakness in any areas of writing, rely on the support of others. In the translation process, after you translate the text, there's an editing and a proofreading step. You might consider working with others to do these tasks for you, especially when it comes to assignments that have a tight turnaround time. The intimate relationship you develop with the text you're translating might blind you about some mechanical issues of language. Always make a sound plan to review your work.

Procuring Essential Tools and Resources

Setting yourself up to be a translator is exciting. Although knowledge of your language doesn't take up much physical space, you'll want to pull together tools and resources as you get started. Pay attention to them as you grow as a professional.

Space

If you're an independent, or freelance, translator, you'll benefit from identifying a space to work. Most translators don't meet in person with clients in an office on a regular basis; they handle most of the work via email or other online methods. This means you don't need to have an office space where you'll receive clients. This could, of course, change over time. Your designated workspace can be part of a co-working space in your town or city if you work best when you're not at home. If you do plan to set up your office in your home, try to have a spot that is all yours where you can work comfortably for long hours in front of the computer. A door is also nice so that you can close it if you need privacy while you're working to meet a deadline or have a video call with a client. Ideally, you'll use the space exclusively for your work.

If you work as a full-time translator for an organization or you have a job that requires that you translate on occasion, you need to have a designated space where you can do your translation work undisturbed. If you're trying to meet a deadline for a translation assignment and you're also the family liaison in a local school district, for example, it will be challenging if not impossible to get a translation assignment done if people are interrupting you to complete other tasks. Going to your translator space will let your coworkers know that you're dedicating your time to that task.

Equipment and access to resources

Once you've identified where you'll do your work, you're going to have to be sure you have a stable and strong internet connection. You'll need the internet for checking email, having video meetings, accessing tools, and searching openly on the internet for information as you create your translation solutions.

If you're working as a translator for an organization, be sure that there aren't restrictions on your ability to do research on the internet. Many times you'll be checking webpages in other languages. These don't always make it through security features set up on an organization's computers.

Having access to a printer will also be helpful. Depending on the assignment, some translators find it necessary to print a hard copy as part of their review process.

Having a second monitor also makes looking at multiple documents easier.

And because translators spend a lot of time at a computer, consider looking into a height-adjustable desk and a comfortable chair.

Translation tools

In addition to your computer, office furniture, and some dictionaries, you'll want tools that are designed specifically for translators. Keep an eye on what the market puts out and what other translators recommend. Investment in a translation memory database can save you time and identify repeated terms, which can offer consistency when you're working on a large project. Translation memory is a database that pairs segments of texts in the source language with their counterparts in the target language. You, as the translator, need to build the memory. Over time, you'll enrich the database with new content.

It's worth asking any language service provider you work for whether or not they have term bases, too. This can help clarify how they want you to translate certain terms, when multiple translations may exist, as well as define the term and give you more context so that you can better understand the source text.

Style guides are often a resource to look out for. Some organizations might have their own translation style guides for identified languages. Organizations develop these style guides to help translators know how the organization represents itself visually and textually. They identify preferred language elements, such as how to write dates and times.

Planning and time

You'll need to plan well how long an assignment will take you. Be realistic with your estimate. If you don't have the time, you can't produce an effective and complete translation. Although each project requires its own solutions, at the beginning stages of your career, try to track your time so that you'll know how to plan and how much time certain texts will take to translate. Whether you're an independent, freelance translator or working for an organization, having a sense of how long translation takes will allow you to share realistic expectations with clients and colleagues.

Financial support

If you haven't inherited a fortune, you'll need to consider how much you need to earn as a professional translator and what kind of work it's going to take to get you to that level of income. You'll need clients who pay you according to the agreed-upon terms.

Mentors and colleagues

Although translators spend a good amount of time working alone, they need colleagues and mentors to help them get the job done. Make an effort to meet other translators through professional organizations or classes that you might take. You'll want to bounce ideas off them. Having a mentor will also help you navigate your career growth and goals as a translator.

Advocates and allies

If you're a translator for an organization, it'll be important to have advocates and allies. These are coworkers who understand what you do and what you need to do it well. Maybe they've even read this book! They'll spread translation education throughout the organization and look out for you to make sure the translation requests aren't unrealistic.

Texts to translate

Finally, to be a translator you need texts to translate. Where might you get them? If you're working on your own, it'll probably take some time to establish a client base. If you're at an organization or an agency, you'll be given texts. The trickiest part in this scenario could be managing your time and making sure the expectations are clear about what you can translate (if the organization you work for gives you texts to translate, you might not be qualified just yet to translate all of them) and how long it's going to take.

Taking a Proactive Approach

For most organizations, translation is an afterthought. This means that they've worked hard to make the source text just as it should be, perhaps taking three full weeks to do so, and then expect the translation to be created in less than 24 hours. Other times, even though translations are needed, that step is completely absent from the project timeline.

Neither of those scenarios creates favorable conditions for effective or high-quality translations. Remind your clients to share details of the project with you from its conception. This can help you as a translator to plan, get in the mindset, and identify any possible resources that you'll need to consult for the translation.

Getting involved from the start of a project

Translators have a certain vision of the world. They see it as a multilingual place. This is often something that non-translator authors of texts don't have present when they're writing. Translators can detect the difficulties and time expectations, and weigh in on whether the content works for the intended audience.

For instance, maybe you're translating for a school and you receive an assignment that consists of translating a flier about a book club for parents that is intended to strengthen connections among parents. The target languages are Portuguese and Spanish. However, you notice that all the books that are part of this book club have never been translated into Spanish or Portuguese. You wonder how the book club will then be appealing to those target audiences if they might not be able to read the books in their preferred language. If you'd been involved with the organization of the event from the get-go, you might have suggested a book that was available in all three languages or thought of a completely different event to bring parents together.

You also noticed that the flier didn't indicate whether interpreters would be available at the event. Because of your translator's vision of a multilingual world, you would have suggested that that info be added to the flier and planned for.

In short, even though the translation might not take place until later on in the process of document creation, it can be effective to have you involved from the start.

Knowing the intended use of the translation

Knowing how a translation will be used will help you offer the best services. For example, if a document translated into Chinese is to be posted on a website and the website is in English, will Chinese readers know how to get to the translation? This is something you'll need to point out to your clients.

If a museum translates an exhibition text into Haitian Creole and then never advertises or promotes in Haitian Creole that the exhibition is available, how will the members of the Haitian Creole-speaking community know that the exhibition is accessible to them? Connecting all these dots and identifying the gaps are things that you as a translator will be able to help your clients with.

Doing More Than Translation

As a professional translator, you won't just translate. Even if you could just translate, it's complex work. On the one hand, translators, because not much is known about translation and the profession, are often called upon to perform tasks beyond just translating. On the other hand, as translators' skills develop and their experience grows, they learn of other professional tasks that they can offer to the world.

Writing your own texts

To contribute to educating audiences on the work of translators and advocating for your profession, you could write blogs, articles, and even books about translation. You might not get paid for your writing, but you could get recognition and additional clients. Writing will also be your own opportunity to think through some of the things in your profession.

Educating clients

Translators always find themselves educating their clients on what translators do and how translation works. Here are the things you'll find yourself repeating over and over again:

>> **Translating and interpreting are different.** Many who approach you will request a translator when they really need an interpreter:

"Oh, I need an interpreter and not a translator!"

"Yes, you're looking for someone to provide consecutive interpretation during a meeting between a teacher and a parent."

>> **Translation takes time.** Many more will ask, "Why does translation take so long? I need it sooner." Pointing out to clients that you'll need to write an Arabic version of their 30-page document that took them three months to compose will give them perspective on why their overnight deadline won't work for you as the translator.

>> **The translation should be as good as the original.** When clients need translations in a rush, they might tell you that "it *doesn't* need to be as good as the English. It just needs to get the point across." While you want to please your clients or whoever requested the translation, you still might need to help them understand that the recipients of the translation deserve a text that is just as strong as the original. Public service documents and documents from community organizations should all be of the same quality because it's the equitable thing to do.

>> **Discuss the different dialects of the given language.** Some clients will know that a language has several dialects, but they might not know how to talk about them. Unfortunately, they might use vocabulary that suggests that one dialect is better than another. Help them give you as many details as they can about their target audience so that you can help them determine which dialect of the language would work best for their project.

>> **Receive files in an editable format.** Clients will often send you PDFs. Although you can convert them to Word or another easily editable format, it's much easier if you can get those files in editable format from the start.

As you grow as a professional, it's helpful to keep a list of the things you find yourself repeating to clients so that you don't have to write them over and over again.

Advocating

Since you see the world through the eyes of a translator, you'll be able to detect when translators aren't recognized or treated fairly. You'll also be able to spot when an audience needs translation and when the quality of translations needs to improve. With translation, it is not the thought that counts. Translations need to be done well! You'll probably want to speak up in defense of translators and translation when there is room for improvement.

>> **For translators:** Although the work of translators is all around, it's work that goes unnoticed and taken for granted. Translators' names are often left off the covers of books, and in general translators aren't compensated enough. Advocating for more recognition and better professional conditions is part of your job as a translator. You can do this through small regular efforts and by joining professional organizations to work collectively toward improved conditions.

>> **For audiences:** You might also find yourself advocating for better professional services for intended recipients of translations. This could especially be the case if you work for an organization that wants to translate material for a certain audience and you realize that the organization isn't using professional services.

Teaching

Once you gain a certain level of experience and expertise, you might find that you're prepared to teach translation. You could look for teaching opportunities at established institutions such as community colleges, four-year colleges, and universities. There might be opportunities as an adjunct or a full-time instructor. Your local high school might even be looking for a translator to teach an elective. Some translators offer their own online or in-person educational opportunities. Perhaps you'll decide to go for something on your own, such as teaching a customized class for an organization or at a community center. This is another service you can charge for as a professional.

Editing

As a translator you learn how to pay attention to and use every word precisely. These skills also lend themselves to editing and proofreading translated texts, which is another service you can charge for. These edits might be translations from other translators, translations from clients, or edits in the language you usually translate into.

Educating and advocating are tasks that you'll often find yourself doing as a translator. Teaching, writing, and editing are activities that you might eventually grow into and use to further promote yourself and expand your services.

2

Getting Your Head in the Game: Education and Training

IN THIS CHAPTER

» Making reading and writing priorities

» Handling multiple dialects and cultures within a language

» Selecting what you read and write with purpose to build content and translation knowledge

» Building research, technical, and people skills to work smarter

» Using your translator skills to make a greater impact in other fields

Chapter **4**

Building Your Skill Set

There's a widespread misconception that anyone who speaks two languages can translate between them. "Oh, great, you know Chinese. Can you translate this birth certificate from Chinese to English?" Most people aren't aware of all the other skills that translators need to be efficient, effective, and responsible translators. To translate professionally, you need to be aware of and develop the skill set of a translator, which goes beyond knowing two languages.

As you gain a certain level of experience as a translator, you'll notice that you see the world through the lens of the translator. Through this lens you see how, in a multilingual community, translation can't be an afterthought; it needs to be on the radar of all organizations, from the initiation of programming, if it is to have a meaningful reach. Therefore, your translator skill set is even more valuable than the translations themselves.

And one of the most rewarding parts of being a translator is that you'll see that your skill set and your translator's lens have the potential to transform a number of fields, from healthcare and education to literature and the arts.

In this chapter, I'll present you with the skills of translators and how to develop them. They range from linguistic and cultural knowledge, reading and writing skills, translation and content knowledge to research, technical, and people skills.

I'll also let you know about how those skills can be applied to other fields. Just like translators never just translate, your translator skills aren't just for translating. They will shape the kind of professional and person you are and will benefit other professional fields that you might be interested in.

Knowing the Language and Understanding the Culture

To become a translator, you do need to know at least two languages, but that doesn't mean just speaking the languages. Translators technically don't even need to speak at all. They read and they write. What's more, to be a translator you don't need to know each of your languages in the same way. For your language pair, you need to be a sharp reader of the language you translate from, the source languages, and an excellent writer of the language you translate into, the target languages.

It might come as a surprise to you that you don't need to be an excellent writer in both languages. But you do need to know the languages well. You need to be aware of how they work. That happens by constantly being in touch with your languages. You need to read them, listen to them, and identify valuable resources in them as often as you can.

Along with knowing the languages well, you need to know about their cultures. You can gain part of that cultural knowledge by reading and listening. Reading the newspaper regularly is a great way to stay abreast. In addition, you need to watch television, movies, and other programming in your languages. You also need to have networks of individuals who are anchored in those cultures so that you can turn to them when you have questions while you're translating.

If you work with a language that has many speakers, such as English, Spanish, or Portuguese, you don't need to be an expert on all there is to know about English-speaking cultures. Nor do you need to be an expert on every single Spanish-speaking country. You need to choose an area to focus on, even if it's a general one.

As a translator, because you need to find answers to any doubts you have, you learn to ask questions. Those questions will help you gauge your cultural and linguistic knowledge and help you determine what you can and can't translate.

Naturally, over time, you'll gain experience, and through that you'll learn which areas are your strengths and where you'd like to focus. You'll also build a network and fill up your toolbox. Your network and tools will help you build your linguistic and cultural knowledge, and they'll be what you use to dive deeper into the text you're translating or try out what might or might not work for your translation.

Developing reading and writing skills

Translators read a text in one language and write it in another. Translation is primarily about reading and writing. Do you need to be able to do both things equally well in both languages?

No. You do need to fully understand the text you're reading and translating, which means you need linguistic and cultural knowledge to help you do that. But you don't need to write in the language you're translating from. You need to write in the language you're translating into. So, the language you're translating into needs to be one in which you're a strong writer.

>> **Reading:** You need to be a careful reader of the language or languages you translate from. You need to pay attention to every detail, including punctuation and research anything you're not completely sure of. When you do your research, you need to be convinced of the responses you find and, in some cases, look at more than one resource to verify them. You need to ask questions about the text you're going to translate.

Sometimes that requires you to talk to other people about the text and to thoroughly research a topic or the use of a word. The paths that a single text can lead you down might surprise you. That's what's fun about translation — you learn about a variety of topics. You can't effectively translate a text that you don't fully understand.

>> **Writing:** You need to have strong writing skills in the language you're translating into to be a successful translator. Accent marks, capitalization rules, punctuation norms, formatting expectations — all of that is part of being a strong writer in the language you're translating into.

As a translator you're taking all that an existing text contains and how it's expressed and writing it in another language. To transform that reading into writing effectively and efficiently, you need to have a lot of tools in your translation language (your target language) toolbox to manipulate the language and to find the best way to express in that second language what you read in the first one.

You can customize your toolbox. It can include dictionaries, thesauruses, glossaries, word lists, books, computers, websites, phone numbers of colleagues and others in your network, a list of podcasts, translation memory tools and more.

There is really no limit to what you have in there. It's what you need to do your work. It'll grow as you go. Some tools will get more use than others.

A well-stocked toolbox will help you test out different words and determine which one will work best for a specific translation project. You need to know why you choose the words you do and, at some times, why you didn't choose other words. That's something you might not always let your readers or clients know, but it's something you'll carry with you as you translate the text.

So how do you develop your writing skills? Read in the language you translate into. Read the types of texts you'd like to translate. If you'd like to translate novels into English, read as many novels as you can in English.

If you'd like to translate museum guides into Spanish, read existing museums guides in Spanish, preferably ones that originate in Spanish and from Spanish-speaking countries. If you want to translate human resources documents into Portuguese, read similar documents in Portuguese. You want to know your working languages inside out.

TIP

Another task you can do to practice your writing skills is copy texts in the target language. If you want to focus on financial documents for banks, for example, find a text related to the subject area in your target language and copy it. No translation is required; just type the text again. It might sound like a useless exercise, but it will help you absorb the language of that text.

One more thing you can do to improve your writing skills: translate, translate, translate, even if it's not an assigned project. Practice improves your writing skills and gives you pressure-free time to devote to their development. Through that experience, you can also figure out if a type of text you thought you'd like to translate really is one that you enjoy. The best part? You can stop whenever you'd like.

Exploring dialects and language variations

When it comes to translation, which dialectal variety of a language to use can be a big question. Languages have *dialects* that usually signal where a person is from. With English, you can think about American English and British English, and just within the United States you can think about New Jersey English, New England English, and Georgia English.

In some regions of the United States, footwear such as Nikes are called *sneakers*, and in other regions they're called *tennis shoes*.

In the United States, which has many Spanish speakers from all parts of the Spanish-speaking world, often in the same communities, it can be hard to know which dialect to use. As a language professional, you want to reassure your clients and organizations that it's possible to produce a translation that all Spanish speakers will understand.

Yes, the different dialects can seem distinct, and they are, but those who can speak Spanish can usually understand each other. Remember that the documents you translate are attached to contexts. Those contexts will also inform your readers about what the content says.

One of the first things you can do as a translator when addressing dialect choice is to help your clients and organizations move away from saying things like the "correct" Spanish, or the "correct" any language for that matter. No Spanish-speaking country in general speaks Spanish better than any other.

Instead, you want to move into a conversation about knowing more about the audience. Is it a translation that's going to be released to anyone anywhere who speaks Spanish? Is it a translation for museum labels at a museum in a specific city where the majority of Spanish speakers are from Puerto Rico? Once the translator has this information, they'll be able to know if they're the translator for the job and how to do it professionally.

If it's a document for a general audience, don't necessarily aim to write in a "neutral Spanish" because no one's language is completely neutral. Instead, try to make word choices that you know most Spanish speakers will understand. As a language professional, you have an idea of which words apply to a specific audience and which ones don't. Go for language that will be as inclusive as possible.

REMEMBER

As a translator you'll have a network. If your Spanish is from Mexico but you're working on a project that's for a general audience, run your translation by Spanish speakers from other areas of the Spanish-speaking world to make sure the document is accessible to them and to ensure it doesn't include any words that might be offensive.

Keep accessibility in mind. Think about how accessible your document is to the intended audience. If you're translating a school document for a community that's mostly from El Salvador, you might want to use words that are familiar to them as a welcoming gesture and to acknowledge the linguistic landscape of the community, while being accessible to the other Spanish speakers in the community.

In certain texts, you might also be able to call attention to the dialectal varieties of a language by including the different options for certain words. Not all projects will allow for this, which might be seen as a creative act, but some will let it in.

As a translator, when appropriate, inform your clients and organization that dialects can learn from each other. Although the text might not include every word that the reader would readily use, readers can be open to learning how speakers of different dialects would refer to something. Through translation, readers can learn about other communities that they share the same language with.

A few more things to keep in mind. Professional translators should know how to respond to general questions about the treatment of dialects. On your way to becoming a professional translator, lean on your network to answer certain questions you might not be sure of, and look for professional development opportunities to learn more about the treatment of dialects.

Also keep in mind that each project will present its own possibilities. What works in one situation might not work in another, so be flexible with yourself.

You might think that languages beyond those you work with are none of your business. That's not true. As a language professional, your clients or your organization will look to you not only to produce a translation but to answer questions about language in general. So educate yourself about dialects. Find out where the different language communities in your area are from. And if one day you're running an operation that translates into more than one language, you'll want to have that knowledge.

Knowing What You Need to Know — Beyond a Second Language

Now, beyond knowing languages and how to use them, what other skills does a translator need to have? Many people will be surprised by that question because they don't think translators need any other skills besides the ability to say things in two different languages. But there's more you need to know to become a translator and to practice translation effectively and efficiently.

Building your translation knowledge

Beyond knowing two languages, to be a translator, you need to know about translation. This means a general understanding of theory and the issues that practicing translators face.

WARNING

You might meet professional translators who express little interest or need for the theories of translation. You might eventually end up with this frame of mind as well. However, to keep your options open and to learn as much as you can, the theories are tools that can eventually help you with a translation project. They'll also give you a foundation in case you want to continue your schooling in translation. As a beginning translator, don't close the door to theory too early.

You also need to be aware of the practical issues of translation. If you have knowledge about how the profession responds to them and what the solutions are, not only will you feel like your professional decisions are grounded, but you'll be able to support the profession. Some of these practical issues include awareness of market trends, appropriate rates, and knowledge of the code of ethics.

Part of translation knowledge includes knowing about advancements in artificial intelligence and machine translation. It's essential to know how they're impacting translation. The benefits of machine translation tools, computer-assisted translation tools, and other technological supports can impact a translator's scalability and in turn income.

You can use the following techniques to set a foundation of translation knowledge and let it develop:

>> **Talk to other translators.** Meet with other translators. These don't have to be translators working in your language pair. Ask them about their challenges, triumphs, questions, projects, professional memberships, and more. Translators usually love to talk about what they do.

>> **Follow translators, language leaders, other professionals, and language organizations on social media.** Individuals or organizations often post articles and links to other material that's beneficial to translators. If you come across an account you particularly like, see who follows that account and who that account follows. This can be one strategy to help you filter social media worlds.

>> **Watch videos.** In addition to finding interesting articles about translation on social media, you might find videos. Follow the same steps listed in the previous point!

- » **Read about translation.** Look out for news about translation in newspapers. Check out articles in *Multilingual Magazine* and other periodicals and posts on the American Translators Association website or any of the online and print publications from international, national, and regional translator organizations. Read books about translation. There are lots of them, so choose wisely. If one doesn't feel helpful to you in a given moment, note something about it and save it for later reading.

- » **Attend conferences.** If possible, go to conferences on translation and listen to different panelists talk about what they do. To make the most of your attendance at any conference, look at the program beforehand to select which panels you'll attend. Conferences can be overwhelming experiences filled with missed opportunities if you don't plot your route beforehand.

Expanding your content knowledge

You've got your language skills and your translation knowledge skills. Now how about content knowledge? This means the knowledge about the kind of texts you're going to translate. When you first start putting yourself out there as a professional translator, you might choose not to specialize and to be open to any project that comes your way.

That's one way to see what kind of clients you attract and what you might be interested in. Even if you don't choose to specialize at first, you eventually will have general areas that you build strengths in. Some translators will choose to specialize in an area from the start. It all depends on your language pair, your background, and how you got into the business of translating.

And if you work for an organization, such as a school or a hospital, and you become a translator through that organization, your area of specialization will be chosen for you. Just keep in mind that schools can produce a range of documents.

TIP

To stay abreast of your content knowledge, read texts and listen to audio material related to those topics in all your working languages.

Building Additional Skills for Success

As a translator, beyond language knowledge, and translation and content knowledge, you need to develop skills that will help you work more efficiently. Those include research, technical, and people skills.

Developing research skills

Translators need to do research to create a translation. They need to look up terms in the source text, how those terms are used in certain contexts, how frequent those terms might be in a given language, and all sorts of other things. Each project will have its own needs and dimensions. The research happens in at least two languages and might involve more.

You'll conduct research on the internet, so you'll need to make sure the settings on your computer and browser allow you to do a complete search. This is especially important if you share a computer or use your organization's computer. Sometimes organizations fix settings so that you can't access certain websites, including those based in a country other than the one you're working from.

Sometimes you'll have to conduct research in books that exist in hard copy. You might need to look at photographs and other visuals of a certain situation or place to understand how to write about it. Or perhaps you'll need to visit a place so you can participate in whatever activity you need to write about so you can understand the words to describe it. The more you translate, the better you'll be at figuring out what kind of research a project requires. Because you can't effectively translate something you don't fully understand, keep doing your research until it all makes sense.

Honing your technical skills

Translators work with the written word, with texts. Most of those texts are shared electronically as scans, attachments, shared folders and files, and other ways. Those texts are worked on electronically, through a computer. That's one of the advantages of being a translator: it's a portable profession. If the situation allows, you can work from anywhere you want.

Because, as a translator, you'll conduct most of your work using a computer, you need to be comfortable using a computer and with the related technical skills. The skills you need can range from creating a professional background if you're having a video meeting with a client to responding to email and other communication features of your professional account.

When it comes to the translation of the documents, you need to be well versed in word processing programs, such as downloading documents, calculating word counts, keeping track of different versions of documents, saving documents as PDFs and in other formats, attaching files, using shared files and drives, linking documents to communications, and more.

Knowing how to use Excel or another tool to track projects and different aspects of each of those projects will help you stay organized.

Once you master the basics of document retrieval and dissemination, you should start learning about computer-assisted translation (CAT) tools. These are programs that can help you speed up your work, recognize the same word patterns you've previously translated, and be consistent. Most of these software options don't search the internet. Owning a CAT tool usually involves a fee, but the investment is usually well worth it. Talk to your fellow translators about them!

TIP

Translators should also be aware of AI options and how they might help or interfere with a translator's work. For example, ChatGPT as of 2024 is NOT a quality machine translation engine. That said, ChatGPT can be excellent in helping you rephrase translations, shorten them, change the tone of a text, and more. Using these types of prompts can be very beneficial. As a beginner, focus on doing the work yourself because there's so much to learn in the process of translation. AI will be there, and you'll have to navigate your relationship with it. For now, just experiment with it.

Cultivating your people skills

Although translators spend a good amount of time working alone, they do work with others. These interactions usually involve communicating with clients over aspects of a project including timelines, rates, and other details. So you need to clearly state your conditions, advocate for your needs, and be a pleasant person to work with. Working with clients also includes educating them about translation.

You need to be able to explain why a translation of a 40-page report can't be done in two hours and why you don't have a way to just switch the button on your computer to Polish to produce a Polish translation.

Some of these aspects you'll have to communicate in writing, and others you'll need to communicate via phone, Zoom, or other ways that allow you to have a live conversation. You'll have to figure out how to communicate these aspects respectfully and firmly. Keep in mind that you're not only representing yourself and possibly your company. You're also representing the profession.

Putting Your Translator Skills and Mindset to Work in Other Fields

One of the rewards of being a translator is that you get to experience other professionals through your translations. Beyond that, you might think about one day practicing those professions depending on what point you're in for your career.

Because you have many skills that go beyond knowing a pair of languages, as a translator, you can think about how you might take those skills, training, and lens and use them to contribute to other industries. Your practice and experience with translation can be a gateway to so many different professional opportunities.

Understanding, interpreting, and transforming laws

One of the ways of getting involved with the legal field is to specialize in legal or judicial translation. Another way is to become a language access attorney, a lawyer who provides advocacy and leadership in advancing laws, policies, and practices related to language access.

They work to ensure compliance, educate about language access laws and accessing and working with interpreters, partner with advocates and organizations, draft legislation, and spread the word about an individual's right to language access if they're better served in a language other than English. Your background as a translator could be of help as you learn what it means to advocate for others. Additionally, your sharp attention to language will certainly be of use as you scrutinize texts and draft persuasive documents.

Focusing on the written word as a writer or editor

Translators work with language in ways that non-translators don't. You read texts and fully digest them and then write them in a language different from the one you're reading. You choose every word that you use in your translation. Because of this attention to the details of language, translators often make great editors of texts.

If you're interested in adding on this service, this means that you could edit the texts written by other people. They can be translations or not, but they should be texts in the languages you have strong writing skills in. Editing texts for others can help you read in different ways — practice that will also improve your translation skills — and bring in an additional stream of income.

There's even more you can do with your language and writing skills! Something to think about when you choose to become a translator is that you're going to spend your professional life dedicated to making the writing and ideas of others known in a language different from the one they were written in.

In other words, you're lending your language skills and your writing skills to another voice.

This is extremely rewarding, and you do learn a ton and develop both professionally and personally in the process. However, to balance all this giving, you might think about doing your own writing in whatever language or languages you feel comfortable expressing yourself in. You can write about translation or whatever you'd like. Because your writing skills are solid in translation, try using them to express your own ideas.

Promoting social justice

Depending on the types of texts you translate and what your interests are, you might also take your translator's lens to influence social justice efforts. As a translator, you make information and written communications accessible in a given language or languages. It's an effort that promotes accessibility, equity, inclusion, and linguistic diversity.

You can take this effort even further by speaking, writing, or educating about how translation is a tool to promote social justice not only for the people who are better served by the translations but for the people who tune into translation by looking out for members of a given community who rely on translations. As more and more organizations add the provision of language access to their priorities, you might think about being a language access consultant as one of your professional activities. You could advise organizations on how to translate communications so that everyone gets the message in an accessible language and more.

Exploring translator opportunities in healthcare

Translator training and the translation mindset that you might be able to cultivate in the classroom and as practicing as a translator can also help you if you'd like to work in the healthcare field. Options include working as a salaried translator for a healthcare-related organization, specializing in health-related documents and maintaining freelance or other independent status, working in hospital language access centers, and becoming a healthcare professional with knowledge of how translation works. This last option will help you distinguish yourself and allow you to take better care of your patients.

Finding your place in education

As schools increase and systematize their language access efforts, they'll be looking for more and more language access coordinators, managers, and directors. In other words, schools need qualified and experienced individuals to run these programs and, as a translator, you'll have the knowledge of what it takes to get the job done.

If you're looking for a salaried job involving translation and language services, keep your eyes on schools.

Scoping out opportunities in communications

As organizations move to provide more and more language access to their audiences, they'll need to be educated on how to provide their communications in multiple languages.

As a translator you'll know what the process is and how to create one that allows for timely and effective translations. You'll be able to support organizations in moving away from translation as an afterthought to something that's part of the planning process. Bringing that knowledge of translation management to a role in communications can distinguish you.

Chapter **5**

Checking Out University Programs

Y ou don't need a college degree to become a successful translator. Most translators today get jobs based on experience, recommendations, and proven translation skills. However, getting a degree in translation or any formal education and training in translation gives you four key advantages:

» A structured program that prepares you for a career in translation faster and more thoroughly than you may be able to do on your own

» A high-quality educational experience delivered by industry leaders and experienced practitioners and educators

» Credentials in the form of diplomas, certificates, and transcripts that you can use to set yourself apart from competitors and open the doors to more and better employment opportunities

» Connections and community — colleagues, mentors, and alumni — you can rely on to build your professional network and generate leads to rewarding and lucrative opportunities

If you're considering a formal education in translation, your next step is to decide how much of your study will be devoted to translation. Do you want to major in translation, get a minor in translation, earn some sort of certificate, or just take a few courses? You need to know which programs and courses are available and which institutions offer the courses and other resources to meet your goals most effectively and efficiently.

In this chapter, I provide you with the information and guidance you need to make the choices that are right for you and for your educational and career goals. In the process, I offer valuable information for those who are tasked with hiring translators.

Exploring University Programming

On your journey to becoming a translator, it's important to be aware of the deep and wide dimensions of the world of translation, including higher education's role in this world. Institutions of higher education are a place for students not only to practice translation but to think about translation as a product and a process and consider its impact on the world in areas such as ethics, sociology, business, and culture.

At a college or university, you have many program types to choose from. These programs are packaged differently, according to the following factors:

>> **Area of study:** Some universities offer programs specifically in translation. Others locate translation within a language department. For example, you could pursue a degree in Spanish, Portuguese, or Russian but, depending on the program, that doesn't guarantee you'll take translation courses per se.

>> **Type of degree or certificate:** Some programs focus on undergraduate education. Others have only graduate degrees, and some have certificates for full-time, part-time, or continuing-education students:

- **Undergraduate education:** These programs allow undergrads to major or minor in translation or related majors. For example, Kent State University offers a Bachelor of Science degree program in translation with concentrations in specific languages from the Department of Modern and Classical Language Studies. Kent State is the only institution in the United States to offer degrees specifically in translation at all three levels — BS, MS, and PhD.

- **Graduate degrees:** Several universities have postgraduate programs that enable students to earn a master's or doctorate in translation. For example, Binghamton University offers an MA in translation as well as a PhD in Translation Studies, which was the first PhD program in the United States.

If your working languages are Spanish and English, check out the Graduate Program in Translation at the University of Puerto Rico. It's one of the first in the field!

- **Certificates:** Several universities offer certificates in translation. For example, for full-time university students, the Comparative Literature Program at the University of Massachusetts Amherst offers an undergraduate Translation and Interpreting Studies Certificate that consists of six courses. Two are required courses that focus on translation and interpreting; two are advanced courses in a language other than English; and two more courses require substantial writing in English. The same program offers a certificate with an identical design for full-time graduate students. This is an in-person option for UMass Amherst students as well as students from the surrounding colleges of Amherst, Hampshire, Mount Holyoke, and Smith.

The preceding examples are from US universities. If you can, look outside the United States. Universities in Canada, the United Kingdom, and Barcelona and other parts of Spain, for example, offer excellent translator programs at both the undergraduate and the graduate levels.

>> **Presentation:** Some programs are fully online, others offer only in-person education, and some are hybrid. You can also find *asynchronous options*, meaning you do all the work on your own time whenever and wherever you desire while meeting program milestones.

>> **Curriculum:** Some programs offer courses that are more practice-based, whereas others are more theoretical. Practice-based courses include those with names such as Medical Translation; Legal Translation; Business Translation; and Translation, Media, and Technology. Theoretical courses are those with names such as Introduction to Translation Studies; Theory and Practice of Translation; Race, Gender, and Sexuality in Translation; and Translation and Global Society. (See the next section, "Distinguishing theory from practice in translation programs," for more details.)

Programming can change, so be sure to check university websites and confirm with departments, especially if translation program offerings are deciding factors in your choice of university.

What you decide to do for your translation study will be driven by your own interests and goals, what's available to you, and how it fits with your lifestyle.

For preparation to become a literary translator, look into programs at the following universities: University of Iowa, Boston University, Columbia University, University of Rochester, and University of Arkansas. And don't forget that you may find a suitable program abroad, such as the Literary Translation program at the University of East Anglia.

Distinguishing theory from practice in translation programs

As you're exploring university translation programs and courses, be aware of the differences between a curriculum that focuses on theory versus one that focuses on practice. Theory courses could look at how translation, as a phenomenon, affects meaning across years and cultures, whereas a practice-based course looks at how to translate specific types of texts or develop other skills such as working with translation memory and building terminology banks and glossaries. It's the difference between *trying to understand* the many aspects of something and actually *doing* something. To study translation, you don't need to know more than one language. But to translate you do. (By the way, knowing more than one language is beneficial!)

University programs called "Translation Studies" might lean more toward theory or may seek to balance theory and practice. Knowing the difference between the two, you're better equipped to choose the program suited to your educational and career goals. If you're planning to build a career as a professional translator, you'll want to focus on the practice and learn about the tools to support your practice. If you want to be a researcher or professor, you'll need a graduate degree, often a doctorate. Also, you'll usually need exposure to both theory and practice, and you'll need to determine an area of scholarly interest in which you'll become an expert.

>> **Professional translator:** As a professional translator, you'll be spending most of your days translating texts — reading a text in one language and writing it in another — usually your native tongue or the language in which you have stronger writing skills. If your goal is to become a translator, you'll want to lean more toward courses that develop your language and translation skills.

>> **Researcher/professor:** As a researcher/professor, you'll be spending your days studying, writing, and teaching about translation concepts. A number of scholars in Translation Studies don't translate, although it's not unheard of that a professor would do so.

WARNING

Translation Studies programs, which may be heavy on theory and light on practice, may not be the best choice if you're planning to become a professional translator. Carefully research a program before applying to ensure that it has the right balance of theory and practice to meet your goals.

Understanding Translation Studies

Translation Studies is an interdisciplinary field that deals with the theory, description, and application (practice) of translation. The term was coined in the last quarter of the twentieth century by the American-born translator, poet, and scholar James S. Holmes (1924–1986). What's important to know is that it does include the practice of translation and much more. Have a look at some of the main areas:

>> **Translation theory and methodology:** Studying the principles and approaches of the translation process, such as equivalence, literal translation, and cultural adaptation.

>> **Linguistics and language analysis:** Understanding the rules and structures that govern both the source and the target languages.

>> **Cultural studies:** Examining how differences in cultures (customs, beliefs, and social norms) influence the translation of a text from the source to the target language.

>> **Literary translation:** Exploring the challenges of conveying literary elements, such as style, tone, and literary devices from a source to a target language.

>> **Technical and specialized translation:** Addressing the translation of specialized texts in fields such as medicine, law, and engineering.

>> **Historical and comparative studies:** Analyzing the development of translation over time and comparing translations of different texts — often literary — across different time periods and cultures.

TIP

For more about Translation Studies, I recommend starting with the following three books: *After Babel: Aspects of Language and Translation,* 3rd Edition, by George Steiner, Oxford University Press, 1998; *Translation Studies,* 4th Edition, by Susan Bassnett, Routledge, 2013; and *The Translator's Invisibility: A History of Translation* by Lawrence Venuti, Routledge, 2017.

Balancing theory and practice

As you're establishing yourself as a professional translator, you may not have time to dedicate to reading books on Translation Studies because, if you're an independent translator, your income will be based on the number of projects you're able to translate. The more words you can translate and the more projects you can responsibly accept, the more money you'll earn. In contrast, most Translation Studies scholars are professors who earn a fixed salary provided by the institutions that employ them. Contributing to the field through scholarly activity is part of their job.

If you decide to study translation at the university level, some of your professors may list Translation Studies as one of their research interests. However, as you establish yourself as a translator, awareness of Translation Studies and all its activity can help you continue to expand your knowledge and skills as a translator, provide you with knowledge that you can fall back on as you grow as a translator, and help you discuss translation on a more sophisticated level. All these benefits can help you win the bid for a large translation project and expand the services you offer as a translator.

At some point in your career, your interests may shift from the *hows* of translation to the *whys* and the broader impact of translations. You might decide to devote some of your time to studying and teaching translation — in practice and in theory. Your knowledge of Translation Studies can help you do that.

REMEMBER

Keep in mind that not all scholars of Translation Studies translate. At the same time, beware that not all translators follow or contribute directly to Translation Studies. In fact, some translators don't find the fruits of Translation Studies helpful to their work. Also, as professional translators, they may not even have time to dedicate to activities beyond translation and the communications with clients around their work. You don't need to take sides. But you should be aware of the overlap and interplay between the theoretical and the practical aspects of translation.

Finding Translator Programs in the US and Abroad

Demand for translators is alive and growing, and institutions of higher education play a key role in meeting that demand through their language and translation programs and courses. After you've decided to pursue a career in translation, you're ready to start scoping out what's available.

REMEMBER

Awareness of the institutional positionalities on translation can help you understand the larger context of the profession, navigate your own development, advocate for translation and translators, and manage expectations — your own as well as those of future employers and clients.

Unfortunately, if you're studying in the United States, you can't just contact a university's Department of Translation for information about available programs and courses. Not one of the approximately 4,000 colleges and universities in the United States has a Department of Translation. To find a program that meets your needs, you'll need to do a little digging. You may even need to cobble together your own plan of study. In this section, I provide guidance on where to look for translator programs in the US and abroad.

Knowing where to look in the United States

If US universities and colleges don't have departments of translation, then where do you go in the US to study translation? Start by looking in language departments, linguistics departments, comparative literature departments, and English departments, as explained in the following sections.

Understanding language departments and translation

The most obvious place to look for courses that prepare you to become a translator are language departments — departments with names like Spanish and Portuguese; Asian Languages; Modern Languages; and Romance Languages.

MAKING THE CASE FOR A DEPARTMENT OF TRANSLATION

Given the current and forecasted need for translators, not to mention the academic and civic benefits that translator preparation offers to students, you may be surprised to discover that not one of the approximately 4,000 colleges and universities in the United States has a Department of Translation. Among those same institutions, you'll find departments of Art History, English, Linguistics, Management, and Marketing, but not one Department of Translation.

Why have a department dedicated to translation? Because a Department of Translation can deliver the following benefits:

- **Provide clarity for students and advisors as students plot their academic paths:** Departments have their own signage and their own curriculums, making it easier for students to find information about programs, courses, and resources specific to the department.

- **Support faculty teaching and research:** Forming a department enables a university to gather a significant number of faculty members who work in the same field. Universities may have qualified professors, but when they're scattered across the university in separate departments such as languages, linguistics, and sociology, their work isn't centralized, and their collective potential is diluted.

- **Promote the profession:** A dedicated department has a greater opportunity to promote translation as a serious area of knowledge and as a profession. Beyond the university, when graduates become doctors, lawyers, educators, scientists, and administrators who need translators, they'll approach translators as highly skilled and knowledgeable professionals.

As a student and translation professional, developing a deeper understanding of translation in the broader context of translator preparation helps you understand your options, the profession, your translator colleagues, and how your non-translator colleagues are likely to interact with you. If you're a professional in some other area of academia, business, government, or a non-governmental agency who works with translators, increasing your understanding of translation, both as a theoretical and practical discipline, can improve your working relationship with translators and the outcomes and products of your collaboration.

You may find it encouraging to know that professors, authors, and other professionals are working to spread literacy about translation. To develop your own understanding and take a small step to promote translation literacy, read and recommend the book *Demystifying Translation: Introducing Translation to Non-translators* by Lynne Bowker (Routledge, 2023).

Within these departments, you're not likely to see many, if any, specific programs with *translation* in their names. Instead, you'll find programs and courses on specific languages, such as Spanish, Portuguese, and Chinese, along with higher-level courses in more specific subject areas, such as literature and culture, film, linguistics, and language courses for specific fields such as medicine or law. Translation, if it even appears in the course catalog, will only be one course or category of courses among a broader selection.

As you and your advisor work on formulating your plan of study, choose courses that prepare you to read and write in the languages and fields in which you plan to build your career as a translator. For example, if you plan to translate from English to Spanish, you'll want to load up on a variety of courses in the Spanish language, including writing, advanced grammar, literature, culture, and so on. If you'd like to specialize in a certain field, add to your list a language course focused on that field, such as Spanish for the Health Care Profession.

REMEMBER

Don't overlook the need to develop strong writing skills in the language you plan to translate into. For example, if you plan to translate from Spanish to English, in addition to the Spanish courses, take courses designed to develop your English writing skills or engage in self-study to sharpen your skills. Strive to improve your understanding of all aspects of the written word and build your vocabulary. A Spanish to English translator needs to be the best reader of Spanish and the best writer of English.

Take a look at these examples of course titles from the Department of Spanish and Portuguese at the University of Texas Austin:

>> **Linguistics**

POR 330L: Introduction to Language and Linguistics in Society

SPN 364L: Linguistics and the Spanish Learner

>> **Literature**

POR 352: Brazilian and Spanish American Literature

SPN 352C: Contemporary Caribbean Literature

>> **Grammar**

POR 327C: Advanced Grammar and Writing in Context

SPN 314: Spanish Conversation and Culture

>> **Culture**

SPN 357D: Cultures in Contact in Medieval Spain

SPN 369C: African Diasporas

>> **For the professions**

SPN 367C: Spanish for Health Care Professions

SPN 367D: Business in Hispanic Life and Culture

SPN 357E: Spanish Translation and the Social Sciences (the only course listed on the website that focuses on translation)

REMEMBER

University webpages don't always reflect the most up-to-date offerings. Be sure to check in with any departments directly about their course offerings, especially if they're your main motivation for attending a specific university.

Course offerings in translation have the potential to transform as the demand for quality translation grows, student interest in translation increases, and programming deepens and expands. Look to language departments for translation courses. Ask your advisor for additional guidance on courses that will prepare you for becoming a translator.

Searching for translation in English departments

English departments, like non-English-language departments, haven't always had active programming that addresses translation. Nevertheless, as you work toward become a translator, the English department needs to be on your radar, especially if English will be one of your working languages. The English department is the place to go to improve your English reading and writing skills and to receive feedback on structure/logic, grammar, syntax, mechanics, and other aspects of written communication.

THE IMPORTANCE OF INCLUDING TRANSLATION IN LANGUAGE STUDIES

Although translation has a rich history, language departments, in recent years, have delayed the preparation of translators by allowing students to use only the language they're learning in the classroom. Such a practice eliminates opportunities for translation because translation proper requires two languages.

Translation courses are often reserved for the upper-level courses for students with advanced language skills, with little mention of translation before students reach that level. Introducing translation earlier in language studies can be a useful tool for writing and for stimulating students' interest in the profession in general.

You won't find many translation offerings in an English department. At best, you're likely to find survey courses in world literature that examine literary works from different languages, typically all of which are translated into English with little to no recognition that the works are translations. For example, *Fictions*, the English translation of *Ficciones* (1944) by Jorge Luis Borges is taught as if it were first written in English, and not Spanish, with no regard to the fact that a translator chose all the English words that are being read in the English version. If you're reading *Fictions* in English, you're reading the English words that Andrew Hurley chose.

Looking at programs outside the United States

While US universities are still waiting for their first Department of Translation, these departments have existed in universities outside the US for many years. Check out what you'll find in other countries:

>> **Spain:** The Department of Translation and Interpretation at the Universitat Autònoma de Barcelona traces its origins back to 1972. Also in Barcelona, the Universitat Pompeu Fabra, founded in 1990, has a Department of Translation and Language Sciences. Many of these programs' offerings are in English.

Studying translation in Barcelona can be interesting because it's a bilingual Catalan-Spanish city with a multilingual backdrop, which means you get to see translations all around you. That alone is an education in translation!

>> **United Kingdom:** The University of East Anglia offers a BA in Translation and Interpreting with Modern Languages and an MA in Applied Translation. These programs are worth checking out, especially if you're looking to earn a graduate degree in translation.

>> **Canada:** The University of Ottawa has a School of Translation and Interpretation, founded in 1971. It was the first Canadian institution to offer professional translation courses at the university level, starting in 1936. Consider the University of Ottawa if you're looking for a bilingual French-English experience because it's a bilingual university that operates in Canada's two official languages. It offers undergraduate and graduate degrees, along with certificate programs.

You may also find that if you directly enroll in a university abroad, costs can be less expensive than programs in the United States.

Exploring the Depths of Undergraduate Programs for Translators

As you explore university programs, consider your level of commitment and desired level of expertise. Are you seeking to earn a bachelor's degree, an associate degree, or a certificate? Do you want to major in translation or a related field or major in an entirely unrelated field and pursue a minor in translation or a language? Or do you want to merely dabble in translation by taking a course or two that piques your interest? In this section, I guide you through your options on the undergraduate spectrum.

Going all in: Getting a degree in translation or a related field

If you're enrolling in an undergraduate program with a goal of earning a degree, you have two decisions to make — the type of degree you want and the field you want to major in, beyond the university's general education requirements.

First decide on the type of undergraduate degree you're going for:

>> **Associate degree:** This is a two-year degree that you can earn at a community college, a junior college, or an online university. Some four-year colleges also offer associate degree programs. An associate degree in translation is usually intended as a *ladder program*, meaning that it serves as a foundation for eventually working toward a bachelor's degree. Here are a few examples:

- Translation and Interpretation (Spanish/English) AA at Monterey Peninsula College in California

- AA in Modern Languages with a specialization in Spanish Translation and Interpretation at the Borough of Manhattan Community College of the City University of New York

- Spanish/English Translation AA at LaGuardia Community College of the City University of New York

WARNING

Associate degree programs expose you to the field and the skills necessary to be successful, without having to make a four-year commitment, but they don't ensure that you're ready to take on a range of translation assignments. If you already work in social, legal, medical, or government services and you're sometimes asked to translate documents as part of your job, these programs could be a starting point.

>> **Bachelor's degree:** This is a four-year degree. Many jobs for translators have the minimum requirement of a bachelor's degree. Translation requires a solid use of language and critical thinking abilities, among the many skills that translators need. You develop those skills on the road to earning a bachelor's degree.

Only a couple universities in the United States offer bachelor's degrees in translation, which usually requires 35–45 credit hours of a 120-credit hour degree. Programs at Kent State University (KSU) in Ohio and the University of Iowa are places to look:

- KSU offers a Bachelor of Science Program in Translation through the Department of Modern and Classical Language Studies with concentrations in Arabic, French, German, Russian, and Spanish. This program focuses on providing majors with the skills and knowledge they'll need to become translators.

- Since 2022, the University of Iowa has offered a 33-credit Bachelor of Arts in Translation through the College of Liberal Arts and Sciences. By building awareness of the practice of translation and its related dimensions, this program prepares students to serve as translators in the global workplace.

Regardless of whether you decide to pursue a two-year associate degree or a four-year bachelor's degree, you eventually need to declare your major. If your university of choice doesn't offer a major in translation, you'll have to look a little deeper into existing majors and work closely with your academic advisor to craft your own path through language studies. Here are a couple examples of how you can use broader majors to pursue a degree in translation (or its equivalent):

>> At the University of Massachusetts Amherst, the Comparative Literature Program offers translation as a track within the Comparative Literature major, which enables students to include translation courses in their study plan.

>> Also at UMass Amherst, the University Without Walls program has an online BA in Interdisciplinary Studies in which students design a degree, such as in translation and interpreting. University Without Walls provides students and their academic advisors with tremendous flexibility. It allows students to take online, blended, on-campus, and asynchronous courses, and it can accept up to 105 credits from prior coursework, learning, and work and life experience.

>> The Department of Spanish and Portuguese at Rutgers offers a five-year BA/MA in Spanish Option in Translation (150 credits). The program develops students' professional translation and interpreting competence and prepares them for entry-level jobs in the field and for professional assessment exams.

These are just three examples among many to give you an idea of what's out there. Translators need to be able to do research, so digging into these programs, determining what they have to offer, following up with them, and deciding which one will work best for you are all part of your translator preparation.

Dipping your toe into translation: Minors and other opportunities

If you found translation after you declared a major, you can't commit to a major in translation, or you're not at one of the universities that offers a major in translation, you may consider shorter programs that allow you to engage with translation in an academic classroom. Shorter programs include minors, concentrations, and certificates, as described in the following sections.

Minors

At the undergraduate level, a minor at a US institution is usually around 18 credits or six courses. A minor allows you to study a particular interest a bit more with the guidance of professors and interactions with other students. A minor in translation gives you some exposure to the field and can be a nice companion to any major because all fields in some way communicate with multilingual communities.

For example, the University of Iowa offers an 18-credit minor in translation for global literacy. It includes a core course; two translation courses; two language, linguistics, literature, and culture courses; and a capstone course (for demonstrating your expertise in your major near the completion of your studies).

Concentrations

Concentrations are similar to minors and can be a bit more or a bit less work than a minor depending on the institution. If you're already enrolled in a university program, take a look around to see if it offers a concentration in translation or something similar. If the university doesn't offer a concentration in translation, try creating a minor on your own or with the assistance of your academic advisor. More and more, universities give students the opportunity to customize an area of study. By knowing about minors and concentrations at other universities, you may be able to find an opportunity to create translation opportunities at your own university. Here's a sample of a concentration offered by Smith College:

>> One gateway course, "The Art of Translation." A gateway course is the first credit-bearing college-level course in a program of study.

>> Two electives in language, literature, and culture

>> Two electives in translation

>> Two practical experiences, which can include a semester abroad, an internship, and an independent research project

>> Capstone

Certificates

Certificate programs are another way to study translation at the undergraduate level. Certificates in translation vary widely among universities. Here are a couple examples:

>> At the University of Massachusetts Amherst, the Comparative Literature Program offers a certificate in Translation and Interpreting Studies. It's made up of six courses, two of which are specifically about translation and interpreting.

>> Rutgers University offers a certificate, open to undergraduates and members of the community, through its Department of Spanish and Portuguese. It requires a specific grade point average in the courses (about seven total) toward the certificate.

REMEMBER

Finding or creating your own track toward achieving your academic and professional goals as a translator is all about assembling the right mix of courses and experiences (such as study abroad opportunities or internships). Searching through programs, understanding their rationale, and using them to guide your selection of courses is the best approach for closing in on your goals. Additionally, awareness of what kind of translator preparation programs are out there will help you better understand fellow translators and potential employees should you one day have your own translation business. The more you know about the field, the stronger you'll be at positioning yourself for employment and for success.

Getting down to the nitty-gritty: Individual translation courses

If you're very lucky, you found a translation program to meet your needs and an academic community to help you select courses and pursue other educational opportunities over your two to four years of study. You have a path from point A to point B — the point at which you should be prepared to work as a professional translator for an employer or as a freelancer.

However, the path may not be so clear, and even if you have a well-defined path, you may need to make some choices when it comes to specific courses. As you choose courses, keep in mind that you need to develop four general areas of expertise:

>> **Source language:** The source language is the language you'll be translating from. At the most fundamental level, you need to be able to read and understand general texts in the source language. You may already have some expertise in this area from past education and experience, but you can develop it more fully by taking university-level courses. For example, if you're planning to translate from Spanish to English, you'll benefit from Spanish-language courses that cover advanced grammar, literature, and culture. These tend to be courses at the 300 level and above.

>> **Target language:** The target language is the language you'll be translating into. If you plan to translate into English, this is where you can tap into the English department to develop your communication skills. Any courses that improve your logic, organization, and ability to read and write in English can make you a better translator.

>> **Translation knowledge, skills, and tools:** Even if you know two languages, you may not have the knowledge and skills necessary to produce high-quality translations. This is where translation courses play a key role, providing valuable conceptual understanding along with more practical guidance through courses such as the following:

- Theory and Practice of Translation
- CAT (Computer-Assisted Translation) Tools
- Translation, Media, and Technology
- Multilingualism and Translation

>> **Specialized vocabulary and conceptual understanding of specific disciplines outside translation and language studies:** If you plan to translate in a specific field, such as medicine, law, or engineering, additional study is needed to build vocabulary and conceptual understanding through courses such as the following:

- Legal Translation
- Medical Translation
- Courses related to the field of interest in the target language, such as courses in law or medicine

REMEMBER

Even if you don't pursue a major or a minor in a language or in translation, you can benefit from taking one or two electives in translation or a related subject area. Even a single course can change the way you look at and use language and deepen your understanding of the world. Also consider that many translators didn't study translation per se at the university. Translation skills can and often are developed outside the four-year university degree.

Taking a Deeper Dive

If you already have your bachelor's degree in translation or a related field, congratulations! Now, you have the knowledge and skills to tackle higher-level courses in translation. In this section, I guide you through graduate programs in translation, along with more expansive programming.

Exploring graduate programs in translation

If you already have an undergraduate degree and you're thinking about returning to college to study translation, you have options! If your goal is to become a professional translator, a master's degree and constant practice should be enough. If you want to teach translation at the university level, you'll probably need a PhD or a graduate certificate to accompany your PhD if it's in another related field.

Master's degree programs

If you're looking into a master's degree in translation, you'll find many more options than at the undergraduate level. Some of these programs are about preparing you to be a professional translator and focus on practice; others are more theoretical and can be steppingstones to a PhD program. Here are a few examples:

>> Kent State University has an MA program, as well as an MA/MBA, with onsite and online offerings. You can choose from six language combinations and aren't required to have any prior knowledge of translation.

>> Binghamton University offers an MA in translation as part of its Translation and Instruction Program.

>> Hunter College, Carnegie Mellon University, New York University, and the University of Texas at Dallas all offer MA programs in translation.

>> The Middlebury Institute of International Studies at Monterey offers at least three different MA programs in translation with in-person and online options.

MFA programs

If you're interested in translating literature, consider pursuing a Master of Fine Arts in Literary Translation. Literary translation can be a competitive field, and literary translators are constantly working to improve their professional situations regarding compensation, contracts, and recognition. Some translators comment that this is a career for people who don't need to bring in a regular paycheck.

Although compensation is a valid consideration, some literary translators have made a decent living doing what they love. Check out the following universities if you're interested in an MFA in Literary Translation. Most of them are for translators who translate from other languages into English:

>> University of Iowa

>> Boston University

>> Columbia University

>> University of Arkansas

PhD programs

If you'd like to become a university professor or are deeply in love with translation and have the time and resources to commit to earning a doctorate in translation, look into universities that offer a PhD in translation or a closely related field. Usually if you're on this path, you spend four to six years working on the degree, which includes time for coursework, exams, teaching, a dissertation proposal, and writing a dissertation. Full-time students usually don't pay for a degree but instead teach to cover the cost of the program and earn a stipend. It's a serious commitment!

Some of the leading PhD programs in the United States are at Kent State University, Binghamton University, the University of Dallas, and the University of Massachusetts Amherst. Although it's important to be part of a program, you'll also want to carefully look at the professors at each institution to make sure a professor is available to support your research interests. Finding the right advisor could be just as important as or even more important than finding the right program.

Certificates

Another route to obtaining graduate-level credentials in translation is to get a graduate degree from a language program and enhance it with a certificate in translation. Depending on your experience and coursework, this path could make you employable as a university professor able to teach undergraduate translation courses. As translation programming at universities expands, so will the need for professors who have some expertise in translation.

TIP

If you're set on getting a degree in translation, consider programs outside the United States. Check out the options in Canada, the United Kingdom, and other European countries. See the earlier section "Looking at programs outside the United States."

University translation centers and other innovative projects

Just because so few universities offer undergraduate academic majors in translation doesn't mean that universities haven't thought about centralizing translation in some way. If you're on a university campus, look out for centers and other projects devoted to translation. They often offer innovative programs and opportunities for students because they operate beyond the constraints of academic departments. In the following sections, I shed light on translation centers and innovative projects that promote and drive the development of translation.

Translation centers

Several universities established translation centers in the late 1970s when the field of Translation Studies was young:

>> **Center for Translation Studies at the University of Texas at Dallas:** Founded in 1978, the Center for Translation Studies educates and supports people who practice, study, or have an interest in translation. It's anchored in literary translation. The Center also offers workshops, courses, and events bringing together students, scholars, and translators. It's the home of *Translation Review*, a peer-reviewed journal in Translation Studies.

>> **The Translation Center at the University of Massachusetts Amherst:** Founded in 1979, the Center offers language services from a public research university while providing educational opportunities to university students. It offers a range of language services in most languages, works with clients from near and far, and draws from a large network of vendors and experts. It provides students with work experience supporting project managers and contributing to other translation education projects.

>> **The National Center for Interpretation at the University of Arizona:** Also founded in 1979, this Center offers a range of language services and is known for its interpreter testing and training programs. It aims to promote social justice for language minorities and advance professionalism in the field.

Conduct your own research into centers for translation and interpretation. The three listed here are just a sample of centers available in the United States.

Projects

In lieu of creating centers at universities, which can take a long time, some campuses have created smaller but no less meaningful projects. Here are a couple examples:

>> Since 2015, Bennington College in southern Vermont has been celebrating Bennington Translates, a translation and interpretation project that spans literary, humanitarian, medical, and legal translation and interpretation. It focuses on conflict zones and involves the entire campus in a variety of ways. Visit the Bennington College website (www.bennington.edu) and search for *bennington translates* to see what they offer each year and to be inspired by the many ways people talk about and interact with translation.

>> The Translation Studies Initiative at Rutgers is an effort to foster "intellectual and creative exchange among students and faculty engaged with translation in its many forms across the Humanities at the university."

REMEMBER

You don't need to have the information about all these centers and programs and the ones not mentioned here at your fingertips. Nor do you need to participate in any of them to be a successful translator. But knowing about the opportunities they offer, how they're designed, and what they do increases your awareness of what's out there in the world. They enable you to see how translation engages and interacts with society. They're inspiring whether you see them from afar or as a participant. They're places to refer to as you grow as a translator.

Chapter **6**

Expanding Your Options with Non-University Programs

n the United States, translation is largely unregulated in terms of who needs what to translate what. In most cases translators don't need a university degree in translation or a certificate in translation to be hired for work. What's more, a university degree in any field isn't a required minimum to be a translator.

Some places might hire you to translate without even asking you anything about credentials. However, practicing translators and trainers of translators will argue that you need the language skills that a university degree in any field gives you. Not to mention that a university degree is a credential that will distinguish you and give you a foundation on which to build more opportunities as you grow in the field.

Although some countries have more regulated ways of dealing with translation, others have unregulated ways of attracting and hiring translators. A lot will depend on what kind of document you're translating and for whom.

This chapter looks at alternatives to university degrees when pursuing the qualifications to be a translator or other professional development opportunities in the translation field.

The Value of Establishing Credentials

As you begin pursuing your career in translation, don't be surprised if you meet professional translators who tell you they've never been trained as a translator. This might be especially common among literary translators. It shouldn't discourage you from seeking training. Training elevates the profession. A lot of your growth as a translator will happen on your own, but don't turn your back on formal training. It will help you get to where you need to go faster, make you more competitive and mobile, and introduce you to more professional opportunities and networks. It will make the job easier in many ways.

Because of the lack of general knowledge about translation and what it takes to provide a quality translation in the United States, an employer or an organization often hires you to translate documents for them without even confirming your language skills and without some other indication that you do indeed have translation skills. So if employers aren't prepared to put forth solid translator requirements, how do you prepare yourself to be a translator?

Even if you can get a job as a translator without credentials, if you want to succeed and grow in the field there are many compelling reasons why you should invest in more formal training. They are similar to the ones listed in Chapter 5 "Checking Out University Programs," which include faster and more thorough career preparation, guidance from experienced practitioners, a credential that could lead to more opportunities for better employment, and connections.

Some of these learning opportunities might be longer-term foundational opportunities that will help you get started as a translator while introducing you to translation's sister service: interpretation. Others are shorter-term opportunities that just focus on translation. If you know that you want to focus on translation and have no interest in interpreting, you might need to curate your own selection of training, which could be fun. Remember as I mentioned in previous chapters, translation and interpretation are not the same thing. Translators work with written documents and interpreters work with the spoken language. Being one doesn't automatically make you the other. I bring this up because there are non-university programs that combine the two.

Rest assured that you have options, and new ones keep sprouting up since the profession is one of the largest and fastest growing in the world. According to the Bureau of Labor Statistics, the field will grow 4 percent from 2022 to 2032. Search for what you want, ask more experienced translators, and be open to carving your own way through existing opportunities.

Also remember that things change. Years ago the internet didn't exist, and organizations that needed translation largely worked with translators in their immediate geographic area. Translators also worked on paper. Now you can send documents that need to be translated anywhere in seconds, and translators can work from anywhere thanks to the internet. This also means that employers can look near and far for translators, so work to prepare yourself, and take advantage of structured programming. Programs educate you, help you meet others, and offer other kinds of connections.

Non-University Programs

Maybe your university years are behind you — you've already graduated or you don't have plans to enroll in a degree program — and you run into translation as a career option. Or perhaps you're juggling many things and want to look at opportunities to be trained as a translator outside a traditional university program. How can you get the training you need to be a responsible translator? You'll be glad to know that non-university-affiliated opportunities are available, as well as programs, housed at universities, for the extramural community that are open to nonmatriculated students.

When you start getting into translation, you might hear about academia versus the industry, practitioners versus academics, and theorists versus translators. These divisions exist throughout the world of translation, although efforts are being made to bridge them. For example, universities open their doors to industry experts to come in and give talks and other presentations about translation-related challenges and initiatives. Companies and agencies might invite university-student or recent graduate interns into their spaces to gain work experience.

If you're not working toward a university degree but want to develop translation skills, you might find yourself deciding whether to enroll in a university translator certificate or similar program for nonmatriculated students or to take advantage of training offered by a company or other non-university organization.

Possible advantages to a non-university affiliated program are greater ranges of start dates, more affordable programming, easier sign-up processes, and the flexibility of online, and sometimes totally asynchronous, learning. On the other hand, universities are becoming more and more flexible and eager to meet the needs of the public looking for nontraditional university programming. Explore your options, and make sure you know what you're getting into and how it will serve your goals.

Another take on looking at translator preparation from the industry perspective is that if you find yourself already in a job within the translation industry, your employer might be able to cover your cost of taking a certain training. This could happen with a language pair that isn't as common or for which there is a large need, or a rapid increase in need.

Training for translators

When you're looking for a training program for translators, one of the first things you might notice is that most programs, at least those in the United States, focus on interpreting or combine translation and interpreting. What should you do? Interpreting and translation are two different skill sets. So consider the following when you make your decision:

>> If your heart is set on being a translator and you know that interpreting isn't for you or at least not in your foreseeable future, see if the program will allow you to choose your courses. In that case, only choose the courses or workshops related to translation.

>> If the program offers a range of courses, classes, or workshops, take the ones that are mainly focused on translation, and take a few on interpreting. It helps to know about interpreting if you're to be a well-rounded professional. Clients will confuse the two all the time, so being able to educate them about what service they need and how to get it will be a big help. This introduction to interpreting might also encourage you to add this service to your professional portfolio when the time is right.

Something more you might notice is that these programs, even the ones at universities, are usually online, and they usually allow participants to enroll in the entire program — a certificate program — or to take individual classes. Because translators working in the United States have a lot of room to create themselves, you can consider piecing together a selection of classes from several programs to get your focus on and practice in translation.

With this option, though, you'll have to consider the pros and cons: selecting courses from several programs might get you the training you need but might not lead you to completing a certificate program. Would that certificate be a nice credential to add to your resume? Or are there indications that you'll be successful without it?

Online offerings

If you're not too sure about how to identify the quality of an online program, selecting one can be a bit tricky. University programs have the credential of being part of a university. In most cases university offerings for nonmatriculated students go through a vetting process within the university by trained scholars and have an infrastructure that supports the offerings.

Language service companies and small businesses

If you look beyond the university, you can find some language service companies or small businesses that offer translator training. Do your research and find out what the company or business is all about. Can you get an outline of the training before committing to it? Can you talk to previous participants? What can you find out about the expert who's going to lead the training?

Training with an accomplished translator

Also in the realm of opportunities outside the university, you might come across the chance to train with accomplished and well-respected translators. It's not unusual for independent translators with years of experience to offer their own trainings. Their experience and credentials often include owning their own business, service to professional organizations, occasional teaching with university programs, speaking and publishing on translation, and more.

Here are a couple of opportunities to check out:

>> A successful translator, later-turned interpreter, and business owner Corinne McKay, author of *How to Succeed as a Freelance Translator*, has a "Training for Translator" platform that serves students via online courses, master classes, and challenge groups. She's an American Translators Association-certified French to English translator and a Colorado court-certified French interpreter. www.trainingfortranslators.com/

>> Check out Helen Eby's Gaucha Translations. Eby, who works in Oregon and Washington, is an ATA-certified English to Spanish and Spanish to English translator working with texts related to government, law, medicine, and education. She's also a certified Spanish court interpreter and medical interpreter. Eby offers a range of translation instruction. www.gaucha translations.com/

University offerings for nonmatriculated students

You can find a sampling of different programs for nonmatriculated students at universities. They range from a robust program that's open to all languages paired with English, to a translation certificate that focuses on Spanish and English with traditional areas, to one that's open to all languages paired with English with a focus on working in the education setting.

THE UNIVERSITY OF MASSACHUSETTS AMHERST

This university offers an Online Certificate in Professional Translation and Interpreting for nonmatriculated students. In other words, you don't need to be accepted as a full-time student to UMass Amherst to be part of this certificate program. Students need to have advanced proficiency in English and at least one spoken language besides English. Students can take the entire 15-credit certificate or only one course. Because the program covers both translation and interpreting, if you want to focus on translation, you have to select the offered courses that focus on translation.

Also check out the offerings at the UMass Translation Center. The university center offers regular and customized training and professional development opportunities.

THE UNIVERSITY OF ARIZONA

This university offers a non-credit Online Translators Certificate that focuses on Spanish and English. The program has three areas of translation: business, legal, and medical. Each course is 16 weeks long and is offered once or twice per year.

THE UNIVERSITY OF GEORGIA

This university offers a professional translator in education certificate that's a total of 30 hours of training. It has no prerequisites to enroll. Students must be able to read and write fluently in both English and another language.

Looking Into Mentorship Programs

You can combine taking courses or workshops with getting involved with a mentorship program. This is a great move for early-career professionals or for professionals trying to make a switch in their career, such as pivoting to offer new services or new business configurations. Mentorships are usually with established programs, which are great because they add a new credential to your resume. Also keep in mind that you can informally look for a mentor once you start getting to know people in the profession. Translators usually love to talk about what they do and how they do it. Having a mentor is important, especially if you work with languages that don't have too many practicing professionals.

Within professional associations

If you're interested in becoming a literary translator and you translate into English, check out:

>> **American Literary Translators Association:** ALTA has several options for early-career literary translators. https://literarytranslators.org/mentorships

- **Emerging Translator Mentorship Program:** This ALTA-sponsored program pairs experienced translators with emerging ones in which the two work on a translation project that can be completed during the year of mentorship. It's a competitive program to which emerging translators must apply.

- **Travel Fellowship Program:** ALTA awards early-career translators with funds to help them attend the annual ALTA conference, which attracts literary translators, writers, students, teachers, publishers, and other professionals from across the United States and all over the world. It usually lasts for about three days. You can attend panels, literary readings, and other events and browse publishers' tables.

>> **National Centre for Writing:** This center has emerging translator mentorships. Emerging translators are usually classified as translators who have not yet published a full-length translated book. Although the National Centre for Writing is run out of the United Kingdom, translators don't need to live in the UK unless a particular strand of the mentorship program requires it. Check out this webpage to learn more about this program and the related BCLT Summer School, another opportunity for literary translators: https://nationalcentreforwriting.org.uk/get-involved/translators/etm/

If you're interested in translating texts other than literary ones, check out what one of the largest organizations in the United States has to offer:

American Translators Association Mentoring Program: This ATA program isn't for beginning translators. As the ATA states, it's a program for "experienced translators with a specific goal or career focus in mind." It looks like you need at least two years as a practicing professional for this program.

Also, look within the professional associations to identify translators with whom you might be able to work in a mentoring situation.

TED Translators

Have you ever watched a TED Talk? Those short videos have so many great ideas expressed in brilliant ways. TED Translators, a global community of volunteers, spreads those ideas by adding subtitles to these talks. To do the work, you need to be a native speaker of or someone who's fluent in the languages you want to work with, and you need to fill out an application to volunteer your services. The application involves sharing your language information, watching a video, and taking a quiz. Once accepted. you can choose a short video to work on. After you submit it you get feedback from an experienced translator. A language coordinator then approves and preps the talk for publication. You receive credit on ted.com.

There's been some controversy among professional translators about this program. However, there's no requirement about how many videos you do. At the same time you, as a beginning translator, get feedback on your work.

TED Translators also accepts individuals who can provide transcriptions. The process is the same. https://www.ted.com/participate/translate

Scoping Out Customized Skill and Educational Opportunities

Even once you have many years of experience as a translator under your belt, you'll need to keep in touch with learning opportunities so that you keep developing professionally. The more experience you have, the better you'll be able to detect where your shortcomings are, what support you need, or what you'd like to learn more about. It's about developing your skills and gaining new ones. A great way to do this is to enroll in stand-alone educational opportunities offered by colleges and universities or with agencies or professional organizations.

Whatever learning opportunity you decide to go for, be sure to add it to your translator's resume. Be sure to note exactly what the experience is: the title of the course or workshop, the organization or institution that offered the course or workshop, the date or dates on which you participated in the experience, and, if not obvious, how long the experience is. A two-hour workshop isn't the same as a 24-hour workshop series.

Also, if participating in such a program involves a cost, which it most likely will, ask your employer if they can cover it, especially if you do the translations for the organization you work for. If you're working as a freelance translator, the fee might be tax deductible or a business expense. That's something you'll have to work out with your tax preparer.

If translation is a way in which you want to earn a living, the skill development and educational opportunities are investments. If they're quality programs, your skills and knowledge will advance, and you'll work smarter.

TIP

For one-time and short-term trainings, keep your eyes on at least three areas. The first could be looking out for trainings organized by associations for translators in general at the national and regional levels. The next would be for translators working in your area(s) of specialization. Finally, check to see if opportunities are available to participate in trainings with other translators who work in your language pair. In sum, keep your focus on translation, area of specialization, and language pair.

Once again, look at what the **American Translators Association** has to offer. Follow this organization, and check out the seminars and workshop programming. The organization has a lot to offer to translators working with English around the world. ATA follows the trends and knows what to offer to its members to advance the profession. It holds webinars and houses an archive of previous webinars. It also offers live events, touching on a range of topics from finance issues for freelancers and physical well-being (remember translators sit down a lot!) to developing translation and related technical skills. Furthermore, the ATA has divisions for individual languages.

New England Translators Association is an example of a regional professional association that offers one-time webinars on hot topics at an affordable rate. Other areas of the United States and the world will have their own regional associations, so check them out for training opportunities.

Keep in mind that particular organizations and associations focus on certain areas of translation. The **American Association of Interpreters and Translators in Education** (AAITE) is one of those. It has a professional development series that gives members the opportunity to learn more about certain topics related to translation and interpretation in the school setting.

Translators, like any successful professionals, are committed to lifelong learning. You can find opportunities of all kinds in the United States and abroad. As you make your way through the world of translation, take note of them so that when you're ready to advance your skills or to learn more, you'll know where to look for them.

Chapter **7**

Focusing on Specialization, Certification, Certificates, and Professional Development

When you start dabbling in translation, you might practice translating different types of texts to see what it is you enjoy and just to gain more familiarity with the whole world of moving between your languages in written documents. You might even continue to do this as you establish yourself as a professional because you'll need to make enough money to support yourself or because you'll want to see what kinds of projects come your way.

Even if you do go through this phase, always reject projects that you can't responsibly or ethically translate. Accepting all projects won't be sustainable, and at some point on your road as a translator you should choose a specialization so that you attract the kinds of texts you enjoy translating and that you translate well.

Yes, you'll be a Spanish to English or an English-to-Portuguese or an English-to-Haitian Creole-translator, but this won't necessarily mean that as a working professional you can or should translate anything and everything that's written in your source language into your target language.

This is where specialization, certification, certificates, and professional development — the subject of this chapter — come in. Determining your specialization and obtaining certification or certificates to qualify you for certain jobs will help you focus your skills as a translator and build your career path, which you will then want to solidify with continuous learning through professional development.

This chapter looks at how you can refine and establish yourself as a translator with a particular credentials and knowledge base. I also emphasize how to keep that knowledge developing so that you can establish yourself as an expert in a given area.

Determining Your Specialization

You need to consider many questions when becoming a translator. One of them might be whether to be a general translator or to specialize in a particular area. If you translate between a common language pair and don't narrow down the kind of texts you translate, you might get lost or find a hard time distinguishing yourself from other translators. Specializing if you work among a common language pair can also lead to more work. You can determine the texts you specialize in translating in several ways.

If you're not a freelance or independent translator but rather got into this business because of an organization such as a school or a legal agency you already work for, then your area of specialization might already be determined for you. Hopefully, it's one you enjoy! Even if you're comfortable in your area of specialization, there's always more to learn and ways to grow.

REMEMBER

Translators, like other professionals, evolve over time. Although you might choose one specialization in your early years, you might curate a list of related specializations that you add to over time. No matter what your specializations are or how many there are, you'll want to keep nourishing them with professional development opportunities.

If you're already working for an organization, such as a hotel or a school, and you translate documents for that organization, that will probably determine the kinds of texts you translate. So in these cases it would be hospitality and school-related texts. However, keep in mind that these are dynamic organizations, and as a translator, especially in your early years, you might not be able to translate all the texts that each one of these organizations creates. A school can have special education documents that have technical language and legal implications attached. It takes a person with specialized knowledge to translate these texts. A bilingual school district superintendent, if untrained as a translator and lacking in specialized knowledge of the special education terms in the target language, wouldn't even be able to do an efficient and effective translation of the document.

If you're starting out on your career path to becoming a translator and don't already work for any specific organization, you might have a bit more freedom when determining which areas you'll specialize in as a translator. Think of the subjects you like and are knowledgeable in. How can you use those interests to create an area of specialization? It's fine too if you don't feel ready just yet to determine your area of specialization. Another helpful starting point could be identifying which areas you don't want to specialize in. You can pass those projects on to another translator and then work your way through the projects you do want to keep and find the threads to identify a specialization.

TIP

You might hear that translators who work with common language pairs or high-volume language pairs, such as English and Spanish, are the ones who get to specialize, while translators of other language pairs with a lower volume must take on all projects. This is something to be aware of, but it's not always the case. It depends on where you're working and how you work, the contacts you have, and your experience. Take a look around, think about your interests and the needs of the kinds of clients you'd like to have, and strategically mark your specialization.

Although all kinds of documents are translated out of urgent need and proactive accessibility to diversity promotion and creative projects, there is seemingly a limited number of areas for which you can find readily available specialized training. The areas that you hear about and for which you can usually find marked trainings or programming have traditionally, in the United States, been divided into the areas of legal, medical, literary, and business translation. At least these are the areas in which academic courses and professional organizations tend to land a specialized focus.

Legal

Power of attorney, by and between, terms and conditions, any and all. Do you know how to express these phases in your languages? Have you ever closely read the lease to your apartment or the contract you signed to get a cell phone? Do you understand the legalese well enough in English to translate it into Portuguese, abiding by all the conventions of legal writing in Portuguese?

Because of the large demand for translation of legal documents and because it's a specialized field with legal implications, legal translation usually gets many courses and other trainings dedicated to it. For instance, you'll see *legal translation* more often as a course name than you would a course on horticulture translation.

Legal translation involves translating contracts and agreements, legal proceedings, internal communications, real estate leases, witness statements, corporate legal documents, intellectual property documents, and more. Many documents with legal implications need translations according to established timelines. Translators of legal documents need to know specialist terminology and the genre conventions of writing in two legal systems. Accuracy is also a must in the translation of legal documents. Legal translators work with documents ranging from small to large law firms and corporations, among other places that furnish documents with legalities attached. Many special education documents generated in schools have legal implications.

It's said that the best legal translators are lawyers who become translators or translators who have studied the law. Legal translators, like those who work in other areas, need to commit to a lifetime of learning because they have to build up knowledge of systems, terminology, phraseology, and style.

Translators of legal documents often develop transcription skills as well so they can offer this service to clients. Professionals working in this area can transcribe and often translate recordings as part of a legal case and testimonies.

If you want to get on this path and your college years are ahead of you, think about majoring in the language or languages you want to work with along with pre-law or legal studies.

Medical

When searching through translator training programs and courses, you'll come across medical as another area of specialization. Medical translators translate training and other educational materials, information between providers and patients, journal articles and manuscripts, regulatory documents from government agencies, sales materials for medical devices and all kinds of products, and documents on pharmaceuticals. To be a medical translator you need, as with any kind of translation, a high level of language proficiency, knowledge of medical terms, and possibly familiarity with statistics and statistical terms.

Being a medical translator is a way to be knowledgeable in and contribute to the world of medicine without all the years of medical school and possibly accumulating all the student financial debt that a medical degree can cost. As a medical translator, you get to learn a lot about the medical field without being a doctor or nurse.

As a medical translator you need to know the terminology as well as how to deal with delicate medical information. Work is available on a contract or full-time basis, and the requirements can depend on where you work. You'll have to take some kind of test to determine your language and translation skills. Being a prepared medical translator combined with having ATA certification, if available in your language combination, can help you get a full-time job as a translator for clinics and hospitals. Figure 7-1 shows the ATA seal.

FIGURE 7-1:
How translation
broadens
horizons!

TIP

Be careful when you're researching medical translator programs on the internet. Some programs appear to be trainings for medical translators, but they're actually programs for medical interpreters. Some providers of trainings use both translators and interpreters for their interpreter training programs. This is a reminder to carefully research all aspects of any program. In a profession that's unregulated in the United States, it can be hard to determine the quality of the training program from online information alone. Do the research, ask the questions, follow up, and know what you're getting into before you commit!

With medical and legal translations, the documents tend to be straightforward, so machine translation can be leveraged more in these areas than in others. However, because medical and legal are such high-stake areas, you must have a human involved in all the stages of the translation process.

Literary

Although people rarely train in a formalized fashion to be literary translators, this area of specialization stands out, especially among university programs. This could in part be because translation programs or courses usually live in language and literature departments, which employ scholars with degrees in literature and language who translate literature as part of their scholarly contributions to the world.

Literary translators read a literary text in one language and write it in another. Doing this well requires reading a lot of literature in both languages of your language pair, having vast knowledge of the language you're translating into, at the very least, and practicing and exchanging with other readers and translators.

To train to become a literary translator, you could take a course or two in literary translation or apply to emerging translator programs and mentorships. Look out for workshops and events offered by the American Literary Translators Association and other organizations (See Chapter 6 "Expanding Your Options with Non-University Programs"). Be on the lookout for residencies. Most of them are based outside the United States. Some are for specific language combinations, while others are for all language combinations.

Being a literary translator as your full-time job, especially if you live in the United States and have no trust fund, is difficult. Many literary translators are also full-time or part-time educators or have some steady income stream from another source.

There's no one single profile of a literary translator, just like it might be hard to say there's one single profile of a writer.

That said, literary translation is one of the few fields that will likely continue to require significantly more human input. Because of the creative nature of poetry, prose, and other literary texts, AI isn't really capable of edging out humans there.

Other ways to specialize

If you want to carve out an area of specialization, you don't have to specialize in one of the legal, medical, or literary areas. But seeing how each of these areas is organized helps you get a sense of the components of a specialization. Over time, anticipate shifts in the way specializations are organized due to the development of technologies and translation needs. For instance, a specialization in translation-related software and hardware is a growing area to look into.

By now you're getting the sense that translators are creators and that you can create your own professional profile and specialize in whatever area or areas you'd like. Just be sure it's one for which there's a need and that will attract work!

To explore areas of specialization or to get inspired, scan professional association offerings and think about your own profile. What do you know best? What do you like? You could specialize in human resources, environmental issues, fashion, electric cars, video games, sports, or any number of things. Specialization could require knowledge about localization strategies.

Specialization has no limits. You can move from medical to pharmaceutical texts and texts on well-being and mental health. You can move from texts related to the hospitality industry to texts on real estate.

TIP

Parallel texts can be your friends as you develop your translation skills to translate texts in a certain area. They're texts of the same subject matter available in the target language. For example, you can read financial texts in French to help you translate banking texts from English to French. Reading parallel texts isn't only a way to advance your language and content skills, but can also be incorporated as part of the research process of translation.

TIP

Translation memories can be very helpful because they allow you to build out a corpus that specializes in one area. You can then use them in computer-assisted translation tools to leverage/recall segments that you've previously translated in other jobs, which in turn makes your translations more consistent and efficient.

In general, specialization requires mastery of subject matter or being highly skilled in an area. If you're majoring in Spanish and electrical engineering, you might one day decide to further contribute to engineering by being a part-time or full-time translator. All of this adds value as a translator or as an engineer.

You won't be limiting yourself if you choose a specialization. You can very well get more work and better paid work.

Pursuing Certifications and Certificates

Along with specialization, at some point on your translator career path, consider whether certification is available and needed. Certification can have a few different looks depending on your language pair or pairs, your specialization, and the country or countries in which you practice as a translator. If a client or an employer asks you if you're a certified as a translator, it's important to understand exactly what they're talking about. They could mean that they just want to know you have training and experience. They might not be referring to any type of certification. From the translator's point of view, you need to know that just holding a certificate doesn't mean you're certified.

Translators love to think of every word critically. And *certifications* and *certificates* sound like serious words and maybe even ones that can put a halt to your path to becoming a translator. But these words shouldn't get in the way of your first steps to becoming a translator. You might even find out that a certification or a certificate is never going to be necessary for you to be a successful translator, depending on your language combination, where you work, and the kind of work you want to attract. Certifications and certificates are an investment of time, money, and effort. In many cases, you can decide what you need.

CERTIFIED TRANSLATION

A client might ask for a *certified translation*. Just because you might be an ATA-certified translator, for instance, doesn't mean that every translation you make is a "certified translation." A certified translation is a translation, a document, that has been certified, usually by a notary or some other official. What's considered a certified translation can vary from country to country. In some countries it can mean working with a lawyer and paying hundreds of dollars. In the United States it might mean getting a notary to put a stamp on a translated document for less than $5. In sum, find out what type of certification, notarization, or apostille is needed before agreeing to move forward with a project. An apostille certifies the authenticity of the signature, seal, and position of the official who has created, issued, or certified a copy of a public document. It allows for a public document in one country to be recognized in another country. Because these are things usually required by a large organization, chances are they're already being systematized, and with a few phone calls or a visit to a website, you can figure out what exactly is needed.

Certifications

Certifications mean different things in different countries. Depending on which country you'd like to translate documents for or in, do some research among experienced translators or with translation associations to have a better understanding of what certification means in that context.

Certification isn't a requirement to practice as a translator in most contexts, so don't see this word as an obstacle as you get started on your path to becoming a translator.

How do you get certification?

Certifications often come through getting certified in your language pair. For example, you can be a certified Spanish to English translator. In some countries a certified translator is called a *sworn translator*, which usually involves a government certification program granting you the right to officially sign your translations.

Certifications usually expire after a period of time. Or, to keep them active, you need to take a certain number of hours of continuing education every year. It all depends on how you're certified and what it requires.

When researching translator certification, don't trust what you find on the web. Many organizations call interpreters translators. Be sure that the certification program you're looking at is an opportunity in translation, if that's what you're going for.

If a client wants a certified translator, that usually means they want someone to have an official translation certification from an organization like the ATA or the equivalent in a country outside the United States. It could also mean that they have no idea what they're talking about, and they just want a capable translator. You have to ask questions to find out more about what clients want and need.

If you're certified as a translator, you usually need to meet continuing-education requirements to keep the certification. The organization that certifies you will let you know what those requirements are.

Organizations that offer certification

In the United States, for better or for worse, there aren't many opportunities to get translator certification. One of the only organizations that certifies translators is the American Translators Association.

Testing

If you're a translator working in the United States, the most common way of becoming "certified" is to take the American Translators Association (ATA) exam. The ATA offers certification exams in language pairs. They don't have a certification exam for every language pair.

To take the exam you need to be a member of ATA, and that has a price attached to it. It also costs money to take the exam. If it's in your plans to take the exam, it's recommended that you first take a practice certification exam. And, yes, that's another fee.

The passing rate for the exam is 20%. If you don't pass the exam the first time around, you have to pay for everything all over again.

The benefits of certification

Certification is proof that you know your language pair well. Having certification could mean that you're the first translator a potential client will contact. Certification could bring you more work because some clients might require it, and others might prefer it. Others, as you can imagine, will have no idea that it even exists!

Certification could earn you more money on a single project or overall by bringing you more clients. The more you're in demand, the more you'll be able to pick and choose your clients.

If you're certified, put it on your resume, your social media sites if you use them professionally, your website, and on your business card if you have one. If you're certified by the ATA, you get to use the initials CT after your name.

Certificates

In the world of translation, you can be awarded a certificate for the completion of a university academic program that required several semester-long courses. This could be a certificate in Translation Studies, for example. You can also get a certificate for attending a one-time online workshop during which you minimally participate.

This range of opportunities that offer certificates isn't a reason to turn your back on certificates. And it doesn't mean that certificates don't mean anything. You need to be aware of what each certificate you go after means and what value it holds. In a sense, the value of a certificate is determined by the program's recognition and quality.

Certificates aren't certifications

One thing to get straight and not lose sight of is that certificates aren't certifications. In this profession, you'll repeatedly hear people ranging from clients to novice translators mistaking certificates for certifications. You might hear some people say that a translator is "certified" because they took a university translation certificate program. This means that they have a certificate, not that they're certified. You might hear a leader say that his team is certified as translators because they participated in a one-time training. This isn't true. Taking a one-time training doesn't mean you have certification.

Certificates are just proof of completion of a certificate program, course, or whatever it is that you completed. It's a credential but not a certification, so don't mess up the terms, and help your clients and non-translator colleagues use them correctly.

Nonetheless, certificates are a credential and can be extremely meaningful depending on the program you participate in. If you did get a certificate from an impressive program, be sure to find an opportunity to describe it a bit more than just listing it when you're presenting yourself.

The range of certificates

A university might grant you a certificate for completing and passing a range of courses in a translation or translator program. An organization or company that offers some sort of training might also offer you a certificate for doing the same sort of thing.

If you're at a college or university working on a degree, the certificate might be something you can do in addition to your major or minor. If you're not enrolled in a degree program, sometimes you can just enroll in a certificate program for continuing-education students. These certificate programs can be online, in person, or hybrid. Check out what your local universities and community colleges might have in store for you.

In addition to the successful completion of an academic program, a certificate can be granted just to prove that you attended a training, workshop, conference, or event.

All the efforts you make to maintain the integrity of the profession are valid. Keep a record of the professional development opportunities that you attend. Review them periodically and pinpoint any gaps.

Also plan for the kinds of professional development you'll focus on in a single year. Keep in mind that you want to continue to develop language, translation, and your area of specialization. Ideally, you'd continuously be touching on all three of these areas.

3

Creating Translations

Organize a process for accuracy, consistency, and effectiveness.

Think about incorporating machine translation into your work.

Understand why a translation is not exactly the same as the source text.

Look at the ethics you should maintain as a translator.

Chapter **8**

Adopting an Effective and Efficient Translation Process

Although the act of translation is about reading a text in one language and writing it in another, the work of a translator includes much more than these two activities. This is especially true if you want to do this work in a professional setting either as a freelancer or for an organization.

A translation process is more than creating a document in a language different from its current language. On the one hand, you need to consider the entire process the document will follow, from before the translation is made through what to do with the translation once you have it in your hands. On the other hand, you need to think about the actual translation process of that document.

This chapter, while laying out a process to follow for translating a document, isn't intended to be a how-to translate chapter. When you understand the bigger picture of where translations come from and where they need to go, your translations have a greater chance of being more effective, and you can finish them faster.

Gathering Information Before You Translate

Before you get texts in your hands to translate, consider what you need to know before and after you translate. Sandwiched in the middle is a multistep process to follow while you translate a text. A lot happens when you translate, so you need a plan in place to keep you on track. This will help your translation achieve accuracy and consistency. You don't want some paragraphs to flow well and make beautiful sense while others seem like a clumsy first draft. A path to follow will save you time and help you create the best translation possible.

Some fellow translators will share the details of the process they always use. Others will tell you they have a process but will share only parts of it with you. You might hear experienced translators say they don't follow any particular process.

TIP

As you read through this section, you might be thinking "Wow, this is a lot to hold onto as a translator," but the sooner you become aware of the webs and networks of the translation process, the stronger you'll be as a translator and the more helpful you'll be to your clients. This is a way to distinguish yourself from a machine translator.

If you ask multiple translators to tell you about their processes, you probably won't get the same answer twice. Some processes might be similar, but no two will be the same. Many might follow the same general steps, but if you dig deeper, you'll find there's a moment when they differ. They'll also differ depending on what kind of text they're translating.

REMEMBER

Translation is writing. There are many ways to write, and each text demands its own kind of process. The process is also affected by a translator's experience, available tools, and time, among other things. Sometimes as creators of texts, as translators, we're not fully aware of all the steps we follow.

As a novice translator, one of the ways you can help yourself is to establish a process. This way, you'll keep track of all the things you need to do to create a translation. The more you follow this process, the more you'll internalize it, maybe even to the point where you'll feel that you have no process. You can also add steps to the process if that helps you. Make it yours. Create several processes!

TIP

Ask your client or the person who requests the translation if the document they're sending you to translate is the final version. The question might sound silly or obvious, but sometimes people send drafts of a text they'll eventually want translated thinking it will speed up the translation process without telling you it's a draft. Although it can be helpful to prepare for a project that's coming your way in terms of theme, time, length, complexity, and schedule, don't start translating a text until you have the final version.

The translation brief

Before you start reading the text you need to translate, make sure you understand the directions that the client or the person requesting the translation gives you. This is sometimes referred to as a *translation brief*. The translation brief is a set of instructions that helps the translator learn about the project to fulfill the client's needs.

Beware that not all clients or requestors of translators will send you a translation brief. Many don't even know what one is or know the complexities of translation. You can help your clients give you the information that would be in a translation brief by asking them for this information via a form through which you would have clients or requestors send you a project, or by other means.

The translation brief should include the elements discussed in this section.

Basic information about the project

Not all projects will fit your profile or your workload. Gather the information you will need to identify the best approach, if it's a project you're able to take on. Be sure the following aspects are clearly defined and agreed upon:

>> Who requested the translation? You need to know who to contact if you have questions about the project.

>> Does the project have a name? This will help you keep track of the multiple projects you might be working on for the same client.

>> What kind of project is this? Is it an academic text, a series of fliers, or a legal translation?

The purpose of the translation

Why is the client translating this text? What will the translation be used for? If it's an academic text, will it be published in a journal? If it's a series of fliers, that's important to know because you might allow yourself as the translator to change the text in a way that will make it more likely for your target audience to pay attention to it.

Knowledge of and access to these materials will facilitate the translation process. Be sure you understand, at a minimum, the following points:

>> **The target audience:** Who's the target audience? What can your client share about their age and education level? What other details seem relevant to the way in which they might read a text? The more you know about the target audience, the more effective your translation will be.

>> **The target language:** You might think it's a given for clients to let you know what language to translate a text into, but that isn't always the case. If you translate into more than one language or work in two directions, be sure it's clear what the target language is for each project. For some clients it will be clear, but if you work for a fast-paced organization in which translating is only one of your duties among many, you'll want to be sure the dimensions of the project are clear to everyone involved.

REMEMBER

A client might send you a text to translate into Spanish. There are many dialects and variations of Spanish in the world. You might hear a client or industry professional use the word *locale*. *Locale* refers to a combination of language and the place where it is spoken. When translators know the locale of a particular project, they can take in the culture, conventions, and preferences of a particular region as they translate. There are commonly used codes for locales. Some examples are:

- en-US = English (USA)

- en-GB = English (Britain)

- es-ES = Spanish (Spain)

- es-MX = Spanish (Mexico)

Does the client know where the target audience is from? Is it mostly a Puerto Rican Spanish-speaking audience? Mexican? Spanish? If it happens that the audience is mostly from Puerto Rico, you'll want to be sure the translation works for them. This means you'll want to avoid the use of words that could mean something you don't want them to mean in the target language. You don't need to be a Puerto Rican Spanish-speaker to do this. This is when you'd translate the text into Spanish and then have a Puerto Rican Spanish-speaker with up-to-date knowledge of Spanish and strong language skills review your work.

- **The amount of text:** Are you supposed to translate the entire text? Again, this sounds straightforward, but it's best to confirm rather than assume, especially when your time and energy are involved. Sometimes a text or a document will have several parts. Ask if you're supposed to translate all of them.

- **Additional material:** Does your client have a glossary or word list they can share with you? Have they had any issues with translating this kind of text before? Are there existing translations of previous versions of the text that their target audience might be aware of? Do they have a CAT tool they want you to work with (See Chapter 4) for this kind of text?

A submission date

Before beginning any translation project with a client or requestor, be sure you've agreed on a submission date or due date. Because requesting a translation is often an afterthought for some organizations, due dates are often ASAP. This isn't an effective practice. It's best to be clear about when translations are expected to be finished and submitted.

When calculating a realistic submission date, consider:

- The length and complexity of the document to be translated.

- Whether you as the translator need to make any desktop publishing or other significant formatting adjustments.

- Other projects you have going on. If you're working on five other projects, you won't be able to work on this new project all the time. Factor that into your proposed submission date for this new project.

- Any scheduled time off. If you have a doctor's appointment or any other previously scheduled appointments or events, that's time away from your desk. Don't forget to factor that in as well.

TIP

If taking on a project is doable, but not comfortable because of your other work commitments, you can charge a rush fee if the client wants the project prioritized. (See Chapter 16.)

Further information

Following are some additional questions you need answers to before you begin to translate to facilitate the process and keep everyone satisfied:

- **Is the document in an editable format?** Sometimes a client or person requesting the translation will send you the document as a PDF or as a beautifully laid out file in InDesign, or they'll drop a hard copy of a flier or handbook on your desk and ask you to translate it. All of that makes things unnecessarily difficult. Ask for the file in an editable format such as a Word document or a Google document, for example. Being able to edit the text will make your life as a translator much easier.

If the client doesn't have any format other than PDF, you can usually find PDF readers, like Adobe Acrobat Reader or ABBYY FineReader (one of the better ones in the industry). However, some PDFs are flat and may contain hand-written text, and so on that the readers simply cannot pick up. A lot of translators would reject flat PDFs.

>> **Does the translation require desktop publishing?** If your client is expecting the translation to look like the original version that was created with desktop publishing, consider charging extra for this service. If you can't do it, let your client know that they'll have to get that done elsewhere and perhaps offer to review the document that incorporates your translation before it's distributed. You can offer this review at no charge if it's a short document that won't take you too much time. If it's a longer document, charge an additional fee.

>> **Does the design of the document allow for language expansion and some flexibility?** Remember that not all languages are the same. In some languages it take a dozen words to say what can be described in another language in seven words. And not all languages use the same script! Some will take up more space than others. It's also been said that translations, regardless of language or script, are often around 20% longer because of the possible explanations that need to be added to the text.

>> **Where will the translation be published?** If you're a freelance translator who's working for a client, you might think that it's not your responsibility to know where the translation will go once it's done. In principle, that's correct. However, with little effort, it's a question you can ask that might help you distinguish yourself from other translators, including machine translators, especially as you're getting started as a translator. The answer you receive might affect your translation and its success.

For example, if you work as a translator for a school and you find out that the Haitian Creole translation of the newsletter is only going to be published on the school's app, it might not have much success reaching the Haitian Creole-speaking families. You know that most Haitian Creole-speaking families don't access the app regularly or don't yet have access to it because it's in English. The newsletter has a better chance of reaching them if it's emailed as an attachment or circulated in print format.

>> **How will the translation be distributed?** This question is like the previous one. What you're looking for is how the target audience is going to know that the published translation exists. This could mean advising your clients to put

notices about the translation on all language versions of the document. If you translated a letter from the superintendent into Portuguese for a school district, the English version of the letter should indicate in English and in Portuguese that a Portuguese version of the letter is available. If this letter is distributed electronically to families, you can create links to both versions of the document.

Compensation agreement

Once all questions about the project have been cleared up and you have a solid idea of everything the project entails, agree to compensation with your client or the person requesting the translation. You want to know you're going to get paid and for how much. This can be a per-word rate or an hourly rate. You also want to charge for any major tasks, such as formatting, that go beyond the translation of the document. For more on this, see Chapter 16.

The translator's lens

Translators have a special way of looking at and reading a text. That's true not only because they read it imagining its presence as a text that doesn't yet exist in another language, but also because they envision how that text will exist in the world once it's in that other language. With this in mind, as a translator, you're able to note things about this future translation that the author of the source text might not realize. This translator's lens allows you to see certain things such as the following:

If the text you're going to translate is a flier for an event, does the content indicate that interpreters in the target language of the translated document will be available at the event? If they're not, this is also helpful to add so that the audience knows what to expect. It's respectful, and it will likely affect whether they decide to attend the event. You wouldn't want people to take off work, schedule a babysitter, and travel across town to attend an event only to find out that the event has no interpreters.

If the document you're translating refers to other sources such as websites, texts, and films or videos, are those available in the target language of the translation?

If the target audience is instructed to call a number or to contact someone via email, will those communication lines be available in the target language?

Other aspects might come up depending on the translation project. Understanding all you can about your project before you start to translate allows you to make your client aware of these necessary additions to the translation as they strive to make their content available to the target audience.

Reading and Understanding the Text

Once you have all the details you need about the text you're going to translate, it's time to focus on getting that text into its target language. Finally! Make sure you're ready to concentrate and aren't distracted. Reading for translation is different from reading for other purposes. When you read for translation, you're reading with an eye for having to write the entire text over again, but in another language. You can't do that and provide a quality translation of a text if you don't fully understand it. Get ready!

First, carefully read through the text. The goal is to make sure you fully understand it. At this stage, don't get too caught up in looking up all the words you aren't sure of. Instead:

>> **Underline** words that you're not completely sure of.

>> **Circle** any parts of the text that you think you'll have to pay extra special attention to while making your translation. These could be repetitions, idioms, or references that might not readily make sense to your target audience. It's anything that jumps out at you not because you don't understand it, but because of the way it's expressed.

>> **Take quick notes** about anything you want to remember to do as you create your translation or things you need to verify about the source text.

The idea at this stage is to keep a reading pace that allows you to get an idea of the entire text, while identifying things that you'll have to pay extra special attention to when you translate. Your reading skills and knowledge of the language and culture, will let you know what those things are.

It's often said that the translator is the closest reader of a text and the one who often knows the text better than the person who wrote it. That's exciting!

Asking Questions: Analyzing the Text

In this next stage, you're going to dive deeper into the text. You'll start looking at all those parts of the text you identified and uncovering what they mean and how you will understand them so that you'll be able to translate them.

>> **Look up the words that you underlined.** Search for them in a monolingual dictionary of the source language. Find them in a bilingual dictionary. Look them up in a dictionary of the target language. Seek synonyms. Write down

all the possible choices. At this stage consider not only the *denotation* of the words (the dictionary meaning) but also the *connotation* of the words (the ideas, feeling, and associations a word might evoke beyond its dictionary meaning). Sometimes a word's connotation in the target language requires you to eliminate it as a choice for your translation.

>> **Focus on the parts of the text you circled.** Why did you circle them? Is there something in them that you must figure out? Is there an acronym you're unsure of? Are there some things you need to clear up by doing research? Are those things you can research online, or do you need to reach out to someone?

>> **Review the notes that you took and what they will mean for your translation.** Like circling certain words, do you need to learn more about certain topics in the source language? If so, dive into them. Are there translations of proper nouns you need to look up in the target language? If so, you want to find official webpages or other reliable sources where you can find out if they're indeed used by the target culture. Don't just throw something into Google Translate and think that because it gives you a translation, it will be acceptable in your translation for the target audience. You need to see it in a reliable document that readers of the target language use.

TIP

Try seeing who might be able to help you in forums like Proz and WordReference. In these spaces translators ask questions about terminology and other language-related questions. There's a lot there to see so it's worth taking the time to browse them to see how they work. They can be a huge help!

>> **Talk to trusted people in your network who can help you understand an aspect of the text you're unsure of.** Don't be scared to expand your network if need be. Professionals are usually eager to talk about their areas of expertise, and people, in general, are usually happy to talk about their languages.

>> **Identify any parallel texts.** Parallel texts are ones in the target language of your translation that cover the same topic as the text you're translating. Preferably they're original texts, not translations, written well by a native speaker. For example, if you're asked to translate a cover letter from Spanish to English for a humanities professor from Madrid who's looking for work at a university in the United States, you'd look at the standard format of cover letters written by US-based scholars in English for work at US universities.

>> **Do any other research that will help you fully understand the source text and what it means to translate it.** For example, if it's a letter, it most likely follows a different format in the target language. Also, in English, dialogue is usually indicated by quotation marks, but that's not the case in a French text. It's important to determine the structural expectations of a text in the target language.

This is the moment when you're figuring out all the answers to the questions you have about the text so that you have a full understanding of it.

TIP

Reading to translate is different than reading for the sake of reading. Don't be surprised if as you grow as a translator, you find yourself reading a sentence, somewhat unconsciously you start to simultaneously translate it. Oftentimes, and even more so if a sentence has multiple clauses, you'll need to move words around in your translation. As you translate, try not to get too caught up with maintaining the same word order.

Translating the Text to Produce Your First Draft

Now for the big moment. It's time to translate the document! Now you will start creating your target text. Make sure you have all the necessary tools with you and get comfortable. You're going to bring many of your translator skills together in this moment to create your translation.

>> **Have the source text available and create a digital file.** Clearly label it as the translation. You might decide to create different files for each draft of your translation, so come up with a naming and tracking system that you'll be able to follow.

>> **Have all the necessary tools available on your desk or on your computer.** This includes having online dictionaries open on your screen and any physical dictionaries you use piled on or near your desk.

Accessible glossaries, word lists, and translation technology are also included in this step.

>> **Get comfortable.** You don't want to start translating and then need to use the bathroom or get a drink of water right away.

Take care of all that before you sit down to start translating. Some experienced translators even have translation rituals they follow before getting to work!

>> **Move between reading and writing at a consistent pace to translate the text.** At this stage, you want to keep the translation moving, so if there are still words or parts you need to look up, highlight them in some way rather than stopping the process to do research.

However, keep in mind that the consistent pace will be slow because you don't want to overlook any details that you're unsure about.

Devise your own system of colors or symbols to track anything you still need to figure out. You can come back to them to research more after you have a first full draft of your translation.

>> **Give yourself a break!** Depending on the length of the text you're translating, don't expect to complete your first draft in a single sitting. Let the text sit if you're feeling like you need a break.

Between longer breaks, you might want to go back and go over what you already worked on to refamiliarize yourself with the text and to advance the work you've already done.

>> **Repeat this until you have a complete draft.** Then keep going over it to clear up anything you identified as needing more attention.

Clearing up any doubts: Revising your translation

Congratulations! You have a complete draft, and you're ready to move on to revising your translation. At this stage, look at your translation, comparing it to the source text to make sure everything is there.

Focus on whether the content is accurate and expressed as you'd like it to be. Limit your distractions as you move back and forth between the source text and your translation.

Read your translation aloud. If any parts sound clumsy or you stumble through them, you probably need to revise them further.

Iron out any parts that sound unnatural or unnecessarily awkward. You want your translation to sound as natural as possible, and this is the time to do it.

Polishing it: Editing your translation

You should do all of this without looking at the source text. At this point your focus is getting the translation to be a stand-alone text. It's the moment when you focus on these details:

>> Punctuation

>> Spelling

>> Capitalization

>> Numbers

>> Addresses, website, emails

At this stage you can also look at word choice and make the language tighter.

This is also the time when you might invite another professional who has strong writing skills in the target language to be part of the process. If you can, don't dismiss budgeting for a professional editor to edit your translations.

The expertise of an editor and another pair of eyes on your translation can improve the quality of your translation and maybe even speed up your process.

Considering Post-translation Tasks

Now that you have an excellent translation that has met its due date, make sure the world — or at least the people who need it — can see it. In many cases, your client will take care of this. However, that's not always a given. Some clients who are new to going multilingual might not think of this. In addition, if you translate as a part-time or full-time employee for an organization, your non-translator colleagues might not be fully familiar with how to get translations into the hands of the people who need them.

Manage the translation

Once you're finished with the translation, know where it needs to go. Does everyone have it who needs it?

This might be a simple question to answer if you're just turning translations into a single client, but if you translate for an organization, such as a school, you might need to do more follow-up to ensure that all the people who need to know about the existence of the translation in fact do.

Disseminate the translation

If you're not turning the translation into a client, but rather using it for your own organization, you might need to manually disseminate the document yourself:

>> Print and send it out or post it.

>> Share it on social media.

>> Include it in newsletters.

>> Think about where else the target audience might look to access the translation. You don't want your hard work to go unnoticed.

Archive the translated document

Before you wrap up a translation project, be sure to label and archive the translated document.

REMEMBER

Translation means change. Your process might change according to several factors:

>> The kind of text you translate

>> Who your client is or the organization you work for

>> Time with experience

>> The use and development of technology

REMEMBER

Being a translator requires you to be flexible while staying committed to the provision of quality services and maintaining ethical standards.

IN THIS CHAPTER

» Understanding what machine translation is

» Looking at the past and present of machine translation

» Gaining a basic understanding of how machine translation works

» Using machine translation critically and responsibly

» Seeing machine translation's role in the bigger picture of translation

Chapter **9**

Inviting Machine Translation into Your Office

Machine translation is one of the most common tools that beginning translators turn to other than dictionaries and that many non-translators use when they need a translation. Machine translation is known everywhere because it's easy to use, accessible, and free. For most people, it's not so much a question of how to technically use it, but how to critically use it.

Machine translation, also referred to as MT or *automated translation*, is a translation that a machine produces automatically, without the help or involvement of a human translator to immediately get the translation, although the translation is technically produced based on texts that were created by humans. It's helpful to think about machine translation as you're becoming a translator because it's one of the most common tools that beginning, novice, untrained translators, and uninformed organizations use. Some examples of machine translation tools are

Google Translate, ChatGPT, DeepL Translator, and other instant translation that's produced as the result of the push of or the click of a button.

Although people and organizations that are not aware of how machine translation tools works, might misuse it, there are a number of very well informed organizations that use machine translation and know how to properly harness it and combine it with machine translation post editing (MTPE).

Machine translation is one of the resources that translators can have among their translation environment tools and in their toolbox. But machine translation and translation environment tools aren't synonyms.

This chapter digs into what machine translation is (and isn't), how best to use it, and why humans still need to play a significant role in assuring the accuracy and quality of machine translations.

Getting Up to Speed on Machine Translation

You've probably heard a lot about machine translation. Maybe they've been conversations about whether machine translation is good or bad. Or maybe it's been a question of whether human translators will survive if machines can translate.

In general, it's not a question of whether you're for or against machine translation. It's more a matter of understanding what it is, how it works, when it might be fine to use it, how to use it, and letting people know that you've used it. In other words, it's more than just using machine translation, but using it critically. It's more about being machine translation literate as you're becoming a translator than it is deciding whether you're for or against machine translation. You can have those opinions, but you need to understand machine translation first.

It doesn't matter whether you're planning to become an independent translator, a full-time translator for an organization, or someone who occasionally translates for your organization, manages translations for your organization, or just wants to learn about translation. You need to understand how one of the most common tools accessible to everyone works.

WARNING

You need to know this because regardless of how you feel about machine translation, you're going to have to explain to clients, colleagues, and many other people in your life what machine translation is, how it works, and why it needs human involvement to have responsible translations circulating in the world that are worth reading.

Origins and major moments of machine translation

To understand machine translation today, it's good to have an idea about how it all started. Researchers have been working on machine translation since soon after World War II, sometime in the late 1940s. So it's probably a lot older than you think it is.

Early machine translation systems focused on words from dictionaries and grammar and tried to translate the way humans do. Dr. Lynne Bowker, a professor and Canada Research Chair in Translation, Technologies, and Society at the Université Laval, says that didn't work too well. A different approach needed to be developed. In the early 2000s, these systems moved away from rules and developed into data-driven systems based on number crunching and pattern matching.

TIP

Check out Dr. Lynne Bowker's Machine Translation Literacy Project at `https://sites.google.com/view/machinetranslationliteracy/`.

These tools today are created using a lot of data, or examples of texts. These examples are usually human-translated documents from a specific language pair. This means that English and Spanish texts can't train a tool destined to translate Ukrainian to Catalan.

The same thing goes for content. Engineering texts can't train a tool to translate texts about human resources. What's more, machine translation tools aren't equal for all languages. One tool might translate a certain kind of text better within a given language pair than it does for another topic in another language pair. And these tools and the data used to train them do get updated. So the result you get today from a tool might not be the result you get tomorrow.

WARNING

Another hot topic regarding machine translation is the biases in machine-produced translations. For example, if a machine translation is trained with texts that mostly use the Spanish masculine, singular form abogado for the English *lawyer*, it's more likely that the Spanish translation of lawyer, even if the lawyer in English is female, will be translated as *abogado*. That means that language that's not in the source text is introduced in the target text or the translation.

Developing machine translation literacy — meaning, knowing how machine translation works, recognizing how it can be useful in some but not all contexts, and acknowledging the implications of using machine translation for specific translation projects — is the key to ensuring that it's a tool used for good and not harm.

Machine translation today

One thing many people probably don't know about contemporary machine translation is that it's based on texts that humans have previously translated. Human translators today are concerned about these systems using their texts without permission to create a tool that could potentially put them out of work.

Fear of job loss due to machine translation is on the minds of people who are considering getting into translation. It's such a big question that even other people who aren't even interested in becoming a translator think about. Ideas about machine translation are even the reason why some people don't want to become translators and why they're no longer motivated to study languages. Fear not. The need for translation is so huge that there should always be a place for translators even if the way they work changes according to some assignments and clients. Some experienced translator colleagues might even share that they're busier than ever.

In today's world, you need to consider whether machine translation is the right choice for all or for some of a project, and what your interaction with the project will be. Will you adjust the source text before using machine translation? If that would seem appropriate, what might you have to do in the post-translation editing phase to get a quality translation?

As a translator, what might be on your mind most is deciding how and when to use machine translation as a tool and how to talk about it with others.

Understanding What People Mean When They Talk about Machine Translation

The term *machine translation* is used in several ways. Some people — especially those who aren't yet experienced in translation — use it to mean any time a machine is involved with translation. For them, there are translations strictly done by humans, and there are translations done by a machine, and the two don't work together. You do one or you do the other. But that's not right.

Then there are others who think that machine translation means using any kind of machine tool, or what Chapter 14 introduces as translation environment tools. That's not right either.

Some people use these tools right away without even considering that they could produce wrong, error-filled translations. Others are transparent about the use of these tools. Others get involved with using machine translation as part of their process, one in which a human is checking the translation's development along the way.

As a professional translator, you're probably going to spend some time helping non-translators understand what machine translation is, how it works, why it's not reliable, and why for professional purposes a human must be involved. You're going to have to understand the judgments and decisions a human can make that a machine translation can't. Some of these include decisions according to context and the distribution of a translation, among other factors.

Options

Google Translate, launched on April 28, 2006, is the most popular machine translation engine (MTE). You might also hear about DeepL Translator, Microsoft Bing, and Naver Papago. Many others are attached to apps and other programs on electronic devices. As a user you don't see how these tools work because you just type in or copy and paste a word, and a translation appears.

TIP

Just because Google is the most popular machine translation engine, it's not necessarily the best one. Part of inviting machine translation into your office means experimenting with different machine translation engines to compare the results. You might end up liking one for certain texts more than another.

Always keep in mind that machine translation is only an option and not a necessity, and it can't be used without your involvement when you're working professionally.

Depending on your language pair and the subject, machine translation tools might slow you down rather than help you translate faster. You might hear translators say that it's more efficient to translate a text from scratch than it is to edit a machine translation.

Beyond this, certain machine translation engines are objectively better for specific language pairs and text domains. DeepL is known for being one of the better machine translation engines for translations between English and French, in both directions. Google is arguably the overall most "well-rounded" machine translation engine, simply because of its age and the sheer quantity of data that is used to train its machine translation output, but obviously it will perform differently for different language pairs based on how much data was used to train each machine translation engine. Machine translation outputs can also be scored on quality, and some popular industry metrics include Chrf3, BLEU, TER, and COMET.

Keeping up with developments

If you're on social media and following any of the major industry news sites such as https://multilingual.com or https://slator.com, you probably won't miss any new developments regarding machine translation. Some updates also make the general news. If you're an involved translator, it's hard to miss discussions, debates, and developments regarding machine translation.

Providing Human Input for Machine Translation

Many non-translator users of machine translation don't realize that machine translation engines are based on translations that humans created. There was once a story going around in the translators' community that Google produced a beautiful English translation of the opening of Gabriel García Márquez's novel *Cien años de soledad*. Of course, Google did this because it's a search engine, and it found the beautiful translation made by the human translator Gregory Rabassa (1922–2016). So the result tells us that Google was able to search well, but not necessarily translate well.

The following sections look at the role humans play and what criteria you can use to determine whether a project is suitable for machine translation or would be better served by a human-only translator.

The responsibilities of humans in machine translation

Beyond producing most of the texts that are used to produce machine translation corpora, the texts that go into building the machine translation engine, humans play other roles when it comes to the existence of machine translation.

As a translator you can decide whether to use a machine translation tool and how — perhaps running an entire text through a machine translation tool or perhaps not.

WARNING

Once you make the decision to use the tool, be careful if you're planning to cut and paste. Many errors are made with cutting and pasting. You don't want to introduce errors in the process of using machine translation.

Machine translation success stories come from a human's involvement at all stages. Some of these success stories come from formulaic texts that are written in a way that creates favorable conditions toward using machine translation. These kinds of formulaic texts wouldn't be poetry, as you can imagine, but might be some kind of guide or contract. But again, those kinds of documents could have legal implications, so be sure a human translator reviews them.

Humans should be sure the texts are written in conditions that are favorable to garnering a successful automated translation. Also, for these translators to review the automated translation, they're reviewing a familiar formula that they've seen repeatedly. They can predict its actions in translation.

Another piece to be aware of here is familiarity with the source text. When the translation process is lost and the text is swiftly transferred into the target language, it might seem accurate to you upon review because the source text is present. You're reading the target text, but as a reader who has knowledge of both the source and the target language. As a result of this speedy process, you might not be as sensitive to mistakes. This is certainly the case if you're working under a lot of pressure. If you find yourself in this situation, be sure to have another reader of the target language review the target text.

In short, if machine translation is accurate and effective, it's usually because a human was involved in some way.

Deciding when to use machine translation

There's no global answer to this question. As a translator, you should consider whether a free online machine is a good choice for the particular text you need to translate. If you're translating a text for your own personal interest, such as an email to a friend or a website, then a free online machine translation might be fine. But for professional services, you need to think carefully about using machine translation.

WARNING

No matter the purpose — personal or professional — if the text contains sensitive or confidential information, such as personal information, addresses, or anything that can identify a person, think carefully about machine translation. If you're going to use it, remove the sensitive and confidential information before putting it through a machine translation tool. Many of the free online tools keep the texts that you put into them so they can reuse them.

If the document has legal implications or is about health and safety, it shouldn't go through a free online machine translation tool. If it does, be sure to have a human involved in the process. This means reading the source text before it goes through machine translation, removing any sensitive or confidential information, and fully understanding the source text. After the text goes through the machine translation tool, you need to make sure it's saying all it needs to say and does so accurately. Keep in mind that the target reader might not have access to the source text as you do, so your reading of the translation can't be coated by your understanding of the source text. With a text that has legal implications or discusses health and safety measures, the consequences of getting an inaccurate translation can be severe.

Don't use machine translation without human involvement for texts that are part of your public image or an organization's website. If you run those through a machine translation engine, be sure to have someone check them. Don't post them without notice that they've been translated by a machine. It's important to be transparent about when machine translation was used and how.

TIP

If your organization decides to put the Google Translate feature on a website, this doesn't mean the organization has fulfilled a language access obligation. Your organization can't be sure that Google's translations are accurate and effective. What's more, if your organization does put this feature on its website, be sure to note somewhere in the target languages that the website is being translated by Google Translate and might be inaccurate. If the reader has questions about anything read in a target language other than English, they should contact the organization and provide their contact info.

If you work as a translator in a school system and your school serves students and their families who speak languages other than English, it might not be productive to run coursework through a machine translation engine. It's quite possible that the students or the educators receiving the machine translation won't be adequately served by the it. See Figure 9-1.

Compared to being an independent translator, machine translation might be more often your go-to tool if translating is only one of your many roles at your organization. If that's the case, you definitely want to understand how to work with machine translation. This is because you might be working with tight deadlines, urgent announcements, or other pressing matters. If something urgent needs to be communicated and machine translation is your only option, it's especially important to let people know that you've used the tool and that a human didn't look at the translation.

Translation Transparency Label	Use	Translation
This text was translated by a professional person.	-Include on a translated document.	És testu foi traduzidu pa um tradutor profissional.
This text was only machine translated. If you have any questions about what it says, please visit the school or contact: 📱 CALL ✉ EMAIL	-Include on a translated document.	És testu foi traduzidu só pa máquina. Si nhôs tem qualquer pergunta sobri informaçon qui sta na és testu, por favor nhôs bai té própiu escola ou nhôs contacta: 📱 TELEFONA ✉ MANDA EMAIL
This text was machine translated and reviewed for accuracy by a person. If you have any questions about what it says, please visit the school or contact: 📱 CALL ✉ EMAIL	-Include on a translated document.	És testu foi traduzidu pa máquina e é foi inspecionadu pa um pessoa pa podi corrigi qualquer erru qui é tem. Si nhôs tem qualquer pergunta sobri informaçon qui sta na és textu, por favor nhôs bai té própriu escola ou nhôs contacta: 📱 TELEFONA ✉ MANDA EMAIL
This app uses machine translation to produce text in languages other than English. Its translations are not always reviewed by a professional translator. If you have any questions about what this app's translations say, please visit the school or contact: 📱 CALL ✉ EMAIL	-Include on communications about the app. -Could be included in a signature on the app or a parent portal page.	És app (aplicativu) ta usa traduçon feitu pa máquina pa escrevi testus na otru línguas pa além di Inglês. Traduçons qui feitu di és manera nem sempri é ta costuma ser inspeccionadu e corrigidu pa um tradutor profissional. Si nhôs tem qualquer pergunta sobri informaçon qui stá na testu qui foi traduzidu pa és app (aplicativu), por favor nhôs bai té própiu escola ou nhôs contacta: 📱 TELEFONA ✉

FIGURE 9-1: A translation transparency label.

Putting Machine Translation to Work for You

If you'd like to experiment with machine translation tools as a beginning translator, you have to determine if it's going to work for the kinds of texts you'd like to translate and your language pair. The quality of machine translation tools isn't the same across languages or across subjects.

If you've determined that you'd like to use machine translation in some way, don't overlook the translation process. If you're working to be a professional translator or you translate as one of your many duties for an organization, be sure to read and analyze any text you're going to translate before it goes through a machine.

Once you get the machine automated translation, you can revise it. This means checking to see if things are translated correctly and ensuring that everything is there. Pay special attention to the parts that you anticipated would be tricky in your analysis of the source text. While doing this, if you're starting to find that it's time consuming and a lot of work, you might just trash the machine translation and have a go at the translation on your own.

TIP

To save time and money, clients might try to send you machine translations to revise. Many professional translators won't accept this work because it usually takes more time to review something produced by a machine with no human involvement than it does to translate the text from scratch on their own.

You probably have the best chances of getting a quality machine translation if you use short, simple sentences and plain language. This means clear sentence structures and no metaphoric language. Of course, this kind of language might not be the best choice for all texts.

REMEMBER

Machine translation or its use can introduce errors, create bias, or misinterpret a text, which can cause, among other issues, legal repercussions. If you do rely on machine translation in any capacity in your work, be sure you review it with a careful editorial eye and if you don't have enough time to review it to get it to the quality you'd like it to be, add a note in which you let your readers know the text was translated by a machine translation tool.

Developing Machine Translation Literacy

If you're going to use machine translation in any way, you need to know how it works. To do that, develop your translation literacy. Study resources, such as the ones by Dr. Lynne Bowker on machine translation literacy. These are excellent to have on hand because it's not only *your* machine translation literacy that you need to develop, but that of the people you work with and for.

In your personal life, if you use machine translation to try to communicate with a new friend or you're traveling to a country where you don't speak the language, you should make it apparent that you're using machine translation. You can probably do that by showing the person the automated translation on your phone or by telling the person this language isn't yours but that a machine translation tool helped you.

If you're an independent translator who's hired by clients and partners to translate a document, your clients and partners aren't expecting you to use a machine translation and hand it over to them untouched. They're expecting a professional translation that's effective and meets all their communication requirements. A current or potential client or partner might ask you how you use machine translation in your work. To prepare yourself, you might want to come up with a statement about how you use it.

If you're employed by an organization as a full-time translator or you translate along with some other roles, you might be asked to translate under certain constraints that encourage the use of machine translation, or you might have to produce translations in language you don't know. Of course, for the latter, you'd have to use machine translation. If this is the case, be transparent about how the translation was produced. To do this, consider using a translation transparency label (Figure 9-1 is an example). Just be sure that the labels are in both the target and the source languages and that a human has verified the text of the labels.

Meeting the World's Translation Needs

Human translators and machine translation engines can and should work together to meet the world's translation needs. Think about all the people who move around the globe due to natural disasters or human-provoked situations that cause people to leave one place and move to another. When people move, they most likely need translations to get all the information they require in a language they can fully understand. There probably aren't enough working human translators in all the needed language pairs to fulfill the demands.

The need for translation doesn't just have to derive from what might be called an "essential" or "vital" document. The world also needs translation of literature and texts related to the arts and culture.

Just think about a single school. A school produces countless communications to families and the community every day. If that school alone translated all its communications into all the languages of the community, it would be a huge amount of work, though things should operate this way at schools. The work involves setting up a system that allows this to happen in a timely fashion and in which quality translations are produced. Managing all those texts, even if some kind of human-involved machine translation process occurs, is a monumental task. In short, working together, machine translation engines and human translators can increase accessibility and equity efforts.

Of course, there are questions about who will finance all these translations and who will identify the translators and compensate them accordingly. And there are unknowns surrounding technology that's rapidly being developed and made available to end users. You must consider the uses and the ethics surrounding these new tools.

As a translator, you'll inevitably need to work with machines in some capacity. Identifying translation needs, understanding how to work with machines, and overseeing the entire process might be part of the expanding role of translators. Continuing to learn about how machines will be part of the translation process and how humans will interact with them can bring forth new opportunities for productivity and innovation.

Chapter **10**

Accepting That Translation Changes Everything

W hen novice or untrained translators start translating, they often say that they want to make their translation the *same* as the text they're translating. It sounds like a fine idea. In most cases, translators can't turn a notice to city residents about recycling into a poem just because they feel like it. Nor can they make a school principal's welcome-back-to-school letter to parents become an invitation to a party. Although those moves might be more effective in getting the point across or to celebrate a certain date or event, the translation of a document isn't the time to shake things up that way.

Translators have ethical and professional responsibilities that guide them as they translate. For example, the "Code of Ethics and Professional Responsibility" from the American Translators Association (ATA) states that members of the ATA "accept as [an] ethical and professional duty" "to convey meaning between people, organizations, and cultures accurately, appropriately, and without bias, depending on the context of the source, purpose, readership or audience, and medium."

To read it in other terms, look at "The National Code of Ethics and Standards of Practice for Translators in Education." This code for translators who translate documents in the school setting lists "accuracy" as the first ethical principle, stating that "[t]he educational translator faithfully translates written text from the source language into the target language."

Beyond codes of ethics, most translations are evaluated according to how they effectively communicate the meaning of the source text, follow grammatical and other linguistic conventions, use accurate terminology, keep the style, and consider cultural factors.

Although translators are tasked with conveying accurately, appropriately, and without bias, sometimes things can't stay the same in translation. Different languages do different things, look different, and read in different directions. Everything changes in translation because you, as the translator, are writing the text in another language. In fact, the translator, theorist, and historian Lawrence Venuti, in 2013, titled his book *Translation Changes Everything: Theory and Practice*.

Although some texts in translation will allow for great change and others allow for a lesser degree of change, sticking to the former will ease the process and acceptance of what translation does. Accepting change helps you get into the translator mindset as you become a translator.

Translation not only changes everything, but challenges everything. As a translator, you can't have any doubts about your translation. If you believe you know the definition of a certain word, but at the moment of translating it, you need to look it up to be sure, you're challenging something you thought you knew. If you're not 100% certain about the way business letters are formatted in English, you have to research it. Likewise, if you're not sure how addresses are written in Mexico, you have to look it up.

This chapter looks at how and why language changes in the process of translation. Translators need to be aware of these changes so that they can have a better understanding of all of the aspects of a text that they must change in addition to their power in a multilingual world.

Abiding by Language Conventions

Beyond writing the text that you're translating in another language, you need to know, as a translator, what that kind of text does in its new language. How does it act? How is it written? As a translator, you need to abide by language conventions.

Look up *convention* in the Merriam-Webster dictionary, and you'll find these phrases associated with the word: a principle or procedure, usage or custom, a rule of conduct or behavior, an established technique or practice. Translations need to adhere to the expectations that readers have of certain texts to be effective. Language conventions include the following:

>> **Tone:** In the source language of an event invitation, it might be fine to have a casual tone, but the target language audience expects a more formal tone. If the translation doesn't abide by that convention, the target audience could find the invitation odd and believe it to be something they don't want to or need to attend.

>> **Grammar:** Each language follows its own grammatical conventions. These include things like spelling, punctuation, and capitalization. They help make writing clear. If you're unsure about spelling, you need to be sure to look it up. Punctuation counts. Periods and commas will cost you a job. The same thing goes for capitalization. You can't not capitalize the names of days and months when you're translating into English. And you need to know whether those words are capitalized when translating into Spanish or Portuguese.

>> **Addresses, dates, and measurements:** Parts of text that involve numbers also change across languages. Not all languages write addresses, dates, and measurements the same way. As a translator, you're responsible for knowing what the conventions are and for finding solutions that work in your translations. Measurements can be interesting to work with depending on where the audience of the translation is located.

>> **Line breaks and alignment:** Beyond the details of the text itself, you need to pay attention to the way it looks. Some languages and types of documents prefer line breaks to happen in a certain way. Not all languages use the same alignment standards for an essay, for example. As a translator you need to know how different types of documents look in different languages.

Not abiding by the conventions of a given language can create unnecessary distractions in your translation, make the text's message misunderstood or less effective, and cost you a client and possibly your professional reputation. Take the time to be sure you know the conventions, or team up with another professional who does. Remember: translators don't need to work alone to get the job done.

WARNING

Keep in mind, though, that the translation of marketing, advertising, and other creative content might present a greater range of opportunities for the target text. In other words, for those kinds of texts to do all the things they need to do in another language, the changes might be greater and move into what's usually called *transcreation* or *creative translation*, which adapts content and concepts to the target culture.

Expecting Translation to Change the Space and Look of the Text

Beyond changes to letters, words, and punctuation, you need to be ready for the changes to the look of the text and the space it takes up in a document. The number of words in a text, a language's reading order, and the script of a given language will affect the way a text or a translation looks and how it uses space.

Even if you work with a language pair that doesn't involve transferring to another script or reading order, it's important to be aware of which languages read in which direction and which languages use a different script. It's likely that, as a translator, clients and coworkers are going to look to you not just as an English to Spanish translator, for example, but as an expert about how all languages work. What's more, if you have this knowledge, you can more easily take on multilanguage projects and hire other translators to work with you or to better support your organization in its language access efforts.

Word count

Not all languages use the same number of words to express the same thing. *Julia's house* has fewer words and characters than *la casa de Julia*. Two words versus four words and thirteen characters versus sixteen characters. If several of these instances happen throughout the translation of a flier or a booklet, for example, the flier or the booklet in translation will be longer than the source text, sometimes adding new pages to the document.

If you're just responsible for translating the text in a word processing document, you might not even blink at this change. However, if, in addition to the translation, you're responsible for formatting the flier or the booklet according to the original layout, the expanded text of the translation that pushed the text onto additional pages could present some challenges. What will you do with a flier that's now two pages instead of one? Or how can you get all the content of the now seven-page booklet into the budgeted six pages?

You'll come up with solutions. One of the most obvious might be to reduce the font size of the translation. Some people will say that the font size of the translation should be the same as that of the original, especially if the original and the translation are being published and distributed together. The translation, in most cases, shouldn't be a footnote, but as long as the quality of the translation is just as good as the quality of the original, give yourself some flexibility with font size and any other solutions you might come up with. Also think about whether there are opportunities to make the text bilingual rather than an original plus a translation. A weaved-together bilingual text, especially if it's for one community, could make more of an impact than two separate documents.

Overall, you need to prepare for the fact that the translation will usually, but not always, end up being longer than the original. Some people say that languages expand when moving from English to Spanish, so a translation from English to Spanish will be longer. However, it's best if you calculate that translations between any language pair will be around 20% longer. Although it's true that Spanish tends to be longer than English, that's not always the case. Sometimes Spanish has words for certain things that English doesn't, so in English you need to explain a bit more, which means adding words. In sum, prepare by anticipating that any translation will be longer than the original. If your original text has 200 words, plan for your translation to have 240 words.

Not only do you as the translator need to be prepared for this expansion, but it's helpful to warn your clients about it, especially if they're the ones who will be formatting the translations or planning to post them in a designated virtual or physical space.

Reading order

The changes continue to add up. Remember that not all languages are read the same way. English reads from left to right. Arabic, Hebrew, and Urdu are read from right to left. This doesn't just make a difference on the page, but in terms of how an entire book will work. A book or brochure in Arabic will be laid out the opposite of an English-language book or brochure, with the front cover in English being the back cover in Arabic.

This also means that you need someone who can read Arabic to do the layout of the Arabic-language document. You can't move things around as you lay out a document if you don't know what the language says.

Even though you might not be an English to Arabic translator, as a translator and someone who works with language, this is helpful information to have, especially if you work for an organization or with clients who work with multiple languages. And in the future if you decide to create your own type of translation agency, you'll need to know about this.

ALL ABOUT SCRIPTS

One more thing to remember for now is that not all languages use the same script. Once again, although you might not be translating into one of these scripts, if you work for an organization or with clients who work with multiple languages and some of them include working with different scripts, you'll want to prepare to have someone who can read the scripts do the work of formatting the translations. If you don't read a script, you probably don't know where you can insert line breaks. If you shift something, you won't know whether you've shifted entire lines. Knowing this happens with language will help you better support your organization and clients.

Understanding Why Translation Changes Everything

Now that you have a grasp of the mechanics of change in translation and what they mean for working with actual documents and text, as you grow your translation mindset as a translator, it's helpful to know a bit more about why so much change occurs in translation. Building up this knowledge of why translation isn't as neat and easy as most non-translators think it is and why it's so fascinating and rewarding requires a dose of translation literacy.

Scholar Brian Baer is a professor of Russian and Translation Studies at Kent State University, a university with a well-established translation program. In his essay "Is There a Translation in This Class? A Crash Course in Translation Literacy" (2022), he says that translation literacy is "an understanding of the nature of verbal translation between natural (as opposed to artificial) languages." He also says that "translation literacy sensitizes students to the workings of natural languages, a sensitivity that can only contribute to their development as astute readers and effective writers." What's more, Professor Baer says that with translations all around us, translation literacy should be "considered a key component of both information literacy and global literacy."

Knowing what happens in translation teaches you a lot. In that process there's so much you begin to understand about language and that will serve you in all your efforts to communicate and get around in a multilingual world.

Professor Baer uses most examples from the world of literary translation, which has much to teach. Take a look at how Professor Baer builds translation literacy on a small number of key components.

Languages don't line up perfectly

One thing to understand is that languages don't line up perfectly. You can't even match up the tiniest word, such as the definite article *the* or the indefinite article *a*. If you're a Russian translator, definite and indefinite articles don't exist. If you're translating from Spanish to English, you don't always need to use the article in English even though it might be in the Spanish original. As the translator, you get to come up with the solution that works for the particular translation project.

Words have many meanings

Another change to be aware of is that words that have several meanings in English won't have all those same meanings in Spanish, for example. Professor Baer presents the example of the word *right*. *Right* can mean being correct as opposed to being wrong, *right* as in the conversative, political sense, and *right* as in the direction. If you're translating into Spanish, it doesn't use the same word for all those meanings as English does. That's one thing you have to consider as a translator.

Words and languages have histories

Professor Baer also points out that translation involves complex and creative decision-making because words and phrases have histories. Over time, words collect connotations and associations, and these connotations and associations aren't the same across languages or even within different dialects of the same language. As a translator you have to be aware of what each word or phrase does in a given language and then determine how you'd like your translation to interpret that word or phrase. These choices don't necessarily fall into the realm of right or wrong, but they do interpret the original.

Context matters

When you share that you're becoming a translator, people might ask you to translate a single word on the spot. Besides the fact that that isn't really a fair assessment of your translation skills, it's an exercise that doesn't really make sense. Translators' contributions to the world aren't because they can translate random words but because they can bring forth texts and other written content that are first written in languages that can't be read. Translators don't just provide a flurry of random words. They help people understand documents and texts produced in other languages.

This kind of exercise also doesn't make sense because, as translators, you translate texts that are part of a specific context that includes a time, a place, an audience, the way in which the translation will be distributed, and all the things connected to those factors. The context will help you make decisions that will go into your translation.

Because the context surrounding the translation is different from that of the source text, it will provoke a certain degree of change. Understanding that change is part of your work will allow you to embrace your role and appreciate its gains.

Chapter **11**

Exploring Translator Ethics

As you become a professional in any field, you'll learn about *professional ethics*, or the standards of behavior expected of a person or group in that profession. When you take formal training to become a translator, ethics will be covered as part of that training. As you continue to grow as a professional, consider taking workshops and other short-term training to refresh and connect with other professionals over ethical questions. New situations and tools regularly arise with the potential to present shifts to the way translators work. Having a solid ethical foundation will help you navigate these shifts and any ethical dilemmas arising in your everyday work with professional integrity.

This chapter covers the ethical standards of practice, and the various situations and circumstances you may encounter as a translator and how to handle them ethically to maintain your professional reputation.

Understanding Ethical Standards

To be an effective, reliable, and responsible translator, you need to understand the ethical standards that guide the work of a translator. In general, these standards to ensure professionalism and ethical behavior encompass:

>> Honestly representing your qualifications. Aiming for accuracy ensures that translations convey the intended meaning without bias, are grammatically correct, and are well-written documents of professional quality. To accomplish this, you have to honestly represent and work according to your qualifications and responsibilities.

>> Divulging any conflict of interest or the possibilities of a perceived conflict of interest arising.

>> Maintaining confidentiality.

>> Being culturally sensitive so that translations are appropriate.

>> Keeping to deadlines and remaining timely with other professional tasks.

>> Using technology responsibly, which involves being transparent about your use of technology, not plagiarizing or submitting solely machine-translated translations to a client.

>> Presenting rates that demonstrate the quality of your work and don't under-cut the profession, and being clear with those rates when a client asks for an estimate.

>> Engaging in ongoing professional development to maintain your skills and knowledge.

The American Translators Association has a "Code of Ethics and Professional Responsibility" that is published on the association's website and "is intended to inspire and guide the ethical conduct of all ATA members in their performance of professional duties." https://www.atanet.org/about-us/code-of-ethics/

The different areas or specializations have their own codes of ethics to guide translators. The codes have some overlap. If you're translating for schools, check out the "Ethical Principles for Translators in Education" released by the American Association of Interpreters and Translators in Education in December 2023. The AAITE presents six areas:

>> Accuracy

>> Confidentiality

>> Impartiality

- » Professional Conduct
- » Professional Development
- » Representation of Qualifications

TIP

It's helpful to know how each area or specialization delineates its own code of ethics, but what's most important is that, as a translator, you're prepared to handle ethical dilemmas that arise in intercultural situations. What's more, although presented as translator ethics, these are ethics that will help you be a better professional in general.

Ensuring You Have the Skills to Do the Job

If you're bilingual or on your way to becoming bilingual, you've probably been asked by a supervisor, employer, community member, or friend to translate a document. If you decided to say yes and did the translation, it's quite possible that it ended up becoming a bigger task than you expected. It probably brought up many questions. You likely became unsure of certain linguistic, cultural, and formatting aspects. You asked yourself questions about commas, periods, and usage of capital letters. And you probably spent more time on the task than you anticipated. You might have told yourself afterward that you'd never translate again.

The person who asked you to do the translation probably had no idea it was going to require so much effort and time. They, also, didn't know too much about translation and thought any bilingual would be up for the task just as easily as bilinguals make it seem when they move between the languages they speak.

If you eventually completed the translation, you might have been left with many questions and felt unsure about the translation you submitted. Perhaps you felt that it didn't adequately serve the people it was intended for. Not a good feeling. . .

This situation, or a similar one, most likely occurred because everyone involved wasn't aware of what it takes to be a responsible translator. Acting as the translator, you probably didn't realize the language skills and other skills needed to carry out a translation that you could present with confidence.

REMEMBER

It's not really anyone's fault that a situation like that occurs. It happens because of a lack of general knowledge about translation and how it's responsibly done. Even though it's no one's fault, this kind of situation needs to be prevented because it really serves no one.

One of the first steps in making sure this kind of situation isn't repeated is ensuring that you have the language and subject knowledge skills to responsibly complete the translation.

The language skills for the assignment

Whether you refer to the ATA code of ethics or the one established by the AAITE, you'll see that both organizations address the representation of translator qualifications:

>> **AAITE:** "Representation of qualifications: The educational interpreter provides an accurate representation of their credentials and of their relevant training and experience, along with truthful professional references."

>> **ATA:** "To honestly represent and work within our qualifications, competencies, capabilities, and responsibilities."

This includes language skills. If you don't have the level of language to write at a professional level in that language, it would be unethical to accept a job that requires you to write in a language at a certain level.

WARNING

Sometimes as a translator, especially if you're just starting your training, you might not even be fully aware of where your language skills are. This can be the case if you've grown up speaking a language at home and in your community and that you feel deeply connected to but you didn't study in a formal setting. Others, and many times monolinguals, might assume that your written language skills are perfect because of the way they perceive your grasp of the language.

If your supervisor asks you to translate, in addition to your other roles, you might get the sense that you can do the job because a supervisor is asking you to do it. This can be complicated. If you find yourself in this situation and you're not sure about your written language skills and have no or little experience translating documents, share this with your supervisor. It's in your best interest, the best interest of your organization, the profession of translators, and the people who rely on the translation for you to be transparent.

The subject knowledge for the assignment

Much of how you think about your language skills can be applied to how you think about your knowledge of a particular subject matter. From the code of ethics examples earlier, even if your written language skills are advanced, if the subject knowledge required to responsibly translate the document is beyond your current ability, you'll have to turn down the assignment for the same reasons as listed.

Keep in mind that many translation projects require you to do some kind of research about things you might not be totally familiar with. To accept a project, you don't have to know everything about the subject. If you have a university degree in English or Spanish, history, or another area of the humanities and you're asked to translate a catalog for an art exhibition for a large museum, you probably have all the skills you need. You'll need to do some research, but it probably wouldn't be a stretch for you to take on this project. However, if you're asked to translate a catalog of supplies for a dental equipment company, you'll most likely have to pass on this project.

Take this into consideration in the general sense. Once a project comes across your desk, you'll know if it's beyond what you can responsibly do. The more experienced you are, the more you'll know your limits and what you can take on, when, and in what conditions.

Knowing the Boundaries of Language

Remember, translation is reading a text in one language and writing it in another. If you don't fully understand the text you need to read, you won't be able to produce an effective and responsible translation of it. To gain that full understanding of the text, you can turn to tools, but if the reliance on tools is impeding you from turning in the work in a reasonable time or the time by which the client wants the translation, it's possible that the project is beyond your current skills.

Understanding your own language and translation skills

How can you figure out if you have the language skills to take on the project? Usually you'll have a sense of whether you write well or not in a language. If you'd like a more defined response to your language skills, you can take a class at your local college or language school. You can search for a language assessment with an organization or find a language coach.

Even if you have the language skills and the subject knowledge to theoretically translate a text, you might not produce an effective translation if you don't know anything about translation. For example, as a trained translator you'd know that you need to "convey meaning," as the ATA says, "between people, organizations, and cultures accurately, appropriately, and without bias, depending on the context of the source, purpose, readership or audience, and medium."

If you're not fully aware that translators should do this or of strategies to do this, then your language and subject knowledge could introduce changes to the text that are ethically beyond the translator task. For example, your expert opinion on something can't introduce what you think are improvements. A trained translator learns how and when it would be appropriate to communicate with the author or client about questions regarding the content of the text they're asked to translate.

Helping vs. hurting

Translations are done for several reasons. One of the biggest reasons is to help an organization reach more audiences. Another is to get an audience access to information. A third is to help share texts with more readers via additional languages. Translations are an aide when they're done effectively and responsibly and will be appreciated by the new audiences that are going to receive them.

WARNING

If you're an untrained translator and you agree to translate a text without being transparent about your lack of training, you could end up hurting instead of helping. The translation might not make sense to the new audience. It might include errors that don't establish and promote intercultural communication, but rather hinder it. They can be offensive and not promote the connection with the new audience that the client is trying to establish. All this can be avoided by understanding that ethical principles ask for professionals to do the work and for them to know when referring a project to another professional is the right route.

Disclosing and Avoiding Conflicts of Interest

Conflict of interest is a big topic in professional spheres. Sometimes organizations have their employees and vendors review a conflict-of-interest document on an annual or a regular basis.

When you're a translator, whether or not you're a member of the ATA, you can refer to the ATA "Code of Ethics and Professional Responsibility," which states:

"to disclose to the relevant parties any real or potential conflict of interest and avoid situations that may lead to perceived conflict of interest"

This includes any personal or ethical values that may affect your performance while translating a document. For instance, if you're opposed to the message of a text that you're asked to translate and think you might alter the language to impact the meaning, then that assignment isn't for you. If you're ethically against a certain practice that's promoted in the text you're asked to translate and you can't translate the text accurately or you might delay the timeline, then you're not the translator for this project.

This could also simply include how and where you get your clients from. If you work for an agency that already has a certain organization as a client and that organization tries to contract with you independently of that agency, that could be a conflict of interest. You would need to tell that client that you can't work with them directly because they found you through the agency, that all work needs to be referred to the agency.

TIP

Depending on the project, you don't need to disclose all your beliefs to a client. You can simply say that you're unable to take on the assignment. If the conflict of interest is real or potential, you should disclose that to your client.

Using Machine Translation Ethically

Machine translation is one of the tools in your toolbox, and you need to use it critically. To use it ethically, you need to have machine translation literacy. The best place to go for an introduction to machine translation literacy is the work of Dr. Lynne Bowker. She and a team created resources, including introductory infographics, on the basics of machine translation literacy that are a must for reviewing and posting in your office. You can find them here:

```
https://sites.google.com/view/machinetranslationliteracy/home/
teaching-resources?authuser=0
```

Knowing how to use machine translation and AI tools responsibly

As a translator who uses technology, you need to know how to employ machine translation and AI tools. Depending on your approach, you can stick to the basics or decide to get more advanced training on these tools. For whatever tool you use, you need to know how it works and seek the appropriate training for working effectively and responsibly with it.

Many novice translators use free online machine translation systems such as Google Translate and DeepL Translator. These tools are storing the content you insert and using it for their own purposes. In addition, what they give you can depend on myriad factors and can be inconsistent and unreliable. So if you're using these tools and not checking your translation, you need to be transparent about that.

Being transparent about the use of machine translation

If you're presenting a text that has been machine translated — this would most likely be if you work as a translator for an organization and you need to release a translation urgently — be sure the audience knows that the text is a machine translation, and let them know by which tool. You can also include a number or other contact information for the reader of the translation to call if they have a question about it. This information should of course be included in the target language. Your organization might make a list of what I call *translation transparency labels* in several target languages and have them ready to go on any documents that are machine translated, especially by a free online tool. (See an example of a translation transparency label in Chapter 9).

Handling sensitive information

Don't put sensitive information into a free online machine translation system. Most of the time machine translation tools are free to use, but they can reuse whatever content you submit. Adding sensitive information to a machine translation tool that you don't protect and control is asking for trouble.

If you work for a company that has a need for translation, inquire within said company to see whether or not they have a paid machine translation or AI subscription. Oftentimes these paid subscriptions do not store your sensitive information per contract, so they can be safe to use.

Honoring Confidentiality

As a translator, you get to learn a lot! Not only in terms of increasing your knowledge in a certain field and expanding your languages skills, but also in terms of confidential information about individuals, companies, and other organizations. Keep in mind that the confidential information isn't yours to share just because you translated the text.

If you're working for a translation agency or direct clients, you might be asked to translate personal documents such as birth certificates, medical records, banking recording, divorce agreements, and all other types of personal documents. Sometimes those individuals will live far away and you'll never get to see them or hear about them ever again. Other times those individuals might be part of your community, and you might know them. Regardless, you don't get to spread that content or even mention it to the person whose work you were translating if they don't already know it.

If you translate documents for a school, you might be translating individual education plans or programs (IEPs) or other special education or sensitive documents about an individual. If you live or are active in the same community, you don't get to use that info to further connect with a parent or students.

Likewise, if you're translating for a company, you can't share protected or privileged information.

While maintaining confidentiality is one of the main ethical principles that translators must maintain, some clients might make you sign a *non-disclosure agreement*, which means you agree not to share anything.

In short, anything you learn during translation work stays in the work.

Committing to Loyalty

Translators are usually busy. A lot will be coming at you: texts, deadlines, clients, other translators, new subject areas, new technologies, and more. In this mix of exciting things, stay professional.

>> **Staying true to your beliefs:** Don't translate texts that go against your beliefs, don't work against what you know is an impossible timeline, and collaborate with your colleagues.

>> **Not complaining about other translators:** The solidarity piece will be appreciated by fellow translators and the profession.

>> **Demonstrating loyalty to the text:** Translator ethics ask you as a practicing professional to translate accurately. This means that you don't give advice through your translations or change the meaning of the message.

>> **Being loyal to your clients:** It's a small world. Don't complain about your clients with specifics. If there's something you need to work through, bring it up with your client and try to solve the situation professionally.

>> **Committing to the improvement of yourself and the profession:** Most translator code of ethics state that as a professional translator you'll maintain and improve your knowledge, skills, and abilities by participating in professional development and continuing-education opportunities. The same applies to other professions. Part of being a professional is keeping up with the changes of your profession. Commit yourself to keeping on top of how your language technology, fields of specialization, and profession might be changing. Read, connect with others, attend conferences, and sign up for learning opportunities. Not only is it the right thing to do, it's inspiring. You'll be a better translator for it!

Letting Your Supervisors Know What's Right

If you're not qualified to take on an assignment and it's your supervisor who's asking you to do the work, it can be tricky to say no. It's even trickier if you work in a fast-paced environment where there might not be much time to sit down and explain and strategize the next move. One way to get into the right mindset about this is to remember that it's about the work and not about you.

Knowing what to say when your boss asks for a translation

If you know that you need to turn down a request and there's time to have a conversation with your supervisor, you can take all the information here and form it into an elegant, professional, and personalized response.

Your response can mention that you're honored to be recommended for the opportunity to do the work, but you don't have the skills required to produce a quality translation. The text, the organization, and the audience deserve a quality translation, and you don't want your translation to prevent that from happening. You could recommend that your boss contact {INSERT PROFESSIONAL} to do the translation.

TIP

Perhaps it's an emergency situation. You're asked to translate a short, urgent message, and you're not confident that your translation is the best it can be. Be sure to be transparent with your audience and state something in the target language that says that "the translation was produced under urgent circumstances and hasn't been fully reviewed. Please contact {INSERT CONTACT INFO} if there are any questions about its content." Include this statement in the source and target languages.

Turning down work diplomatically

Be direct, and emphasize that you want the best for everyone involved. Recommend another translator for the work. If you can communicate this verbally and in writing, for the record, that's ideal. Because if these requests are repeated, you'll want to have that on record.

Supporting the Professionalization of Translators

As a translator it's your professional duty to support the professionalization of translators and the profession in general. You should advocate for professional services, treat the services in terms of the profession they belong to, and support the profession and the individuals who are part of it. As a translator, you're not only representing yourself but an entire profession. Remember that. When you behave unethically, you can affect how clients interact with other translators in the future or how they view professional services. Two tips to support the profession come in the form of proper pay and recommending a professional for the work.

Charging for translations

Chapter 16 touches on charging and getting paid for your work. Your skills and time are valuable, and you have to pay the bills. However, you also need to look at charging for your translations from an ethical point of view. Here are some general things to consider:

>> Do charge for translations because your skills and services deserve compensation. Charging for translation also helps organizations plan and budget for translations.

>> Keep your rates in line with what the average is for your language pair. In other words, don't go too low.

>> Be consistent with your rates.

>> Let clients know if it's looking like a project's final cost is going to be way off from the estimate you gave.

If you're able to offer pro-bono or reduced-rate work, be transparent about that and consider, if appropriate, letting the client or organization know what the professional rate range would have been. Also consider having some criteria for which work you do pro-bono or at a reduced rate.

Recommending another translator if you can't take on a job

If you're working as an independent translator or as a freelancer and you need to turn down a project for an ethical reason, help your clients by referring them to another translator if you know a professional who can do the work. Your client will be grateful, and so will your colleague. Assuming that the outcome of that project is positive, it's likely that the client will return to you with another project and that your colleague will think of you when they can't take on a project.

If you work as a translator for an organization but you're asked to translate because you're bilingual and you know the project deserves a professional translator, be sure to speak up. This isn't only a win for the world of professional translators, but for your organization, the audience for which the translation is destined, and your integrity as a professional in general.

4

Making Translation Your Career or Business

Balance the pros and cons of independent and full-time work.

Broaden your language skills beyond translation.

Determine your work location, space, and the tools you'll need.

Understand how to network and build your professional profile.

Look at how translators are recognized and how they set rates.

Chapter **12**

Choosing a Way to Work: Employed or Self-Employed

Translators are needed everywhere! Because of that, if you're a prepared and professional translator you should have the luxury of being able to choose where and how you work. There are a few main options. You can work as an independent or freelance translator on a full-time or part-time schedule. You can also be employed by an agency or other organization, also on a full-time or part-time schedule. As an independent translator you'd have more freedom over the kinds of projects you take on and the amount you charge for them. If you're employed by an agency or an organization, you probably won't be able to pick and choose your assignments and you'll most likely have a fixed salary for those translation projects. As you can imagine, each situation has its own set of advantages.

In this chapter, I'll take you through some of the main working scenarios as a translator and give you an introduction as to what they each entail and the things you'll need to be thinking about in each situation.

Working for Yourself

Many translators who are freelance or independent translators will tell you that at some point in their careers they had the realization that one of the appealing things about being a professional translator is that they could work for themselves from mostly anywhere, at any time. The flexibility of the working situation appealed to them because the work wasn't entirely dependent on hours or location.

The path those translators took to that working situation varies. Some gradually made the transition from another work situation, and others progressively eased into the situation while taking care of family or other responsibilities. Others established themselves as translators at the start of their working life. Remember, becoming a translator can be like becoming a writer. Ending up in this profession has no set path.

In addition to the flexibility of the work, becoming a translator is immensely appealing because you're usually helping people communicate with each other and learn from each other, and you yourself are learning along the way with each new project. You're learning about translation and how you want to work, and you're learning about new topics or confirming how it is you can say something in a given language.

For instance, if you watch the film *Dreaming Murakami* (2017) by director Nitesh Anjaan, you see that the literary translator featured, Mette Holm, confirms the vocabulary for playing pinball in Danish to effectively translate the Japanese writer Haruki Murakami.

So one way to go about becoming a translator is to plan to work for yourself. This can offer you a lot of flexibility over time and space and freedom to do things your way while still enjoying the rewards of being a translator. However, it also requires discipline, organization, and knowledge to carry this out professionally.

Knowing what to expect as a freelance translator

If you're planning to do this on your own, as an independent translator, you need to know what that might look like before deciding if that route is for you. As an independent translator, you're responsible for taking care of everything on your own. What exactly does "everything" entail?

>> **A network of other independent translators:** Trusted colleagues who have been successful at setting themselves up as independent translators will most likely be willing to share a lot of the how-tos and whens and whys with you.

They'll most likely be able to advise you on what can work well and what to shy away from.

>> **A network or hiring of other professionals:** You don't have to figure everything out on your own. You can think about hiring a lawyer to help you sort out any legal questions you might have. You can also hire an accountant to take care of your taxes and perhaps other financial questions. And a financial adviser can help you get on the right track to setting up a retirement fund.

>> **Making sure you have all the tools, including your space:** Along with setting up a solid foundation for your business, make sure you have all the tools to get the jobs done. This ranges from a space to work in, a way to contact you (email or phone), possibly a website, some print material advertising your services, a computer, plenty of secure storage, and a high-speed internet connection to any translation-specific tools you want to incorporate into your workflow. Some of these tools you can add as you learn more about how you prefer to work and what's needed.

>> **Attracting clients:** If you're an independent translator, you need to figure out how you're going to attract clients and maintain a relationship with them. It involves developing marketing and communications plans. A client is likely to stick with you if your translations are solid and the professional relationship is working out well — even if your rates are slightly higher than another vendor.

>> **Your schedule:** You maintain your own schedule. This ranges from your workday schedule to when you take vacation days or enjoy time away from translation projects for your own professional development. You might find it helpful to strategically plan for those things at the beginning of the calendar or fiscal year instead of arranging for them as you go. Otherwise you might have trouble fitting everything in you want to do.

>> **Accounting:** You'll also have to take care of your own accounting. This can include setting up how you'll be paid, requesting payment and following up if you aren't, and all the other number things, such as keeping track of your expenses and paying taxes.

>> **Translations:** It's no surprise that you have to project manage on your own. This includes receiving the projects, making sure you understand all their aspects, translating the text, preparing it for delivery, and actually delivering it. This might seem straightforward, and it is, but when you have several projects going on, this management piece can present many moving parts into your workflow.

Keep in mind that just because you work for yourself, you don't have to do every single piece of the work on your own. But you do need to make a plan to get all these pieces and possibly more done.

TIP

Check out the book *How to Succeed as a Freelance Translator*, first published in 2015, by Corinne McKay. It's been a classic for freelance translators. You can also follow her on her social media handles and her website for great tips on running your own translation business. Besides *How to Succeed as a Freelance Translator*, she's the author of *Thoughts on Translation: The Translation Industry and Becoming a Translator* (2012).

Starting a business

If you're working for yourself and plan to do so for the visible future of your career, you might consider establishing a business to separate your personal assets from your business. The *For Dummies* book on starting a small business might be a good place to start for the aspects of how to run a small business.

However, you may need to fill in the blanks with some small-business-specific things, which can include the following:

>> **Insurance:** If you're imagining being a translator as a risk-free job because you'll mostly be working from home or a pretty safe location with no large, heavy tools, you might be wondering why in the world you need insurance. It's recommended that you have insurance to protect you from the errors you might make (you're human after all!) or the misinterpretations others can make of your work. (They might think you made an error that you didn't.) Professional liability insurance, also called an errors and omissions (E&O) policy, provides coverage against lawsuits. You might also want a business owners policy for general liability and property coverage. What if someone breaks into your office space? Cyber insurance will also protect you from online hacking incidents and data breaches. Remember, most of your work is done on a computer and online.

>> **Statement about your translated text:** Because the languages you speak and work with as a translator are usually shared with other people who aren't trained translators, it's not uncommon for a speaker of your language to come in and want to edit the translation you submitted to them. People don't use language in the same way, and it's possible that someone might read your translation and think, "I can say that better." You probably don't want to be responsible for post-translation changes. Consider including a note with the submission of your translation that states that you're only responsible for the text you submit to your client.

Negotiating agreements

If you're working for yourself, you'll either have direct clients or work as a contractor for an agency. You still need to consider the latter as working for yourself because you won't be an employee of the agency. They'll be another client in your portfolio. With your clients, if you're an independent translator, you'll have to negotiate your rates and other conditions, including turnaround times and other tasks for which you might be responsible, such as formatting and glossary submission. Each project will be different, so keep an eye on the extras that go beyond the translation of the text.

You should establish what your rates are and know how long it will take you to complete a project. Don't forget all the other things going on in your life and with your business when you calculate the time it will take you to complete a project. Knowing this will help you determine your rate for a project.

Be sure that your overall rate for a project doesn't undercut other translators. Don't go too low just to get a job, or you won't have enough money to pay your bills or take time off. Although you might not know exactly what other translators charge, you'll have a sense of the range of pricing. (For more on pricing, see Chapter 16.)

If you happen to be in a position to take on a project at a lower rate or pro-bono, be sure to let the client know that you're doing that and possibly tell them why. It can be dangerous when a client thinks a cheap or a free translation is the norm. And if you do that, ask for some kind of credit or something from which you'll benefit professionally in return. Check with your accountant to see if pro-bono work is something you'd write off on your taxes.

A client will either accept your rate, not reply at all to the rate you give them, or try to negotiate. You can make it a policy not to negotiate. Making this decision upfront can save you from the back and forth of negotiations.

Not all clients will negotiate with you. Many will accept your rate right away. And if you deliver quality work according to your agreed terms, it will probably be a smooth working relationship.

You might think about negotiating if the project will take a while or if you'll be a client's go-to vendor for translations. Just know what your work is worth, and don't go below what you need to earn.

Whatever you decide to do, try to be consistent with the same client. If you charge one price the first time and another price later for a similar project, it could make your client's bookkeeper raise their eyebrows, and you could spend a lot of time having to explain yourself.

In short, if you should get to negotiations, be clear and know your limits.

Recognition

Beyond compensation, you'll have to determine with your clients how you are going to be recognized for your translation work. Chapter 16 dives deeper into getting recognized for your work. But let's start planting the seed about the importance of recognition.

If the translation project is a book, although the name of the translator has historically been left off the cover of the book, publishers are increasingly in favor of putting the name of the translator on the cover of the book. Be sure to check any contract to see if placing your name on the cover of the book is included, if, of course, you want it to be. Although most translators are advocating for translator recognition, especially when it comes to the publication of books, there are still some translators who prefer to stay off stage when it comes to publicity.

For translation projects other than book projects, translators don't usually have a tradition of being cited as being the translators of their works. This is however, something that the industry or you yourself as a translator might reconsider, especially as AI enters conversations about the provision of translations. In other words, if AI is also cited, why can't the human translator also be recognized as part of the work. If you're working for an agency, they might not be in favor of placing your name on translations. If you work with direct clients, depending on the project this could be something to consider. This is all of course, if you want to. Some translators don't want the attention, although in general, this could be an interesting strategy to advocate for the work of human translators.

Working for Others

A possible path for your work as a translator is to get a full-time job with an employer. This situation might allow you to have steady hours, a fixed salary, health insurance, a retirement fund, and other benefits through your employer. If this type of stability appeals to you, it might be the way to go.

Working for others as a translator could also mean that you do translations as part of your regular job duties, but it isn't your exclusive duty. Read on for a look at what some of those options look like.

Translation agencies

Translation agencies, or businesses that provide language services to clients, often hire full-time translators. The pay can, of course, vary depending on the company, the language pair, the location, and other reasons. Some of these jobs are onsite, others are remote, and others might allow for a hybrid situation. If you're interested in this type of employment situation, identify the translation agencies in your area or the ones that allow for remote work, and browse their website, follow them on social media, and attend professional conferences where agencies might have a representative.

Organizations that hire staff translators

With language access efforts increasing and more and more organizations becoming aware that they need to and want to provide their content in multiple languages to reach all members of their communities and new audiences, they often seek to hire translators directly as employees. This is especially the case for organizations that have many and ongoing needs for translation in a given language pair. Organizations might hire not only translators but also managers, coordinators, and other types of administrators of translations and language access services. In this situation, you'd usually be treated as another employee of the organization. The stability is an advantage. If you're in this situation, you might think about what the available opportunities for growth are.

Translating as part of another job

You might be asked to translate as part of your other job duties. This could happen in the school setting. If you're a Spanish-speaking counselor, for example, you might occasionally be asked to translate some documents. This could also happen at a museum or elsewhere.

This could be a nice option if you're looking for a job that allows you to translate at times. Remember that translators become effective and efficient translators because they translate regularly. So regardless of whether you spend eight, five, or one hour a day translating on your translating days, be sure you have translating opportunities regularly and that all the tools are in place for when you need to do the work.

Checking out the job description

Speaking of job descriptions, if you translate for an organization and that's not what you were hired for, be sure that it's in the job description. If it isn't, you might want to have a conversation with your supervisor about that. You don't want your other job duties to be neglected because you're spending too much time translating. Also, you want to get credit for the translation work you're doing.

Dual-role translators

If you were hired to translate and perform other job duties for an organization, you might want to discuss with your employer what those two roles mean and how they play out in the workplace. For instance, you can't consistently be pulled from performing your other job duties so that you can translate. The interruptions could be counterproductive to your overall performance and negatively affect you down the road.

You shouldn't be held responsible for knowing the content of every document you translate once you submit your translation. Sometimes colleagues want to hold you responsible for that content. You also shouldn't be asked to share the content if it's confidential.

Looking for Work

How you look for work depends on who you'd like to work for. Regardless, you need at least a resume, some kind of statement on the translation work you're qualified to do, a business card or other tangible document you can share with potential clients, perhaps a professional social media presence, and time. The time part might be tricky; while you're looking for another job, you probably need to have some way to bring in money until you land a full-time job or get paying clients. If you're looking for part- or full-time employment, be ready to respond to whatever the potential employer requests. Once you have all the material ready to go, where and how do you look for the jobs? Well, that depends!

Getting ready to apply for jobs

Chapter 15 covers the material you need to have in your portfolio before you start looking for jobs. In addition to a resume, short translation samples, your translator's statement, and testimonials, you'll also need to have the following lined up:

>> **Time:** The job search can be time consuming, so be sure to plan for it. The time it can take often depends on where you live, where and how you'd like to work, and what your language pair is. Perhaps set a certain number of hours per week to your job search so that you can manage your time.

>> **Money:** Be sure to have some money in the bank or a way to cover your expenses because it will take time to find the job or to gain paying clients.

>> **Tracking system:** Have a way to track the clients and employers you've contacted and a way to organize follow-up. If you do get responses that indicate general interest but nothing at the present moment, follow up with those organizations or people in a month or two. Update them on what you've been doing and see if they're interested in working with you.

TIP

Use good judgment when it comes to who you ask about actual jobs. For instance, if a small agency works with only a few translators in your language pair and all of them are already your friends or colleagues, ask them about opportunities with that agency with care. You don't want to give the impression that you're taking someone's work. The same goes for direct clients. It can be helpful to talk to translators of other language pairs about the fact that you're looking for job opportunities.

Finding and responding to job postings

If you're looking for a job as a full-time translator for an agency, you need to identify the agencies you're interested in working for and apply to them directly if they have attractive positions. You can find out about those opportunities on their webpages, sometimes through social media posts and professional organizations, from fellow translators or alumni networks, and from job postings. Look for agencies in your source and target language countries, and use the contact information on their webpages instead of the one you might find in a posting on a third-party page.

If you're looking for a job in a certain field that allows you to occasionally translate, you'd follow the process of any other job search. Think about choosing a variety of words in search filters, such as *translator, translation, linguist, language translation, multilingual,* and *bilingual.*

If you're looking to start out as a freelancer or independent translator, you might be doing work for translation agencies as a contractor instead of working with direct clients. This could mean contacting hundreds of translation agencies. Don't get bummed out if many of them don't respond to you. However, as the need for quality translation increases, this might not necessarily be the case. Contact directly the kind of organizations you want to translate for. If this is part of your approach, you need to spend time researching these organizations and direct clients to show them that you know about them and why you'd be a convincing translator choice for them.

Be sure your network knows that you're looking for translation jobs.

TIP

You need to do all of this in an error-free way. Have a trusted colleague who pays attention to detail review all your material.

Chapter 13

Curating the Range of Professional Services to Offer

As a professional translator, it's possible that you won't just translate. Although just translation alone is a huge task! Translators are often called upon to perform tasks beyond just translating words in one language to words in another. Translators also work as writers, editors, or even teachers.

As translators' skills develop and their experience grows, they learn that they can offer other professional tasks to the world. This can include improving your competency in an already acquired second language or learning even more languages.

For example, as you begin to establish yourself as a translator, you'll have to decide which language you're going to translate from and which language you're going to translate into. Because a translation is a written document, you need to be a strong writer in the language that you translate into. Although the direction you translate into might be clear to you right now, keep in mind that your languages develop with time and grow and transform as you learn new things and acquire more professional and life experiences.

WARNING

Many translators have been taught to avoid inverse translation, which means translating from a stronger language into a not as strong language. Many translators have been taught to go from not as strong languages, usually referred to as L2 or L3, depending how many languages you have, into your strongest language, which is referred to as your L1. These translators are taught to only translate into their L2 or L3 in a pinch. This all makes sense and many translators will stick to this throughout their entire professional life. However, this doesn't always have to be the case. Because the tools translators work with develop and expand overtime, and because the need for translation grows, especially among new language pairs, I believe there will also be more flexibility regarding directionality in translation. My advice is not to limit yourself as you are becoming a translator. See what you're languages can do and where they can take you.

As you become more comfortable in your role as a translator, it will become clearer where your strengths and qualifications lie and what additional skills you can develop to expand your business and professional profile to include additional services or to share your knowledge with audiences beyond your clients and immediate colleagues.

In this chapter you'll learn about determining how to use your languages for translation and how to grow your language collection. This in turn will also increase the amount of services you can offer. Finally, I'll cover how to share your knowledge with the world and to promote your own work.

REMEMBER

The possibilities presented in this chapter aren't intended to overwhelm you but to excite you about the dimensions and directions of the profession. Keeping an eye on the opportunities can shape your daily decisions and connect you to the larger industry.

Directionality: Which Way to Go with Your Languages

People use language every day to communicate in writing via emails, texts, or chats; to communicate verbally via phone, video call, or in person; or to communicate nonverbally, such as by signing.

But because you're reading this book, you likely have an interest and skill in language that goes beyond using it to function in an everyday sense. You likely know more than one language and are interested in seeing how you can apply this skill as a professional translator. You might even love languages so much that you'll be inspired to add more languages to your repertoire.

Strong language skills don't automatically prepare you for a career as a translator. You have to be able to move from one of those languages into the other with the help of the development of additional translator skills beyond being bilingual. When translators talk about language direction in translation, they talk about directionality.

You might, for example, be able to responsibly translate a German text into a professional piece of writing in English but struggle to produce the same quality of writing in reverse. Your best direction would then be from German to English.

This section looks at assessing language skills to determine where your abilities as a translator currently are strong and where they might be improved.

Being qualified to translate "into" a language

Especially in the United States, translators tend to translate from a language learned in a structured setting into their native language. (See Chapter 3 for more on what constitutes a *native* language.) This means that if you grew up speaking English at home and in school and then learned Chinese in high school and college classrooms and during a study abroad experience, you'll most likely translate from Chinese into English. If you grew up speaking and being educated in Portuguese and took English classes at a language academy and in college and then moved to the United States afterward, you'll most likely translate from English into Portuguese.

TRANSLATION LANGUAGES OF LESSER DIFFUSION OR ENDANGERED LANGUAGES

Not all languages have the same level or number of resources when it comes to reliable translation. For example, Chinese and Portuguese are languages with many speakers and many resources, including qualified translators that can go from English into Portuguese and vice versa. But for language pairs for which there are not as many qualified translators, such as English and Haitian Creole, English and Cape Verdean Creole, and English and Khmer, it might not be the case that translators are always translating into their strongest language. In fact, they might move in both directions translating from Khmer into English and from English into Khmer. Ideally this happens with the support of strong editors of the languages they're translating into.

(continued)

(continued)

Languages in this situation are sometimes referred to as languages of lesser diffusion. If you have some kind of existing foundation or interest in learning one of these languages, go for it! The world needs people who know these languages who can become qualified translators. Translators who work with languages that are still developing resources, often receive higher rates of compensation because they are not as in demand.

As we learn in chapter 3, there are people who have different language profiles which make the question of what qualifies as a native language very interesting. In some cases, people speak two languages at home and then attend a school with a dual-language program in those same two languages. So they've been educated in two languages, and have sometimes picked up a third language along the way.

There are other people who might have lived in one country until their high school years and then moved to another, in a new language. While their native language might be the one of their country of origin, by the time they've graduated college, they've had their more advanced years of education in the language that is not their native language.

You have to have a very strong, ideally native level, written command of a language in order to translate into it. This is as a translator, you're essentially a writer. Solid writing is hard to fake, and if you can't write well in a language, you can't translate into it.

Being aware of your limitations in a given language will help you determine what languages you have strong writing skills in. But don't let this discourage you if it is your goal to translate to another language. You can certainly improve your skills to get to the level where you can do so responsibly.

WARNING

It's really important for your credibility to be realistic and transparent about your language ability when accepting a project, and not to claim to skills you still need to work on.

To be a strong writer of a language, you need to not only know all the written conventions of that language, but you also must have a wide range of vocabulary in that language. The wider your vocabulary, the faster you'll be able to find the words you're looking for to make an effective translation. You'll spend less time searching for words and researching about their usage.

To improve your knowledge of the language or languages you translate into:

>> **Listen** to the language on the radio, television, podcasts, and other presentations. You can also listen to the way people speak the language on the streets, public transportation, and in other spaces.

>> **Read** in the language you translate into. Pay attention to word choice and look up words you don't fully understand. Be sure the texts are written well.

>> **Be strategic** about your listening and reading choices. If you specialize in the translation texts related to food and cooking, listen to and read content about the subject. Ask people questions about food, recipes, nutrition, and preferences. All of this will expand your language knowledge.

>> **Talk to people from** different countries with different dialects. The more you can learn about the language as a whole, the better. This can help avoid faux pas.

Subject matter is also something to consider. How well you write about different topics might differ from language to language. If you're a Spanish-English translator who only watches and reads about soccer in Spanish, you might be better equipped to translate articles on soccer into Spanish than into English, while you might prefer to translate other texts into English.

REMEMBER

Translators don't have to work alone. Have people review, edit, and proofread your work before you submit it to a client. Each project will require something different, a different support network.

For example, if you're a French to English translator who specializes in the culinary arts, you might be able to have a friend who is an experienced baker in English review your translations of dessert recipes for content and then have a proofreader look at the translations for spelling and other minor technical errors.

If you translate texts for a local school district from English to Spanish, be sure you understand how the school works since you can't readily apply terms from the school system in Argentina, for example, to the one in the United States. Check in with a colleague who is an interpreter for the same school district and ask the school district if they might already have some Spanish-language resources to support your translation. Then of course have another set of eyes proofread your translation.

Being a translator requires knowledge and creativity. The more solid your language base in the language you're translating into and the stronger your ability to see what a project needs and how you will make that happen, the better your translations will be. A fun part about being a translator is that you're a problem solver.

Although this all might sound like a lot to think about, the more systematic you are about routinely listening and reading in the language or languages you translate into, it will just be something you do. The same goes for knowing what kind of review process each translation will need. The more you translate, the faster you'll be able to identify the most efficient and effective route for completing a project.

TIP

If you offer translation services into what appears to be your non-native language, be prepared to explain to clients what makes you qualified to do the work.

Being qualified to translate "from" a language

Not only will you have to determine which language or languages you'll translate into, but you also need to determine which language or languages you'll translate from. The language or languages you translate from must be languages that you read and are committed to fully understanding. You can't effectively and efficiently translate a text that you don't fully understand.

The language you translate from is usually a language you've learned in a formal setting. You need to be able to read the language and not only understand what the text is saying but be able to determine how it says what it says. It is often said that translators know texts better than any other readers, including the person who authored them.

In your reading of the text, you can't have any doubts. You need to look up everything and ask all the questions you need to ask. Every word counts. Doing your research will impact the quality of your translation.

Here's what you can do to learn to read like a translator:

>> **Practice.** To get good at reading texts in a given language, you need to read, read, read. Read texts in the language you translate from, and read guides to idiomatic expressions and other texts about language.

>> **Have your network.** It's also helpful to have friends and colleagues, people you can reach out to who are native speakers of the language of the texts you translate from. You can consult them when you need to verify something about a text you're translating and with any questions you have.

>> **Listen.** Create opportunities to listen to the language you translate from. The more you are familiar with how people use the language, the more efficient you will be at navigating your way through how it is written.

While it might be hard to add onto the languages you can translate into, don't overlook opportunities to expand the number of languages you can translate from. Remember language skills and translation skills are two separate things. So if you have the translation skills, you might think about expanding your language skills and learn new languages.

Consider learning a language from the same language group. If you already translate from Spanish to English, think about learning Portuguese or Catalan. Or if you have the time, energy, and opportunity to do so, learn a language of lesser diffusion or one with a growing demand. The more language you can offer, the more services you can offer and the more work you'll be able to take on. Just keep your limits in mind. One bad translation can cost you a client forever.

TIP

There's a difference between what you can do as a translator and what you can do as a business. As a translator you might only be able to translate from English into Italian and Spanish, but if you are also a business owner, you might also be able to take on other language combinations and send them out to qualified translators in your network. In this case, you would do your calculations so that you would profit from facilitating such a transaction. The best time to take this step might be after you've fully learned the entire process yourself as a translator.

Translating from unknown languages

You might be surprised to learn that some translators even translate from languages they don't know. Yup! This doesn't happen with high-stakes texts. If you wanted to try this, you'd most likely choose a literary text. Usually this is done to be creative with language, to experiment, to play. It's an exercise that can help you as a translator build more confidence in the language you translate into, into making bolder decisions. But to translate a literary text, a poem for instance, from a language you don't know, you do have to know a lot about other things.

>> **Know a lot about language in general.** Sometimes when you know a lot about language, you realize that sentence structure differs from language to language, time is represented in different ways, and so much more. This knowledge will allow you to ask questions about a text.

>> **Know a lot about translation.** You need to know a lot about translation to translate from a language you don't know.

>> **Know a lot about a specific genre.** When you translate from a language you don't know, try for a text that belongs to a genre you know a lot about. Many times, it's translators of poetry that translate from languages they don't know.

>> **Work with an informant or a text that has several existing translations.** An informant assists you. This is someone who does know the language you're translating from and who can answer your questions. If you don't have an informant, go for a text that has several existing translations. This way you can learn from them, compare, and come up with your own translation.

Editing, Transcribing, and Other Language-Related Skills

Becoming a translator doesn't happen just because you know two or more languages. It happens because you know those languages, how you can responsibly work with them, and because you know a ton about how language works. You are a close reader that pays attention to every little thing in a text, and you can confidently make choices when making that text have a life in another language. All that ability to work with the written word can be applied to language services in addition to translation for which you can charge.

As a translator, you can also think about hiring another person to carry out these services on your own translations. There are often times when translators have worked with a text so much that they become blind to some of the areas that need improvement. Having another set of eyes review your translation is a must! You can try to exchange services with another translator or hire another professional.

Polishing and editing texts

Once you're done translating the text, you'll move to the editing process to get the text as good as can be before sharing a final version. Because of the complexities of translation, the editing stage can also be time consuming. It can range from revising texts for accuracy and completion to proofreading them.

As a translator committed to delivering effective and flawless translations, you'll want to have a solid system in place for doing this stage on your own, or what is even better, having someone else do this for you. At the same time, this is a service that you yourself can offer in addition to translation.

This stage however doesn't need to be reserved for only the texts that you translate. You can also offer this service for texts created by others in the languages that you translate into. These texts can be originals or translations created by other translations. Just remember, you're evaluating writing so these texts have to be in the language or languages that you have total confidence in when it comes to writing.

Revising, editing, and proofreading are sometimes terms that are used interchangeably by clients and even in the industry.

Here is a helpful way to sort out the terms when they involve the translation process.

Revising

Revising is a service you can think about adding once you're an experienced translator. You need to have significant translation experience to do this well. Revising usually involves looking at the source text and the target text to check for accuracy and any omissions.

Be sure to check with clients to see if they are looking for this kind of revising or just a focus on the target text, or the translation. If you are comparing the source and the target texts, it might be more involved so you'll need to charge more.

If you're serious about adding this service to your repertoire, you might search for a course to take on revising or editing in the target language.

With the rise of machine translation and other machine-produced texts, you might want to establish in what conditions you'll revise or edit texts sent to you. Some translators will not edit texts that have been translated by Google with no prior systematized editing in place. With some machine-produced translations, it can take more work to revise and edit them than it does to professionally translate them.

WARNING

Oftentimes agencies and other clients pay less for revisions than for translations. Make sure that when accepting a revision, it's a true revision rather than an attempt to cut corners/costs.

WARNING

Speaking of machine translation, a responsible way to use such tools is not just throwing a text into the program and pressing translation. When professionals use machines to assist with the translation process there is pre-editing performed on a source text and post-editing performed on the target text to get the best result possible. Check out this resource "Machine Translation (MT) Pre-editing" created by Imogen van den Oord and Professor Lettie Dorst, which includes tricks and tips to master the pre-editing: https://drive.google.com/file/d/11InBB4WM8KGaLnTFy8BI9oDo8ZpkHQnG/view

Once a translation is revised, it moves on to the **copyediting** stage. In this step, you identify and fix errors related to spelling and grammar, inconsistencies regarding tone and style, and poor word choice. You also look to improve any awkward syntax, or the arrangement of words and phrases to create well-formed sentences in a language.

Proofreading

Proofreading is a step in the right before you are ready to finalize a text, including translations. In the proofreading stage, you review the mechanical elements of the text such as grammar, spelling, punctuation, capitalization, and possibly issues regarding layout.

For this service, which might in fact sound like many, you can charge by the word or for your time. If you charge by the hour, you will get paid for the time you put into the project. Charging by the word doesn't guarantee you'll get paid for the time spent doing the work, but clients often like to know upfront the cost of the work. Charging by the word allows you to do this.

Since as a translator, you dedicate most of your time to reading and writing, you'll be able to know what a text needs after spending a few minutes glancing at it. You'll be able to offer your best work if you understand the project and the client's needs and wishes. To facilitate things for the client, group these services into one and then provide a rate and timeline once you've seen the text in question.

Remember to establish a network because for some of your own translation projects, you will be the one who might need support from other professionals at this stage.

Transcribing

Transcription involves making a written transcript of an audio or video recording. A transcription is not a translation. It is writing all that is said in an audio or video recording. Most translators can offer this service in their working languages, either source or target languages. This could involve transcribing an interview in Spanish between two parties. This would be one service.

TIP

There are AI transcription tools that produce a transcription and then a human can simply review the transcription. This facilitates the work. I encourage you to look into these options, but also try doing the work on your own so that you can have a better understanding of transcription.

Translators can also offer transcription plus translation. To do this you listen to the audio recording and instead of making a transcript in the source language, you would translate the text while listening to the audio. A police department located in the United States might need this done for audio recordings they have in Arabic or some other non-English language. If this is a service that you can responsibly offer you would charge a different, increased fee from just the transcription fee.

You can take special training to develop this skill. There is even specialized software to assist with this that allows you to use your computer keyboard or foot pedals to do the work. Be sure to check out all the available tools.

Writing subtitles

When you think subtitles, you might think about words on a screen that accompany a movie or television show. With increased accessibility efforts and the availability of screens in all kinds of places, there are many ways in which words accompany the spoken word on the screen. Not all of them are subtitles. Some are captions. Since as a language professional you will come to represent all things language related for your clients, it is a good idea to be aware of the differences between subtitles and captions.

There's so much more to all of these services and they each require additional training and skills. While you might try adding one or all of them to your repertoire, subtitling is usually more attractive to translators because it doesn't happen in real time and because the time and space constraints require the translator creating the subtitles to be highly creative.

Closed captioning

Closed captioning is the audio portion of a television program as text on the screen. They are in the language of the audio and usually provided verbatim, the exact words of the speaker or in edited form. Non-speech information is usually also included. They are called "closed" because they usually need to be activated by the viewer.

Sometimes closed captioning is provided in a language that is not the language of the audio portion of television program. In other words, it is provided in translation.

Closed captioning and closed captioning with translation are often services that happen in real time. They can be provided by a human, by an AI program, or a combination of the two. Like most things language related, quality varies depending on how well educated the provider is about offering the service and how much money is invested in its provision.

Subtitling

Subtitles are different from captions in that they assume the viewer hears the sound, but perhaps doesn't know the language of the audio or for other reasons chooses to enable the subtitles. Subtitles are not transcriptions of what a speaker is saying. They are translations that have to follow certain time and space requirements. They can only have a determined number of characters and stay on the screen for a certain amount of time. Knowing that there are these constraints you probably now better understand why you've read some subtitles in a language you understand to a film in a language you also understand and said to yourself or aloud, "that's not what she said!"

Some other things to be aware of regarding subtitles: It's almost impossible to do subtitles without proper technology. A lot of the time spent on doing subtitling projects can be spent revising the translation to make it fit the constraints. It's almost impossible to do subtitles without proper technology.

Interpreting

As a translator you'll spend a lot of time seated or standing at a desk and in front of a computer. Once you're an experienced translator, you'll know a lot about language in general and have extensive knowledge about the languages you work with. And if you specialize in a certain area, you'll have extensive vocabulary and knowledge about something that most people don't.

At some point in your career you might decide that you can do even more with all these skills and knowledge. You might consider adding interpreting to your collection of services. Interpreting, if done in person allows you to get out. If done via phone or video, it allows you to focus on listening and speaking. You might even be moved to begin to train as an interpreter if you speak a language for which there is a need for qualified providers.

To be an interpreter, you need to be able to speak well in both languages if you're a Japanese-English interpreter, for example. Remember that interpreting requires a very different skill set than translation, which includes:

>> Language skills

>> In-depth cultural knowledge

>> Knowledge of context and terminology, including extensive vocabulary in general

>> Interpersonal skills

>> Memory retention

>> Significant concentration

>> Public-speaking skills

>> Listening and note-taking skills

>> Quick thinking skills

>> Confident decision-making skills

>> Steady oratory

Here are the primary modes:

>> **Simultaneous** In this mode, the speaker speaks in one language and the interpreter listens and then says what the speaker says and how it is said in the target language. This happens almost at the same time. This mode is mostly used for large meetings and conferences and similar meetings, and special equipment is often required.

>> **Consecutive** In this mode, the interpreter listens to what the speaker says in one language, takes notes, and then interprets what the speaker has said during a pause. The exchange carries on like this. This mode is mostly used for small meetings with few parties.

You need initial training and ongoing training to' be an interpreter. Training can be in the form of a certificate program or a masters degree with a focus on conference interpreting, for example. You'll have to do your research and see which program fits your needs. And sometimes a certification or other credential is required.

Interpreters are paid by the hour, usually with a minimum number of hours, or by the day. The pay varies widely and often includes travel expenses as well for onsite appointments. As an interpreter, you can work directly with clients or with an agency.

Sharing Your Knowledge with Other Translators

Most translators are happy to share what they do and a bit on how they do it. In general, translators are generous when it comes to talking about their work. Since it's a profession that is not often understood by people who don't do it, translators embrace opportunities to share experiences and knowledge with others.

You can learn from what other translators have to say by reading books and articles, listening to podcasts and presentations. Bringing together what you learn from being part of the profession with your own experiences as a translator, will help you to carve out your own professional profile.

Educator

Translators often must by ready to educate clients and partners about their services. You can further contribute to spreading knowledge about translation by teaching about translation in a planned fashion. As you grow as a translator, this can happen in several ways, for which most of them will bring you an additional income stream:

- » **Higher education.** Professional translators occasionally join college and community college campuses to teach a course or two on translation. This kind of course would mostly be for students who would like to become translators.

- » **Workshops and trainings.** You could offer workshops and trainings for organizations, clients, and partners who are looking to develop more knowledge on a specific need. For this you could be hired by an agency or offer these services directly to a client.

- » **Write texts on translation.** To further spread translation education you could write blog posts, articles, and even books that address general and specific topics. Writing doesn't only educate the reader, but it will also help you to think through and further explore any professional topics that are of growing interest to you.

It's very exciting to reach a point in your career in which you are prepared to educate the next generation of translators! Their questions and ideas will also inspire you to evaluate often how you do your own work.

Consultant

Once you've acquired many hours of translation experience and have worked with a range of clients, you're going to be well versed in how multilingual projects work. You can also package this expertise as a service as a language consultant or a language access consultant.

You might help a local organization go multilingual by helping them understand how to write texts for translation, work effectively with an interpreter, and identify vendors and request services. Translation and other language services often come as afterthoughts so helping clients to plan for this work will improve their efforts and the working relationship with their language service providers.

You could also help an organization consider which Spanish or Portuguese to translate into and how to be consistent with such choices. While performing this service you wouldn't be doing the work of translation, but you'd be helping organizations decide which work to get done, plan for the work, and follow process to get it done.

Champion

As you develop as a professional, there are many activities you'll do that won't be translating a text or providing any of the other services you add to your repertoire. All these activities will give you a sense of the bigger picture of this large and growing profession, and maybe even help you determine how you want to contribute to it and shape it for future generations. Becoming a champion of translators and translation would mean that you actively seek ways to contribute to and improve the profession. This is also referred to as giving back. Here are some ways to do this:

>> **Join professional translator organizations.** Join professional organizations. If there are gaps in the organizations, think about how you can work with others to fill the gaps in the organization.

If none of the organizations address a need you see in the profession, think about creating your own professional organization or network if that would make sense and doesn't duplicate the efforts of the excellent work that's already being done in the profession.

>> **Attend conferences.** Check out if the professional organizations hold conferences and consider attending them. These organizations are usually happy to have members help organize the conferences as well and that's a great way to meet colleagues and contribute to the profession.

>> **Talk about translation.** Tell your friends, family, and neighbors what you do and why it's important. Everyone should be aware of how translation impacts their lives and also aware that there might be individuals in need of translation services in a community.

When you go in bookstores and libraries, ask where the translated books are. This is how you can help support literary translation and translators.

>> **Write about translation.** Champions, like educators, can also write about translation. Think of social media or blog posts, short articles, news pieces, or even books that you could write that would contribute to productive thinking in the profession.

These activities and your participation in and support of them will help distinguish you and give you greater recognition. You'll also be helping the profession address challenges and create more opportunities for yourself and others.

Chapter **14**

Setting Up Your Work Environment and Choosing Your Tools

Whether you end up as an independent translator, working for an employer, or translating as part of your existing job, you'll need to pay attention to the kind of workspace you have from which to do the translation work and the tools and supports you fill that space up with.

If you're planning to become an independent, or freelance, translator, you're probably looking forward to setting your own terms on where you'll work from, what you'll wear to work, and when you'll work. One of the nice things about being an independent translator is that you can work around your energy levels. You're probably also excited about the ability to work from home with no long commutes. Being an independent translator rewards you with a lot of flexibility, but it also requires you to be disciplined in many ways.

If you work for an agency or translation company, you probably won't have to pay as much attention to setting yourself up, and they might have tools and supports in place for you beyond those included in this chapter. Nevertheless, keep an eye on making sure you're physically comfortable and that you know how to use their tools and supports.

If you work as a full-time translator for an organization, you might be the only one or one member of a small team. Perhaps you're the full-time translator at a bank, a school, or a museum. You might need to treat the setup situation the same as you would if you were an independent translator. Non-translators usually don't know all the things that translators need to get the job done.

And if you do translation on occasion for an organization where you have another main duty, you also need to keep an eye on being sure you're getting all you need to get the job done.

Finding a Suitable Workspace

One of the top reasons you might be encouraged to become a translator is because of the flexible workplace location. If you'd like to become an independent translator, or freelancer, who works directly with individuals, organizations, or agencies as your clients, then you'll probably have the freedom to choose where you work from. Although some clients will want to meet on occasion in person, you'll handle most of your work via email, the internet, and other means.

You can look at your work location in two ways. One would be the country, city, or town that you work from. In terms of the country you decide to work from, you'll have to become familiar with immigration and business laws and related procedures to see how it is that you can work from country A with clients located outside country A. Or how you, as a non-citizen of country A, can work from country A. You'll have to figure out a lot of things about setting yourself up as a business and working from the place where you'll be based.

TIP

If you're interested in learning more about setting up a small business, check out *Small Business For Dummies* by Eric Tyson and Jim Schell.

Even though your business might be based in a single location, because most of the work comes to you through the internet, you can move around and still work. You'll usually just need to take your laptop computer with you. So if you want to take a personal trip, you can do that as long as you can take your laptop and figure out how to get the work done from that place according to the schedule you have to follow while there. Also, if you decide to move from City C to City D, it's likely that you'll be able to keep your job. Isn't that nice? The flexibility that comes with not having to work from a single location is appealing to many.

Once you've decided where you'll be based, depending on your situation, you should start thinking about defining your workspace.

>> **Home:** Working from home is an option. Try to have a designated room or space that you use only for work. Having this space allows you to take a deduction on your taxes.

>> **Rented office space:** You can rent an office space outside your home. This way you can more easily separate your home life from your work life; otherwise, you might feel like you must work all the time. If you're someone who's distracted easily, renting office space can also hold you more accountable for completing your work.

>> **Co-working space:** Check out co-working spaces, where you rent a desk in a shared space. These spaces can have a variety of options, from private and semi-private offices to open area desks. You can usually rent these spaces in a variety of ways, from a daily pass or a monthly pass to a punch card system where you don't need to commit to a regular schedule. Some of these spaces also offer conference rooms if you need to host a meeting with clients or colleagues.

>> **Nomadic:** You can also incorporate working from local libraries or coffee shops into your rotation if you need to change things up or focus in a new way. And if you're a parent and need to be at your kids' sporting events, you can pop onto your computer during downtimes if you'd like.

If you work as a full-time translator for an organization and agency, you might be able to do that work remotely, or you might have to report to an office. If remote work is the case, you can consider all the above that would apply to an independent translator, or freelancer. If you're working onsite, you'll have to follow your organization's requirements.

TIP

Something else to consider: If you're occasionally asked to translate as part of your job, which is not a translator at an organization, try to make sure you have a designated space to translate that works for you when the time comes. For example, you need a computer to translate documents. If your job doesn't give you a computer and you're asked to translate, you'll need to ask them to give you one to use and a space to do the work that's conducive to your productivity. For instance, if you work in a school as a paraprofessional with no personal work computer and are then asked to translate a document, you probably can't do that very efficiently on your phone and in the middle of the cafeteria. You need a dedicated space, an allotment of time, and the necessary tools to do the work at a professional level.

REMEMBER

You do a lot of sitting when you're a working translator. Keep ergonomics in mind. Have a comfortable chair and desk set up. Because of all that sitting, make sure to stay active when you're not at your desk. Your body and mind need it!

Procuring Equipment and Access to Resources

Although you'll have your language skills and your translation skills and the desire to start receiving texts to translate, you're going to have to take some time to ensure that you have everything in line that you need to get the job done, while remaining flexible to the fact that you're a beginner and you might have to add tools and setups to your workspace as you go. It takes trials, consulting with others, and adjusting to find a setup that works for you.

In addition to your skills, knowledge, and creativity, here's a basic list to get you started on collecting your tools.

>> **Computer:** You'll need a computer, obviously. Depending on how mobile you'd like to be, go for a laptop if you're going to be on the move a lot. If you do get a laptop, consider setting up something more comfortable at home that allows for at least one large monitor, maybe two, and a keyboard that you feel comfortable typing on.

>> **Printer:** It's a good idea to have access to a printer because you might want to print a draft of a translation and read it before you finalize it. Other times a client might want a hard copy of a translation in addition to the digital copy. Remember to recycle!

>> **Internet access:** Internet access is a must. If you're working for an organization and doing translation work onsite, be sure that you're able to freely search the internet and in languages other than English. You'll need to do this when you research terms and other items.

>> **Email:** You'll need a professional email address and a solid way to keep all your emails organized. Include a professional signature in your reply messages that has your phone number and other contact information.

>> **Phone number:** Although the majority of your work will probably come through email, you do need a phone number so that clients can contact you. Clients will on occasion want a live conversation, and so will you. You can have a separate line or use your cell phone. Some of them will also want to text. Be sure that your photo, if you're using a texting application that includes one, is professional. Also be professional in your voice mail greeting.

>> **Video calls:** Get set up to use a video calling program such as Skype, Zoom, Teams, or any other one that clients will be familiar with. When on a video call, be sure to present professionally in terms of how you look and how your background appears.

This list isn't totally inclusive. Along the way you'll figure out what you need, what you want, and what you wish for in your office space. Talk to other translators about how they set themselves up. You want to aim to work smarter, not harder!

Gathering the Tools of the Trade

Once again, there's no definitive list of what should be in your toolbox. Keep in mind that usually you work with the tools, and the tools don't work without you. Start with the basics, in no particular order, and then ask around and do your research to see what more you might add and when.

Word count tools

Because one of the parts of calculating how much to charge for a translation assignment is based on the word count of your source text or your target text, you'll want to have help with that so that you don't have to count each word manually. Most word processing programs have word and character count capabilities. Learn how to use them. However, not all projects will come to you in word processing programs. If you need a more advanced word counting program that would help you count words on a website, for example, you can find specific tools online that can help you.

Dictionaries

Meet your best friends: dictionaries. Translators work with dictionaries in many ways. They're your source for verifying that you know the definition of a word and seeking out definitions for unfamiliar words. You'll work with bilingual dictionaries in your language pair, monolingual dictionaries (one for each language of your language pair), and thesauruses.

It's wise to have dictionaries in digital and print forms. Identify helpful online dictionaries, and bookmark those sites because you'll be jumping to them often. Think about installing at least one dictionary on your computer in case the internet fails and you can't use your phone as a hot spot.

TIP

Don't dismiss print dictionaries as a helpful tool. They're great if you're browsing for a word because you get to see all the words around it. You'll also get all different types of assignments. Maybe for one, you'll need a word that starts with n, for example. You can open your print dictionary to the n section and search for that word that will help you make an excellent translation. Translators like to learn words, so just browsing through the dictionary is fun.

Style guides or manuals

Because being a translator isn't just about knowing which words to use and when, but how they look in that language, it's a good idea to get style guides or manuals for the languages you translate into. They'll show you how the languages treat certain aspects of language, including dates, addresses, times, and more.

If you're translating for an organization, don't be surprised if they also give you a style guide or a translation style guide. This might include things like language-specific conventions for numbers, dates, times, addresses, inclusive language, localization of proper nouns, style, voice, and register.

Word lists and glossaries

In addition to dictionaries and style guides, as a translator you'll also most likely want to use word lists and glossaries. A word list could simply be where you keep track of basic, included-in-the-dictionary words and how you'll translate them for a particular client and their needs. If you're working for a school district, this is where you'd keep a list of how you'll say *school bus* and *meetings* and refer to parents in the target language. A word list is especially helpful when translating into languages that have many variations.

You can think of glossaries as more advanced versions of word lists. Glossaries will usually include words and terms that aren't in the dictionary and are more advanced in structure. They usually have several fields, including source language, target language and source where you can find the translation or translations, other possible translations and the source where you found the translation, examples of the term used in context in the source language, and examples of the term used in context in the target language.

You must be careful that the examples of the terms in context are original texts and not translations. Because the internet is filled with non-human verified, automated translations, even on reputable sites, you don't want to promote poor language use.

Translation memory

You'll hear about translation memory, also called TM. Translation memories are repositories of data that are gathered from previous translation projects that you or the users of the specific translation memory did. A translation memory creates a database of previously translated text that you can use again in other translation projects.

CAT TOOLS

The name *CAT tools* sounds attractive, doesn't it? They have nothing to do with felines. They're computer-assisted (or aided) translation tools that help you with the translation process. CAT tools refer to the entire gamut of software that a professional translator uses during their process. Don't confuse them with machine translation (MT), or automated translation. CAT tools help translators achieve consistency and efficiency, manage terminology, and manage projects. You should do your research before deciding which tools to add to your toolbox. Talk to clients and colleagues, and look into training. These tools will cost money, so research them wisely, and consider what their return-on-investment will be.

There's a lot more to learn about tools that will help you be the best possible translator. However, one of the first steps of becoming a translator is to understand how translation works and to master the basics. Once you understand what the work is all about, you can start getting more advanced tools, which are generally referred to as *translation environment tools* (TEnTs), which will help set you up for your career as a translator.

MANAGING YOUR FINANCES AND TIME

When thinking about your workspace and the tools you'll need, don't overlook what you'll need to get the non-translation tasks done. For instance, bookkeeping is not a task specific to translators but it's one that you'll have to do if you're an independent translator. When and how will you get it done?

When you're calculating how much you want to make as an independent translator, pay yourself for the hours you do bookkeeping and other non-translation tasks. Try to work those numbers into how much you need to make as a translator. You might not be charging a client directly for these tasks that you need to do, but calculate how much you'd like to make a year and use that to figure out how much you'll need to work and get paid. Add in these other costs. Set aside time to check out a new tool, an updated way of organizing your project tracker, or to network. All these tasks are working hours. As a professional translator, you should find a way to pay yourself for them.

If you're thinking of becoming an independent or freelance translator, part of the plan is to grow. Even if the work is slow at first or you're just picking up one or two translation jobs per month, keep organized as if you were bringing in a lot more work. This will give you a solid foundation.

(continued)

(continued)

Also in your planning, you should figure out how you'll be paid for your work. The first step is to determine what you'll be paid and when. If you're going with the standard of 30 days after the completion of a project, but sure to invoice your clients as soon as the project is done so that you will be paid on time. Working with clients outside the United States might have different average payment times.

Determine if you'll require a check or a transfer to some online banking account. You might not be able to deposit checks in the United States from countries outside the United States, so be sure to look into that. Keep in mind that your bank might charge you a fee for a wire transfer if you do direct deposit.

Keeping in Touch with Mentors and Colleagues

Translators spend a lot of time alone at their computers translating and working on related tasks. Translators also need to have a professional network of translators, language professionals, people who have high language skills, and more. Each project could be a chance to bring more people into your professional network.

As you begin to build your network, you'll learn more about the unique profiles of your colleagues. At the same time, try to identify some mentors who can offer advice, wisdom, and feedback aimed at the long term. Cultivate these relationships by sharing news items or other content of interest. Meet up with them at conferences and other events. And talk to them in a live conversation while you're taking breaks between tasks. You can phone them while you're on a walk. In other words, just as you'll plan tasks as you're becoming a translator, connecting with mentors and colleagues is something you should build into your schedule. These kinds of conversations can even lead to new projects and ideas that innovate your own work and possibly the profession!

Recruiting Advocates and Allies

Just as all causes need advocates and allies, so does translation, especially for the promotion of quality language, linguistic diversity, and access to information and ideas.

Your professional contacts don't have to just include clients, translators, and language professional colleagues. Translation is needed everywhere! Tell family, friends, and neighbors about the awesome work you do and why it matters. Talk to them about Google Translate and some of the other automated, non-human generated translations and how they can be harmful. Of course, talk to them about other things non-translation related also!

You can encourage people to be advocates for translation by talking about the benefits of translation and language inclusion, pointing out where it's needed, and recommending it.

Encourage them to be allies by listening to and supporting you.

Encourage them to recommend you if a need comes up that's connected to their professional, community, or personal interests. You might be able to translate for them for a fee, or you can refer them to another translator or language professional.

TIP

Unfortunately, translators are often an afterthought. It's common for a translator to be sought only after an entire project and all its content are established. This can make projects complicated. But things don't have to stay this way. The more people know about translation, the more successful you can be as a translator, and the more favorable your working conditions can be for yourself and all professional translators.

Chapter **15**

Breaking Into the Profession

P erhaps you've decided that you want to be a translator. Maybe you've been translating for the organization you work for and now you're actively trying to deepen your knowledge of the profession and perhaps pick up some additional work. Or you're just curious about how translators can professionalize what it is they do. In any of these cases, this chapter provides key insight.

Here I discuss getting experience, meeting fellow translators and people who might want you to translate for them, and packaging yourself as a professional translator who is going to add to this vast profession.

Getting Experience When You're a Rank Beginner

Many practicing translators have become translators accidentally. This means they didn't necessarily set out to become translators, but a particular set of consequences led them to that path and they stayed, survived, and thrived doing it.

You might be finding yourself in that position as you read this book, or you might have proactively decided that you want to become a professional translator. If you've made that decision, congratulations! Translating is a dynamic and reward-ing career.

Now you're an eager, beginning translator, or you're looking to professionalize a task that you've already been doing for some time now. How will you get experience?

The good news is that there's written text all around you. You can pick up a receipt, the schedule for classes at your gym, a flier from your local library, a letter from a local politician or realtor, or a news article and try translating it into your target language. You can practice by translating anything that's around you.

Beyond that, you can look for ways to gain experience that contribute in tangible ways to the making of your professional profile, distinguishing yourself, and making connections.

Find an internship

As in other professions, you can look for an internship.

>> **Compensation:** Sometimes these are paid; sometimes they're not. Your budget and time will help you see which route you should take.

>> **Length of time:** An internship is usually for a predetermined time period and set number of hours per week. Internships can vary greatly. Try to look for something that's no shorter than six weeks but no longer than six months. You want to be sure you have enough time to develop a significant relation-ship with your colleagues, while not committing yourself to something that might interfere with other opportunities that come your way.

>> **Support:** As an intern, you're looking to grow your professional experience. Therefore, as a beginner, if you're set loose at an internship to be the one-person-translation show, that's probably not going to be the most rewarding, productive, and educational experience. A worthwhile experience would include working alongside translators, assisting an experienced translator or organization with project management tasks, and anything else that would give you further insight into how a translator works with available tools and how the translation process works, including the steps before and after a translation is made.

>> **Meaningful experience:** If you're interested in an internship, examine closely what the opportunities are. There's little general knowledge about what it takes to produce effective translations. Plenty of people and organizations

unfortunately think that anyone who speaks the language can be a translator. Those same people believe that an unpaid intern could be the answer to their translation needs. Try to avoid those situations. If you understand what being a translator entails, you should be able to identify a worthwhile internship.

Get a job at an agency

You can skip the internship and go right for a job at an agency that provides language services. Language service providers, also referred to as translation agencies, vary in size and can offer a variety of opportunities, including translator, project manager, language expert, vendor manager, account manager, and periphery support to translators and the making of translations. If you're not ready to apply for a position as a translator, you can gain experience and exposure to the profession and the industry working in one of these other roles. Because so many agencies are available, some more ethical and professional than others, take your time to research them before applying for a job.

Assist a professional translator

To gain some experience as a translator, instead of looking for an internship or entry-level job with a company or an organization, consider working for an established professional translator who considers themselves a freelancer. Many professional translators are freelancers. Freelancers, or small business owners, often have a ton of tasks to complete. You might find one who's looking for an assistant to help with all sorts of duties. If you know a professional translator who works as a freelancer and you think you'd like working with and learning from them, ask if you might arrange something. It could be insightful to see the life of a freelancer up close!

Volunteer

If your budget and time allow, consider volunteering to gain experience. Volunteering can be rewarding on many levels. You can do it in several ways, but keep these two things in mind:

>> Although you're not getting paid for the work, you need to be professional and treat the opportunity as you would any other professional endeavor.

>> Gently remind the organization or person who you're translating for that professionals need to be compensated. Also, if they're going to continuously need translation services, they need to budget and plan for the services. You don't want to undercut your experienced colleagues or the profession.

Now, where will you seek volunteer opportunities related to getting experience as a translator?

Support a translation office or related department

If you work for an organization that has a translation or language access office or, even if not named as such, an office that handles translation and other language access service requests, see if you can spend some time there helping them fulfill or manage requests. Another way to do this — if you don't work for the organization but know that your local school, library, or other community organization needs translations, reach out to them to see how you might contribute to building their depository of quality translations.

OFFER YOUR SERVICES AT A CONFERENCE

Have you ever been to a conference? It takes a lot of time and hard work to make a conference successful. Organizations and associations that host conferences are always looking for volunteers to serve on their conference committees to help put them together. If you don't think helping to put on a conference sounds all that fun, think less about the tasks that you'll do and more about the professionals you'll meet, the insights you'll have exposure to, and how you'll be serving the professionals who are or will be your colleagues.

For some organizations and associations, you might have to be a member to volunteer or serve on the committees. But those memberships, which often have an associated fee, will give you access to member-only resources, meetings, networking opportunities, and more. The conferences could be translation-related conferences for a local, regional, or national organization. Check out their websites to see how you can volunteer and for membership information.

Translation-related conferences aren't the only places where you can volunteer. If you're thinking about specializing in an area for translation, find out what the conferences are in the area, and sign up to be a volunteer at them. If you specialize in coffee, for example, find out where those conferences are and when. Seek opportunities to volunteer, or consider attending them. While you're there, collect all the materials you can about the industry so that you can use these resources in the future.

Remember that, as a translator, you work with at least two languages. You don't have to just attend conferences in English. Try to volunteer at or attend conferences in all your working languages.

Seek feedback from the people you work or volunteer with. Especially if you're volunteering to gain more experience, ask for feedback in exchange for sharing your developing knowledge and expertise. To get feedback that really speaks to you and your strengths or areas where improvement is needed, it can be helpful to not just ask people for feedback, but ask them to respond to specific guiding questions you give them. The people you ask for feedback might not always be able to vouch for the quality of your translations, but they can talk about your professional skills. Use this feedback to improve your service as you become a translator.

While feedback might just be for your eyes only, consider asking for a testimonial. Be selective about who you ask for one. Because a testimonial is a statement that speaks to your qualifications and the experience of working with you, you don't want to ask people who don't really know your work and what it's like to work with you. You want solid statements that give a clear sense of who you are as a professional. With the permission of the person or organization that gave you the testimonial, you can use it on your website, in your online profile, and have it ready when a potential client asks to see samples of your work.

Create your own translation projects

Plenty of things need to be translated in this multilingual world that's constantly on the move. Take a look at your surroundings: the places you normally go to, the social media accounts you frequent, and the newsletters you subscribe to. Would any of these venues benefit from having their content translated into your translation language? If so, think of how you could create a meaningful project that would give you translation experience and the creator of the content a new audience.

You want to provide quality translations, so review your work. Think carefully about what you propose, and don't bite off more than you can chew. In return for your translations, ask to be credited. This will also get you publicity. And if the "client" and you are happy with the work, maybe you can turn this opportunity into one that you'll actually be paid for.

As a translator, you're a creator. Don't limit yourself to this list. Create your own ways to gain meaningful learning and practice experiences that don't just benefit yourself but the networks associated with the translations you create or support. Keep track of everything in a single place.

Networking Your Way to Translation Opportunities

Now that you have ideas for how you're going to get experience, it's time to start thinking about building your network. As one of the oldest, most needed, and fastest growing professions, it won't be that hard to start and grow your network. Although you might hear that translators are hermits who like to work alone, translators need people. You can't be a translator without a network.

Who should be in your network? That's a question that can have many answers. In general, your network is more about professional associations and connections and less about your clients. Although everything's connected, think about your network as the people and groups you'll turn to for advice, support, or the exchange of ideas:

>> Translator colleagues who work in your language pairs and in others.

>> Other language professionals, including interpreters, editors, and more.

>> Professionals connected to your areas of specialization.

>> People who have superb command over the languages you work with. Remember: translation challenges all you know about language. You want people in your network who have a strong command over your working languages when you need to find out which preposition to use and identify the best word for your translation.

Anyone can be in your network. Keep track of who is, and put some keywords by each person so you remember how they can help you. Also remember that a network is never complete. You'll add to it over time as your work develops and expands.

When you think about networking, embrace collaboration over competition. As long as people keep moving around the world, there will be a need for translation, out of obligation or because it's the right thing to do, to be sure that everyone is receiving communications in a language they can fully understand. There's enough translating work to go around.

It's also important to keep the collaborative spirit because, as you grow as a translator, you'll need your network in several ways:

>> A complex or rush translation project might come your way. You can reach out to your network to help you make the deadline or complete something that's difficult.

>> You can involve a translator colleague to edit your translations.

>> You can share tools or resources with a translator colleague.

>> Many times clients will ask if you know anyone who can translate into languages that aren't your target language(s). If you have colleagues in your network who work in other language pairs, you can readily recommend them. They should do the same for you. When you can refer others, your client will consider you an even greater resource.

>> Include interpreters from your network. You could be doing a translation for an event communication or something similar and notice the need for interpreters at the event.

>> With colleagues in your network, you can talk about all things related to working with clients and other work-related items.

Attend conferences

One of the most obvious places to network is at conferences. These can be conferences that focus on translation (in a specific and general sense), language, or your specialization. Attend these events with a business card, postcard, or other tangible item to share with the people you meet. Your card or other item should include your name and contact info and something that will remind those you give them to who you are and what you do. Remember that although conferences can have a laid-back, social atmosphere, they're still professional meetings. Be on your best behavior.

Be present on social media

Think about how you can use social media to connect with and attract colleagues. You can scan the major social media sites for individuals or groups. Some are better than others for the purposes of networking. However, you might discover that a colleague you find interesting only uses one of the sites. If you encounter colleagues who interest you, try to learn more about them by visiting their websites.

Make sure you have a professional account on these sites. By doing so, you won't just be learning about others; you'll be connecting and sharing as well.

Depending on the social media platform, some will make it easy for you to directly reach out to others, and they may even encourage you to do so. If you do want to reach out to someone directly to introduce yourself, it's worth tailoring your message to that person. This is much preferred to coming up with a few standard sentences that you share with each person you try to connect with. In most cases, those requests will be ignored.

As you start to build your social media networks, also think about providing useful comments if certain posts allow it. You could share what you find helpful or consider who might want to view a post. This is contributing to the interaction of your network and the profession.

Seek out local events

You don't always have to trek to a conference to network in person. Look around you and see what local translation, language, or specialization events are happening in your area. Some smaller venue events can be less intimidating and will help you ease into in-person networking.

Also, for in-person networking, embrace your own style. You don't have to be loud or connect with 100 different people at an event. Take notes and reach out after the event with an insightful and pleasant comment. The internet makes it easy to find and contact people. And if you don't find or want to connect with anyone at or as the result of an event, that's fine, too. It's likely that you learned something from listening to others in your professional sphere.

Building Your Portfolio

Building your portfolio is about creating a mosaic of the kind of professional you are. A portfolio should present the range of services, projects, and interests you have. Your portfolio could be housed on your website, your professional social media account, or some other digital format that you could easily share with potential clients and colleagues if they can't readily access it on a public platform.

What should you share in your portfolio? The following are some suggestions in no particular order.

Your resume

This should be a translator resume, not necessarily the resume you'd use to apply for a job as an office clerk. This document could be your first gateway to jobs, so make sure it's as clear, error-free, and solid as possible. As a translator you work with languages, so make sure you don't have any language errors on your resume. Have another person or two proofread your resume. Post it or share it as a PDF so that it can't be easily altered.

Keep in mind that the resume format isn't the same across languages and countries. Do some research to see what the resume expectations are in the languages or countries you want to share your resume with. You can try to locate resumes of other translators. Be sure to look at a few to confirm the format.

Short translation samples

Include selections of your translations with the permission of the client you did them for. This gives a quick look into the kind of work you do.

These need not be paid projects. If you did some volunteer projects to gain experience and give back to your community (through volunteer translation projects) or to the industry (by volunteering at conferences), by sure to package each experience with a brief description highlighting what the project was and perhaps what you learned from it. Include any necessary links.

Your translator's statement

Your translator statement is a brief narrative about you as a professional: why you do what you do, your language pairs, your services, and the kinds of projects you're interested in taking on. It's a statement that can change over time depending on your interests and profession growth.

If you have several specializations, list them and write a brief statement that explains why you're qualified to work in these areas, what you like about them, and what your approach to translating for this area is.

Include a brief statement about how future clients and colleagues can contact you and maybe how long it usually takes for you to respond. This information can be helpful in setting up the minimum communication requirements.

Testimonials from clients

In addition to listing the clients or colleagues you've worked with, include quotes or testimonials from them in your portfolio. This will give viewers of your portfolio a more dynamic picture of you and a sense of what it's like to work with you.

Chapter **16**

Getting Paid and Recognized

What you'll find when you start networking with translators is that many love their job. They love their job because of many reasons including working from home or from wherever they want to, having a flexible schedule, dressing casually most of the time, and not having many long meetings. They also love that translation gives access to content and ideas, supports a multilingual world, saves languages, and in most cases, helps people. You'll agree with most of these things or they might be the reason you're learning more about becoming a translator.

But all this love doesn't mean that you won't think about how and how much you're going to get paid and recognized for your work. In fact, translators can be driven away from the work they love because of low pay and an inconsistent flow of work.

In this chapter, you'll learn about what you need to consider as you determine how much you need to get paid and different models for charging. Recognition for your translation work is also something you don't want to lose sight of. You'll find that recognition helps boost the productivity and quality of your translations.

Estimating Your Earnings as a Translator

How much exactly are you going to make as a translator? This is an excellent question to have as a beginner. And there is not one single answer. There are many things you need to keep in mind to try to get that answer.

The first path to getting that answer depends on how you are employed.

Full-time translator for an organization

If you're a full-time translator for a company, school, hospital, or other organization, then the answer can be simple. You'll probably have a set number of hours you'll work, benefits you'll receive, and salary you'll earn for those hours.

You might receive a higher salary if you hold a credential such as American Translation Association Certification for your language pair, or you work with a language pair that is in high need and not as common. In other words, certain external factors could impact your salary, but in general, if you're a full-time translator at an organization, you'll have a set salary which you'll hopefully be aware of before you accept a job.

Full-time employee with non-translator duties

If you're an employee somewhere and your job duty is one thing which isn't to translate, but you're regularly asked to translate, and that's not in your job description, or you find yourself translating documents beyond your regular work hours, you should consider asking for additional compensation so that you are paid for your skills. Beyond your regular salary, you could negotiate an hourly rate or one that's based on word count and time.

You might also find that if you're looking for a job, some organizations offer additional pay, if you're able to work in a professional setting in more than one language and even more pay for translating as part of that job.

REMEMBER

Keep in mind that some of these ideas might sound foreign to some employers, but there are increasingly more employers who offer incentives for language and translation skills.

TIP

In fact, if you work in Massachusetts, you should know about the Language Access and Inclusion Act, S.1990/H.3084 which states "Any employee who is regularly acting as an interpreter or translator must be reasonably compensated for that additional work."

Also, keep in mind if you do have a full-time job that doesn't ask you to translate, translation is work that you can pick up to do after your regular work hours for additional income.

Independent professional translator

Now, if you're an independent professional translator, or a freelancer, what you charge can depend on so many factors including your language pair (the languages you translate to and from), where you're located, your clients, your experience, and your income needs.

Because there are so many factors that impact your rates, it's difficult to publish a specific number that indicates how much you'll make as a translator. Don't be surprised if you ask a new colleague and they also refrain from sharing a specific number.

First, you need to understand what you're charging for.

>> **Text.** One of the first and most obvious things you're charging for is the translation of a text from one language to another.

>> **Complexity of the text.** Since not all texts are the same and some are more complex than others, you'll want to be sure you charge for complexity as well. A scholarly article or a document that has a literary quality can be quite different from a flier or informational letter. It's not uncommon to increase the rate by a certain percentage to make up for these complexities.

>> **Due date or urgent.** Some clients can plan for translation and others have urgent needs come up. If you get a project with an urgent due date, charge a rush fee or something similar.

>> **Other projects.** Another thing you might want to consider is how many other projects you have in the pipeline. If adding another project will make it impossible to work within your usual turnaround time, that's something you might want to factor in to determining your rate. Will taking on a new project mean you have to work extra-long and hard for a week? If so, charge for that, if your client can't wait for you to submit the project when it's convenient for you.

>> **Beyond translation services.** Take a close look at a project before you present the rate. Are you just supplying the translation of the text or are you being asked to perform other services such as Desktop Publishing. If you're being asked to do a translation plus a lot of formatting, charge for that.

>> **Creating additional resources.** Are you creating glossaries or other resources along with the translation for the client? If so, this is another fee you'll want to factor into the rate of the translation.

>> **Project management.** Sometimes it's the case that clients will have many documents and somehow they end up asking you as the translator to do some management of the documents or a project that seems to go beyond the norm. You'll usually know this kind of work once it starts happening. Address it immediately with a client and see how it can be handled.

>> **Experience.** Your experience will also be factored into what you charge. If you are a novice translator just starting out, then you might prioritize getting the professional experience over getting the highest rate. But if you're already a professional in one field and then decide to translate documents in that field, you could enter the world of professional translation and request a higher fee than a novice would. For example, if you're an art historian who then decided to start translating museum catalogs or exhibition text, you could probably set a higher rate than a novice translator would. But, once again, this could also be impacted by the above factors.

>> **Confidence.** Your confidence could also factor into what you charge. If you're confident about the quality of your work and your ability to stick to the agreement, and you can project that to current and future clients, then you might be able to charge on the higher end of things.

Now, how are you going to measure all of the above? There are different ways, and don't be surprised if there are more than those listed here:

>> **Per word:** One of the most common ways of charging for the translation of a text from one language to another is according to the word count.

You can do a word count of the source text and multiply the total word count by your per-word rate. Don't forget to factor in any other costs. One of the benefits of charging by the source text word count is that you'll know the price before you jump into the project.

You can also calculate the price of the translation according to the target text. If you're charging by the word count of your translation then you'll usually have to provide your clients with an estimate before you get started on the translation. You can use the source text word count and increase it by a percentage since all translations usually have more words than the source text. Give that amount to your client as an estimate, and then once you've completed the translation, you can provide the final cost based on the actual final word count of the target text.

>> **Per hour:** Some translators charge by the hour, although this might not be the most common way to come up with rates for translations. In order to do that, you'll have to have a way of estimating how many words you're about to translate in an hour, and not jump to other tasks while you're translating. To figure this out, you could keep track of how many words you translate per hour when you're working on a practice translation. A drawback of charging by the hour is that you might have to talk about money more than once with a client, especially if you've underestimated the number of hours it will take you to translate a text. All this talk about money could put strains on the relationship.

If editing and proofing are among the services you decide to offer as a professional, charging by the hour might make more sense for those services.

Per word, whether of the source text or the target text, and, less so, per hour are the most common ways translators charge for their work. Those rates can be increased in a systematic way according to the items listed above (complexity and urgency, for example). Keep in mind though, that there could be other ways to charge. For example, you could do all your calculations and then give your client a total rate per project. This could work out well if the project involves more than translating a text.

Think about converting your rates into other currencies if you're positioned to attract clients from several countries.

TIP

When determining your rates, don't think that the lowest rate will win you a job. It has negative consequences that can be hard to shake. In general, if your rates are too low, you'll undercut other translators, and they won't be happy. If you're working for a rate that's too low, you'll be unhappy because you're not getting paid what you deserve. You might have a hard time raising your rates in the future for this client. Rates that are too low can also make clients suspicious. In general, this practice can devalue the entire profession.

So, what's the specific number you should change? You'll have to do some investigative work and then come up with your own in the range of what you hear other translators charge. Ask other translators or in an online forum what's the standard rate for your language pair. Beware that that might open all kinds of debates in a forum so the most efficient way might be to ask a few trusted mentors or colleagues. Do some investigative work. It's probably best not to start out in the top range, although it depends on who you are when you start out. Assuming you're a beginning translator without too deep of a specialization, consider going with a rate that is not too high. You can always increase your rates regularly as you grow and have satisfied clients.

You could determine how much you want to make per year, divide that by how many hours you want to work, how many words you can translate per hour.

TIP

Translators sometimes have to bid for jobs. Don't go too low. The lowest price isn't always the answer to getting a job. Clients usually want quality work and a translator who can meet reasonable deadlines. The quality of the presentation of your bid is what can impress.

When a language service provider or an agency posts a job, they'll often give it to the first language professional who accepts it. Checking in regularly and turning on mobile notifications can help to learn about new opportunities right away.

If a client wants you to offer your services at a lower price or they're a repeat customer, or they come with a large project, they might ask you for a discount. If offering a discount works for you, have a formula for how you're calculating your discount so that you can apply the same discount for the same client in the future. However, you don't have to give the discount. And once the word gets out that you give discounts, you could find yourself having no set rates at all and always having to come up with new formulas for every client. That can get messy. If you stick to your rates and do excellent work, a client will usually stick with you.

If you want to take on pro-bono or work at another rate that is less than what you would normally charge, be sure to let your client know why you're doing this and what the reduction is.

When you give a client an estimate for a specific project, but sure to include an expiration date of your estimate. You don't want to give an estimate and then three years later, once your rates and situation have evolved, a client comes with an estimate and wants to get started on the work.

Once a client accepts the estimate and before you start a project agree on a few things: price, scope, timeline, deposit/payment, on what or how you'll get paid. Some translators request an initial payment or deposit or a purchase order. If it's a large project, ask for payments at certain milestones.

REMEMBER

Keep track of all your projects and billing: who's paid, who hasn't, when and how you sent reminders.

Getting the Recognition You Deserve

You might hear that being a translator is often considered an invisible profession. And if you haven't, that's great! If you are entering into this profession, you should be aware this happens so you're prepared to educate clients, coworkers, family members and friends who don't recognize translations and the work of translators. In most cases no one overlooks translators on purpose. There's just not yet widespread examples or a tradition of people citing translators or recognizing translations as translations. So, get ready to do your best and to help make the profession more visible. Here's what the lack of recognition looks like from several points of view:

From the translator perspective

A translator writes a document in another language. In most cases, there's not a tradition of the translator signing his or her name on the document translation. And there are many documents that translators probably don't want to attach their name to, not because of the content, but just because it's not necessary. However, in not including a name or a note that the document was translated by someone, the fact that a certain person did the work, with whatever necessary tools, is overlooked. Not even when a book is translated is it a guarantee that the translator's name will be easily identified on the translated book.

Another factor: As a translator, you, in a way, lend your writing skills to an existing text and although as the translator, you choose every word that goes into the translation, you aren't actively calling out within the text that you are there as the translator. You aren't showing the choices you had for each word, or the questions you had about certain aspects, or how you came up with the solution to some translation dilemma. With those omissions, which of course if included would make the reading somewhat clunky, another level of lack of recognition is introduced to the translation.

In sum, your name isn't attached to the text as the translator, nor does your writing scream "I'm a translation that went through an intriguing process." So, translations don't recognize themselves as translations, most of the time, nor does every translation get a "Translated by [INSERT NAME]" added to it.

You must know that some translators don't mind all the anonymity and in some cases, this is one of the reasons why they chose to become a translator.

TIP

So, what can you do as a translator to promote recognition? Talk about translations as translations. When there is a document that has been translated, note that it's a translation. When appropriate and desired, you can add the translator's name to the translated document. When appropriate, you could even indicate somewhere a note if it indicates a translator's choice that might educate the reader about translation.

From the reader perspective

When the translator's name is nowhere on the book or the document, readers may not know they're reading a translation unless it's flagged in some other way as a famous work or a poor translation. Unfortunately, it's when translations are poor that translators get attention. In general, when translations aren't recognized as translations, readers might not be aware of all the translations they consume in a single day, for example.

If the text is displayed alongside versions of the text in other languages, then the reader might think more about translation and the existence of multiple languages. But still, how those texts got there might not inspire the reader to think about translators and what it took to produce the translations.

When it comes to translated books, even if the translator's name is included on the book cover, title page, or copyright page, readers don't always realize they're reading a translation. They're not aware that it wasn't the author but a translator who selected every word on the page. This especially happens with books that are bestsellers or classics: since the title, author, or story are so familiar, it often gets overlooked that the book originated in another language.

What can you do as a translator to promote recognition? When talking about books with friends, colleagues, or family members, ask if they're reading any translations, help them note if they're reading translations they might be reading but aren't aware of, and gift translated books.

Others who can recognize translation and translators

Reviews of translated books that get published in newspapers don't always mention the fact that a book is a translation or the name of the translator. Teachers and professors who include translations on their syllabi don't always note that a book is a translation. What is more, they don't always specify which translation to read. And sometimes media outlets and other venues don't note when a book they're discussing is a translation.

Let organizations, newspapers, and other venues know when they've cited a translation but have not credited the translator or the fact that the text is a translation. You can email, call, send a note, or give the feedback in person.

#NameTheTranslator

Have you ever seen or used the hashtag #NameTheTranslator? This ongoing social media campaign was started by the Chinese to English translator Helen Wang in 2014 in response to the tendency of reviewers and other media outlets that mention translated works to not include the name of the translator. When a translated book is talked about in media outlets it is often the case that the author of the original gets mentioned, but not the translator.

Since translators are often freelancers, when their name is mentioned that helps them promote their work, build reputations, and get more work.

An effective practice you can follow and encourage publishers to follow is to name the translator wherever the author's name is mentioned. Translators' names should be mentioned in book reviews, programming at libraries and other venues, festivals, in schools and the classroom, blog posts, podcasts, social media posts, and in online retail spaces.

The Translated Bookmark

#NameTheTranslator was a translator-initiated project. As you work as a translator and become familiar with the field, you might notice where there are big gaps and where more recognition is needed regarding translators' contributions to the world. If you have an idea about how to promote translators and translation, go for it! You will elevate the profession and market the professional you are becoming along the way.

The Translated Bookmark, an item I created in 2023, helps to promote readers' recognition of translators while they're reading a translated book. Even if the translator's name is on the cover of the book, the Translated Bookmark asks readers to write the translator's name on the bookmark and this way the translator's name follows the reader throughout the pages of the book.

The Translated Bookmark was first created in English. I also created a version in French and the Association des traducteurs littéraires de France adapted my version, with my permission, to create their own Translated Bookmark to mark their 50th anniversary.

Translated Book Awards

Beyond social media campaigns and tangible items that promote translator recognition, there are more traditional routes that bring greater translator recognition such as award competitions. Awards can be granted in several categories. The main streams of awards are usually for translated books, mostly literature, through a professional organization or other entity, or industry awards for individuals, companies, or organizations, again through an association or some other kind of professional association. The awards can range in the meaning and importance they have. In general, they're positive as awards bring recognition and attention to a translator's work and efforts. Here are just some examples to follow.

Translated book awards, usually for literature in translation, recognize the work which not only pleases translators and their publishers, but also their authors. Translated book awards also:

>> Incentivize translators to pursue translation.

>> Bring visibility to translations.

>> Create opportunities for readers to identify books in translation to read as readers sometimes look to award lists as their reading guides.

Some organizations that have translated book awards:

>> The International Booker Prize, according to the website, "is awarded annually for the finest single work of fiction from around the world which has been translated into English and published in the UK and/or Ireland." https://thebookerprizes.com/the-international-booker-prize

>> The American Literary Translators Association offers six major translation awards, including the National Translation Award in Poetry and Prose. The other awards focus on debut literary translations and translations from Asian languages, of Italian works, and of works from Spain.

>> The Massachusetts Center for the Book has a translated literature award as part of their Massachusetts Book Award program. The translator must be a Massachusetts permanent resident.

>> The American Translators Association grants several awards in almost ten categories from advocacy and innovation awards to service and student translation awards. https://www.atanet.org/about-us/honors-awards-program/

>> The Association of Translation Companies offers a Language Industry Awards for operational excellence for companies of all sizes and individual industry professionals.

Check out *Multilingual* magazine for the announcement of award categories or special features of translators and other language professionals.

There probably aren't enough awards to give to the professionals who do outstanding work every day. However, these initiatives are motivational and bring attention to the profession and general role of translators and translation in society. Keep your eyes out for these opportunities, nominate colleagues, and check in on them to see who the winners are and what they do. Maybe one day, you'll find yourself on the list!

Staying Active

An indirect way of getting recognized and paid for your work is by staying active in the profession. When you attend conferences, professional development programs, workshops, and courses, you expand your skills, deepen your knowledge, reconnect with or meet new people, and support your profession. These activities can lead you to new clients, partnerships, and even expanded services for which you can get paid!

Keeping your translator skills sharp

As a translator, you must keep your skills sharp. If you keep working with the same toolbox day after day, month after month, year after year, the tools will get dull. You won't be a bad translator, but you might not be working in the most efficient way. New technologies and tools will, if used effectively, help you save time, keep you organized, and allow you to work smarter.

New tools might help you work more effectively with your translation memories. They might help you stay organized in such a way that you can navigate through your files faster or keep better track of your tasks.

You can sharpen these translator skills by reading industry newsletters, following a group of smart translators on social media, listening to podcasts, connecting with colleagues, and participating in structured and focused learning opportunities. As you develop as a professional, you'll find ways to stay in the know, and hear about tools that are helping translators work smarter.

If you can work smarter and more efficiently, you will be able to take on more projects and that will mean more pay for you.

Staying in touch with the profession

While you're keeping your eyes on the new tools that will help you enhance your skills, also think about how you are staying in touch with the profession in a way that allows you to share all you do and make connections with different kinds of people from clients and partners to colleagues and organizations.

You can share what you do by attending and presenting at conferences, looking for speaking opportunities in your local community, getting in touch with appropriate venues for presentations in the places you visit, and volunteering. LinkedIn is also a great way to connect by sending direct messages to colleagues, and reading and sharing relevant material from professions. Translation is needed everywhere. If you can get out there and speak about it, that's recognition for you. That visibility could lead to more paying jobs. Think creatively about how you can market yourself!

5

The Part of Tens

Grow your network and skills.

Check out professional translation organizations, translators, and supporters.

Discover other resources to help with your professional development.

Chapter **17**

Ten Tips for Getting Started as a Translator

You can become a translator in a multitude of ways, so the chance that two translators will agree on a list of ten tips for getting started as a translator isn't too likely. Another translator would probably give ten different tips for getting started, while not denying that the ten tips shared here are important ones.

These tips focus most on the foundations and the mindset of a translator because if understanding how to do the work and making professional decisions aren't in place, the additional tools can only get you so far. Those tools though are game changers. So my bonus on this list of ten would be: Don't be afraid to dive into tools and technologies and tinker around from an early stage.

I share things here that all translators should know and do regularly. The sooner you make them part of your life as a translator, the more they'll be part of what you do.

Consider Your Qualifications

Becoming a successful translator has many paths, just like becoming a successful writer or most anything else. It's one of the things that makes the field exciting and makes it necessary for you to be able to communicate your qualifications to do the work. You can be charismatic and convincing, but at some point, you're going to have to back that up with qualifications and knowledge demonstrating that you know what you're talking about and what you're doing. Here are some ways for you to do that:

>> **University degree in working languages other than English:** If you're a native speaker of English, know Spanish, and want to be a Spanish-English translator, a university degree in Spanish will help communicate that you have the foundations of the language skills to become a translator.

>> **University degree connected to translation:** If you're able to obtain an undergraduate or graduate university degree in translation or a related field from a university, go for it!

>> **Demonstrated capability in working languages:** People who could potentially hire you are looking for solid evidence that you can write well in your target language. But how will they know you can write well in Portuguese if they don't speak it? They might have you take an assessment or perform a sample translation that they'll have evaluated by a qualified person.

>> **Solid textual analysis skills:** Knowing how to analyze a text is one of the skills you need to become a translator.

>> **Critical thinking:** Critical thinking skills help you work through translation assignments and texts. They're a must!

>> **Knowledge of the profession:** Becoming a translator isn't just about language. It's also about becoming familiar with the translation profession.

>> **Awareness of the translation process:** You need to show that you know about the workflow and that there are things that happen before, during, and after a document is translated.

>> **Error-free cover letter and resume:** An error in a cover letter or a resume can cost you a job. Be sure to check these documents multiple times and have other sets of eyes look them over.

>> **Enthusiasm for the use of language:** Knowing how to communicate your passion for how language is used will be favorable when speaking to potential clients.

>> **Depth of knowledge:** Everything you've worked hard to learn as a translator will be evidence that you're qualified to do the work.

Live Language and Translation

Keep reading and listening to your working languages. Keep writing in your target languages. Read and write about translation. Attend webinars, workshops, and conferences. Take some courses. Ask colleagues for recommendations. Never abandon your curiosity to learn more about translation and the languages you use to do it. You need to reflect on what you do and how to do it better.

You can also create your own translation exercises:

Collect texts that you think are interesting and try translating them or parts of them into your target language.

Another exercise is to look at the translated versions of a website and compare those translations to the English-language version, or vice versa. Remember that just because a text is published and printed in translation doesn't make it a quality translation. Use a critical eye and identify what you think was done effectively and what you think could be improved.

Experiment with machine translation tools. Put an original text through a machine translation tool and see what happens. How is the translation? Next, edit another original text to simplify the language and clarify anything that doesn't seem so straightforward. Then put it through a machine translation tool. Is that translation overall a better quality translation than the previous translation? Next try putting another original text through a machine translation tool and then edit the translation it gives you. How does your edited translation compare to the original text? Would you say this is a quality translation? You can keep these experiments going with all kinds of texts. The results can be fun and surprising!

Work with Others

Some people imagine translators working alone, surrounded by dictionaries, in isolation, but that's inaccurate. It's impossible to work alone. As a translator, you need a network. You need to work with others and know how to identify the right people to work with. Have a network of colleagues, and continuously add to it. If you're a French translator, not all your colleagues have to be French translators. You can learn a lot from translators who work with other languages. Add people who have other skills to your network. Those colleagues will give you recommendations, but do your own research. If you're not convinced by their advice, keep looking and make your own informed decisions. Join professional organizations. Beyond professional translator organizations, get involved with organizations whose texts you want to translate. If you dream of translating for museums, be an active museum goer and subscribe to museum memberships.

Talk about Translation

If you want work, you need to advocate for qualified translators and quality translation. Make noise about translation everywhere you go. Ask for recommendations for translated books in bookshops and libraries. Borrow translated books from libraries. Show that translation is in demand. Credit translators in conversations or on Wikipedia pages. Everyone needs to see and understand translation if translators want more work and educated clients. Have conversations about translation with your clients. Talk about translation in an approachable way.

Elevate and Support the Profession

Help your clients use terms correctly. For instance, if a client keeps asking you to be a translator for a meeting, remind them that it's interpreters who interpret spoken languages. Know that if you don't follow an expected procedure or something that might be standard across the profession, you might make it harder for the next translator who comes along. Know how to articulate in an approachable way the complexities of the work. At the same time, don't undercut others by charging low rates just to get a job. Undercutting devalues the work of all translators.

"No hay reglas, solamente casos" — Javier Calvo

Translators often receive general questions about their work. How do you translate this word? How do you translate humor? How do you. . . ? The list goes on. It's hard for a translator to answer these types of questions because every project will have its own needs and context. Calvo says that translation has no rules; it all depends on the situation. Keep this in mind while translating, but also while working with clients. Although it's important to maintain standards and ethics, be aware that each client might need and expect something different. Remember that these are human relationships. Don't be quick to assume that as a translator you know all the dynamics of the project.

"Duda siempre" — Amelia Pérez de Villar

"Question everything." "Duda siempre," says the translator Amelia Pérez de Villar in her book *Los enemigos del traductor: Elogio y vituperio del oficio* (2019). As a translator, you must do your research so that you fully understand a text. You can't translate the text otherwise. If you don't fully grasp or aren't 100 percent sure about the usage of a phrase or what an idiomatic expression means in the source language, ask a trusted speaker of the language. Then verify their response with another source. And don't leave language in the translation that doesn't fully convince you. If you don't know whether you should use "question everything" or "always have doubts," ask a speaker of the target language what they understand those two phrases to mean. Ask them if they have a better option. Likewise, if you aren't sure about a preposition, do more research. Your client, your audience, and your reader will note any weaknesses in the text and move on to the next translator.

Determine How and When You're Credited for Your Work

Translation has often been referred to as an invisible profession, but the good news is that translator recognition and visibility are on the rise due to collective efforts such as the social media campaign and hashtag #NameTheTranslator, created by translator Helen Wang, and individual demands to be recognized as the translator. Many people don't realize that when they take a quote from a famous work of Spanish literature and post it in English, they're usually quoting the words of a human translator. Not all translation projects are the same. For some, your payment will be how you're recognized and credited for your work. All parties will be fine with that. But for others, you might want to be named as the translator. This usually happens if you're translating a book, an article, or some other published essay. Basically, it's when the work has an artistic quality or it's important that readers know they're reading a translation. This won't apply to all projects, but when it's applicable, take the time to figure it out.

BRITISH MUSEUM OFFERS PAYMENT TO TRANSLATOR AFTER PLAGIARISM ALLEGATIONS

The British Museum has offered to compensate Yilin Wang after she alleged that her translations of Chinese revolutionary Qiu Jin's work were used without credit in the China's Hidden Century exhibition. Earlier this week, the museum removed the translations following Wang's claims.

On Thursday, the museum apologized for the "unintentional human error" and offered Wang payment for the period her translations were displayed, as well as for their continued use in the exhibition catalogue, which now credits her work.

The museum emphasized its commitment to copyright permissions, attributing the oversight to an inadvertent mistake below their usual standards. The offered payment aligns with the museum's standard compensation for such work.

The China's Hidden Century exhibition, the result of a four-year research initiative involving over 100 scholars from 14 countries, features 300 objects, half from the British Museum and half from 30 British and international lenders, many on public display for the first time.

Following the plagiarism claims, the British Museum reported that its staff faced personal attacks on social media, condemning these actions and standing by their colleagues. The museum called for an end to these attacks as they worked with Wang to resolve the issues concerning her translations. Curatorial team members received direct email vilification, and academics affiliated with the museum expressed concern and confusion over the incident.

Julia Lovell, a professor at Birkbeck University and a principal researcher for the exhibition, voiced her sympathy for Wang and apologized for the error, clarifying her lack of involvement in the design or permissions process.

Lovell acknowledged the error as an unintended, non-malicious mistake within a complex project, for which the museum has sincerely apologized and sought to rectify.

Wang tweeted that the British Museum informed her it would not reinstate her translations in the exhibition.

Keep Translating

Translate, translate, translate. You get better at translating by doing it. As you're starting out as a translator and establishing your professional profile, you don't need to wait around until paid assignments come your way. In your downtime, volunteer to translate texts you're interested in.

This might be a brochure for a local organization, signs for a public library, or a guide to a local park. Try to find something that interests you.

Also consider doing this work for people of limited means or the organizations that represent them. Of course, regardless of whether you're getting paid or not, don't compromise quality, and let the organization know that the regular provision of translations does require a budget. Be willing to show them how to establish one. If the translation is a volunteer project, ask if you can get credit for your translation with the inclusion of your name. The credit will help you with marketing.

Prepare to Add Your Own Tip to This List

As a translator, you'll get better by tuning into other translators. You'll be able to evaluate and innovate the profession by listening to and learning from others. You, too, can take an active role in determining what it takes to get started as a translator.

What's your own tip for translators who are starting out? Share it here:

_____.

Chapter **18**

Ten Influential Translators and Supporters of Translation

U nderstand the title of this chapter as "Ten Influential Translators and Supporters of Translation," but not *the* 10. Many more names could be added to this list.

The organizations and individuals you find here are generally recognized by most active translators or translation educators and have been committed to the practice and development of the profession for years. In some ways, this list represents some of translation's pioneers and pioneering efforts. It doesn't include companies, software, or other technological efforts that have also shaped the field.

Translators need to understand the foundations of translation as they work with others. This list is in no particular order. As you grow as a translator, update and expand the list. Think about what your description would say if you were added.

American Translators Association

It won't be too long on your path as a translator until you hear someone mention the American Translators Association (ATA). Founded in 1959, it's one of the most referred-to organizations in the field. The ATA was established to advance the "translation and interpreting professions" and to promote the professional development of its members. You need to pay an annual fee to be a member of ATA.

You might hear translators debate about the high membership fee. However, you can get a lot from the ATA without becoming a member. You can learn about education programs, working with clients, events, news, and credentialing just browsing what's readily accessible on the website.

ATA certifies translators if they pass a test in one of the languages paired with English. The certification isn't necessary for most jobs. Testing requires a fee, and it can take ten weeks or more to get the results. ATA also hosts a large annual conference.

If you have the resources, think about attending one year and go to panels and events. In the meantime, you can enjoy some smaller one-time events and webinars.

American Translation and Interpreting Studies Association

Not as large as ATA, American Translation and Interpreting Studies Association (ATISA) is another organization you might hear translators and their interpreter friends talk about.

The American Translation and Interpreting Studies Association was founded in 2002 to foster translation and interpreting research and to be the academic home for translation and interpreting researchers from the United States and abroad based in the United States. Membership has a fee.

ATISA holds in-person and virtual events, including a biennial conference, and sponsors and publishes a leading academic journal called *Translation and Interpreting Studies*, first published in 2006, which engages with various academic and professional stakeholders.

If there's a point on your road to becoming a translator or a moment in your career in which you want to explore getting a graduate degree in translation studies, if you need inspiration, or you want to dive deeper into a certain topic, check out the journal or attend the conference.

You'll get a good idea of what people who focus on Translation Studies think and write about, how they talk about it, and what it means to study the many dimensions of translation.

PEN America

If you're interested in translating literature, you'll probably hear about PEN America. Founded in 1922, PEN America protects free expression of poets, essayists, and novelists (conceived the acronym of PEN) in the United States and around the world. The PEN International network has more than 100 centers worldwide.

Also, founded in 1959, the same year as the ATA, PEN America Translation Committee advocates on behalf of literary translators to promote greater understanding of the work they do and to offer professional resources.

In 2023 the Translation Committee published a Manifesto on Literary Translation, available on the website, promoting the idea that translation is a specialized form of writing, among many other things. The roots of this document go back to 1963.

Even if you aren't interested in translating literature, reading this document will help you build your translation knowledge and understand just how deeply ingrained translation is in everything you do as a translator.

PEN is an example of what translators, writers, and their supporters can accomplish together. Membership levels are available for both professionals and for those who advocate for their mission, which they consider readers.

American Literary Translators Association

Not as large as PEN America, American Literary Translators Association (ALTA) is a nonprofit arts association founded in 1978 by Rainer Schulte and A. Leslie Wilson at the University of Texas at Dallas, where it remained until 2013. It's now affiliated with the College of Humanities at the University of Arizona.

It offers awards, fellowships, mentorships, and an annual conference. Poke around the website for more information.

Translators Without Borders

If you're on your path to becoming a translator and would like to build your professional portfolio while using your language skills to help people, check out Translators Without Borders (TWB). TWB is a community of volunteers who offer language services including, but not limited to, translation, revision, voice-over, and subtitling to humanitarian and development organizations around the world.

In 1993 Lori Thicke and Ros Smith-Thomas founded Traducteurs sans Frontières in France with the intention of linking translators from all over the world with vetted nonprofit organizations focused on health, nutrition, and education.

Almost twenty years later, in 2011 the organization became the US nonprofit Translators Without Borders (TWB). And then another ten years later, it grew even more to become CLEAR Global to further develop the work of TWB.

The organization is known for responding to crisis situations, building capacity in under-resourced languages, and advocating for language services. About 100,000 language volunteers offer their time and skills so that people get the info they need in a language they can fully understand and be heard, whatever language they speak.

You can read their annual report to learn more. You might also consider fundraising for the organization.

National Association of Judiciary Interpreters and Translators (NAJIT)

If you're interested in specializing in the judiciary field, browse the National Association of Judiciary Interpreters and Translators (NAJIT) website. It's the world's largest association of judiciary interpreters, and most of the members hold professional credentials, including interpreter or translator certifications and other credentialing by government agencies and international organizations.

If you're going for these credentials, think about getting a student membership, which can save you time and money. As a member you'll have access to a network of professionals to help you navigate the process. Many of the members of this association work in conference, medical, diplomatic, and immigration settings. Association members also volunteer their time to influence legislation and support other professional issues.

Edwin Gentzler

On the path to becoming a professional translator, it's inspiring to learn about the individuals who have shaped the aspects of the profession that might not be readily visible while you're doing the work. Dr. Edwin Gentzler, professor emeritus of comparative literature, directed the Translation Center at the University of Massachusetts Amherst for more than twenty years until 2015. He transformed it from a small community translation service to a national center that offers most language services in most language combinations while involving students, faculty, industry professionals, paying clients, and other community partners.

The model bridges academia and the industry and gives students practice and exposure to the world of translation at a time when no academic departments in the United States are dedicated to translation. Dr. Gentzler has been committed to expanding resources in languages that lack resources in a given geographic area.

Check out the four books he authored or coedited to learn more about contemporary translation theories, translation and power, translation and identity, and the age of post-Translation Studies. If you decide to teach translation one day or to dabble in Translation Studies, knowledge of his work will give you a good foundation.

Lynne Bowker

As a professional translator, you're going to have to communicate to your clients and non-translator friends and family members what it is you do and how you do it. The work of Lynne Bowker can help you do that. Her book *De-mystifying Translation: Introducing Translation to Non-Translators* (Routledge, 2023), which is an open access publication, is an accessible introduction to the field that builds awareness of and appreciation for translation. Bowker, for many years, was a professor of translation and information studies at the University of Ottawa's School of Translation and Interpretation.

Since 2024 she is Full Professor and Canada Research Chair in Translation, Technologies, and Society at the Université Laval. She's the project leader of Machine Translation Literacy, which creates teaching resources and other research outputs on the topic.

Be sure to check out the introductory infographics in multiple languages that guide translators and those who want to know more about the use of machine translation on how to be a savvy user and how to use it critically.

She and her team also created fun games and activities to test machine translation literacy. Keep an eye on her work to see what else she comes up with!

Lawrence Schimel

Novice translators or people who don't know too much about translation think that translators just translate. Even if a translator holds regular business hours and sticks to translating documents from English to Spanish, by now you know that they're not *just* a translator.

Translators do many things, and sometimes they even add roles to their portfolios. Lawrence Schimel is a literary translator, mostly of poetry, children's books, and fiction, besides a bilingual English–Spanish full-time author and anthologist who has published more than 120 books in a wide range of genres and media.

His own writing has been translated into several languages, and he's won many awards. He started the Spain chapter of the Society of Children's Book Writers and Illustrators.

Most recently he become the senior editor of NorthSouth Books Spanish-language publishing program. A regular at the world's leading book fairs, Lawrence is active on LinkedIn and Facebook, publishing content about his books, travels related to his books, and his reading practices.

You can also search the internet for recorded presentations he's given. Listening to him talk about translating children's literature is a good use of your time.

Ruth Ahmedzai Kemp

As you cruise through the world of translation, try to identify professional translators whose profiles and work you can learn from. Ruth Ahmedzai Kemp is a translator from German, Russian, and Arabic into English. She's also a language educator and activist.

As a translator, she focuses on children's books, contemporary fiction, and literary nonfiction. She has translated or co-translated more than 30 books for children and adults in addition to excerpts, short stories, chapters, articles, essays, plays, and filmscripts.

As an educator, she teaches English as a second language and the languages she translates from, as well as professional development for language students and early-career language experts.

On her website, Instagram, and Facebook accounts, you can get a sense of the range of her activities. Her creative writing workshops in schools inspire students to think about translation and advocate for translation as a creative activity that's accessible even with limited language knowledge.

She inspires language learning, the circulation of translations, and human interaction with language. She really pushes for this with young people, hoping to make language a priority in their academic, professional, and personal lives.

Chapter **19**

Ten Additional Sources to Help You Succeed in Translation

As a translator, you'll never stop learning. Each new project presents new questions about language, translation, the text's subject, and new topics. While you're following the paths of your projects, you can also create your own paths to learn more about being a translator and its many aspects. The following list includes sources that develop your thinking about translation and offer practical advice. Even if you go into legal translation, don't turn your back on other professional translators. Translators across fields share experiences, and there's always something to learn. Don't be overwhelmed by all the content you'll find in these sources. Strategize how you'll interact with each. Get the books on your shelves, bookmark the websites and plan to visit them regularly, sign up for newsletters, think about when you can listen to the podcasts, and note the conferences. You'll discover just how exciting it is to get into this profession!

Brand the Interpreter

As you're becoming a translator, it's inspiring and educational to listen to the stories of other language professionals. Started in 2020, Mireya Pérez's *Brand the Interpreter* podcast feature interpreters, translators, and other language professionals. Guests share their personal stories, experiences, challenges, triumphs, and contributions to the profession. The range of topics includes lobbying, terminology, language competency, leadership, and more. Pérez produces two to three episodes per month. The episodes can last more than 60 minutes, so save them for a long ride or walk, or listen to them over several sessions. You don't have to weed out the episodes that feature translators. While you listen to this podcast, you're focusing on how professional lives begin and transform over time.

Why Translation Matters

Published in 2011 as part of Yale University Press's Why X Matters Series, *Why Translation Matters* (2011) by the late Edith Grossman (1936–2023) is a pioneering book that defines the cultural importance of translation and advocates for more appreciation of the translator role in an accessible and engaging way. Grossman translated into English many of the great literary works from the Spanish-speaking world, including *Don Quijote* by Miguel de Cervantes. In *Why Translation Matters*, Grossman points out the ways translation and translators have been ignored or misunderstood and carefully explains the intellectual work of a literary translator. Although the short, four-chapter book's focus is on literary translation, you'll be inspired and stimulated no matter what field you work in as a translator.

Fundamentals of Translation

Fundamentals of Translation (Cambridge University Press, 2015), by Sonia Colina, Regents Professor at the University of Arizona, is a book you'll want to keep on your shelf. It's a useful, nontechnical, and readable textbook that introduces the central concepts of translation theory and practice that beginning translators and students need to understand. The seven-chapter textbook is ready for any eager student of translation and includes examples, exercises, and practice activities from a variety of languages. You can check your answers to the exercises in the answer key. Take your time working through this book. It's one you'll come back to over and over again.

Words Without Borders

You can't miss the digital magazine *Words Without Borders (WWB)*. Founded in 2003, it's the home for international literature, with a mission to "cultivate global awareness by expanding access to international writing and creating a bridge between readers, writers, and translators." WWB first published some of today's most talked about writers before they became international sensations. WWB publishes contemporary fiction, nonfiction, poetry, drama, interviews, and related multimedia. If you translate literature, you'll want to consider submitting your translations here. If you're a teacher, WWB Campus offers global literature and multimedia learning resources for teachers to use with their students. Poke around the website and sign up for the newsletter.

This Is a Classic: Translators on Making Writers Global

As a translator, you're a lover of language, and you'll never exhaust the questions you have about what happens when languages meet and translators work across languages. To find out more about what happens for certain language pairs in translation, especially when they involve the translation of what's considered a literary classic, check out my anthology *This Is a Classic: Translators on Making Writers Global* (Bloomsbury Academic, 2023). It features the writing of 19 translators in addition to an introduction, epilogue, and translation experiment. Through translators' perspectives, you'll discover how things that are assumed in one language don't always apply to another language. No matter your specialization, this book heightens your awareness of just how much care goes into translation and the depth of translators' knowledge about the texts they translate.

MultiLingual

Since 1987, *MultiLingual* magazine has stressed that translation isn't just translation, but localization that makes a text or other communication appeal to the end user, especially in business. This is a must-read monthly publication to keep up to date about language industry news and developments. You can get a subscription to the digital or the print magazine. Make a plan to regularly visit the website, where you'll find news, a directory of vendors and organizations in the language industry, and resources. Also check out the magazine's podcast *Localization Today*, which has short episodes on language, technology, business, and culture, in addition to book reviews, an events calendar, and a career center. And don't over-look the ads, which give you some company names to explore. The magazine also welcomes article submissions should you ever be interested in writing your own articles about the industry.

Slator

Once you have the language skills and are familiar with the basic terms of transla-tion, if you're interested in the larger industry surrounding translation, you'll want to get familiar with Slator.com. Slator.com publishes news and research for the global translation, localization, and language technology industry. News sections include People Moves, Deal Wins, Technology, Academia, Machine Translation, Translation Management Systems, and more. Headquartered in Zurich, audiences in Asia, Europe, and the United States are familiar with Slator. com. Slator also offers *SlatorPod*, a weekly language industry podcast, and video interviews of the global translation and localization industry. The episodes are usually about 45 minutes long. Slator.com hosts the conference SlatorCon and owns LocJobs.com, the language industry talent hub. If you think you'd like to have a role in this industry beyond being a translator, don't miss Slator.com.

How to Succeed as a Freelance Translator

If the idea of being a freelance translator appeals to you or you want to learn more about how to do it, you'll want to pick up the book *How to Succeed as a Freelance Translator* (Two Rat Press) by Corinne McKay, an ATA-certified English to French translator and a Colorado court-certified French interpreter. First published in 2006 but now in its third edition with over 10,000 copies in print, this is a how-to reference for translators of all stages on a structured approach to having your own business. The 14-chapter book covers in detail an introduction to freelance work, marketing, working with direct clients, your online presence, technology, con-tacts, terms, taxes, insurance, retirement, and more. This should be one of several reference books you own on how to succeed in working for yourself.

Dreaming Murakami

If you're curious about how literary translators work and how literary translation impacts the world, check out the 2017 *Dreaming Murakami* by director Nitesh Anjaan. This film, classified as a documentary, focuses on Mette Holm, who translates Haruki Murakami's literature from the Japanese into Danish. Even non-translators will enjoy and learn from this film. Besides getting a close-up of Holm's life as a translator in Denmark, you'll see the universal struggles of translators and how they work together regardless of their language pair and get an eye-opening glimpse of what it's like to work with a language pair that doesn't involve English. If you don't know Danish, you'll need to rely on the English subtitles, which adds another fun translational dimension to the film.

Smart Habits for Translators

It's never too early to start listening to the *Smart Habits for Translators* podcast hosted by Veronika Demichelis, an English to Russian and Russian to English translator, and Madalena Sánchez Zampaulo, a Spanish and Portuguese-to-English translator. Both are ATA-certified translators and business owners. On this podcast, founded in 2019, you can learn more about habits to help you build a career and have a lifestyle you desire. Topics range from imposter syndrome, healthy exercise and nutrition habits, goal setting, and decluttering to smart marketing, professional development, and much more. The episodes feature a conversation between the hosts or with special guests. And most aren't more than 30 minutes, so they're great to listen to during a commute or while exercising or cooking.

Index

human input for machine translation
  deciding when to use machine translation, 143–145
  overview, 142
  responsibilities of humans in machine translation, 142–143

I

idiomatic expressions, 56
impossibility of translation, 26–27
inclusion, equity, and belonging
  multilingual communities, 39–41
  spreading and offering access to information, 34–38
independent translators. *See* clients; freelancing; professional translators
instruction manuals, examples of translation in, 19–20
insurance, importance when freelancing, 174
interlingual translation, 13–14
International Booker Prize, 226
internet
  access to, procuring, 200
  examples of translation on, 17–18
internships, finding, 208–209
interpersonal skills, 74
interpreters
  consecutive, 193
  non-university programs for, 102, 113
  offering as service, 192–193
  simultaneous, 193
  translators versus, 12, 24–25
intersemiotic translation, 13–14
intralingual translation, 13–14
inverse translations, 53

J

Jakobson, Roman, 13
jobs, in translation. *See* freelancing; professional translators; staff translators

K

Kemp, Ruth Ahmedzai, 244–245

L

Language Access and Inclusion Act (Massachusetts), 219
language access services, supporting, 210–211
language analysis, 83
language conventions, 150–151
language departments in universities, 85–88
language industry, 32
language justice, promoting, 42
language rights, promoting, 42
language service providers
  getting jobs at, 176–177, 209
  offering translator training, 103
  translation industry, 32
languages
  boundaries of, understanding, 161–162
  developing, 51
  dialects and variations in, 68–70
  directionality
    determining, 183–187
    importance of, 53–54
  disappearance of, 2
  endangered, 37, 183–184
  idiomatic expressions, 56
  immersing oneself in, 233
  of lesser diffusion, 183–184
  leveraging symbolic value of, 42–44

misconceptions about translations and, 23–24
as not lining up perfectly, 155
qualifications for working with, 232
reading order in different, 153–154
register in, 52
role in promoting equity, inclusion, and belonging
  multilingual communities, 39–41
spreading and offering access to, 34–38
scripts in different, 154
skills needed for project, ensuring, 160
source, 29, 94
specialization and, 111
spreading ideas of people who write in other, 34–36
target
  asking client about, 126
  defined, 30
  developing, 51
  individual translation courses focused on, 94
  proficiency in, 66–70
  writing skills in, 54–56
translating everything into all, 43–44
translating from unknown, 187
legal field
  career opportunities in, 75
  specialization in, 111–112
legal framework for translation, 41–42
line breaks, language conventions for, 151
linguistics, 83
literary translation
  defined, 83
  by Edith Grossman, 49–50
  MFA programs for, 96

W

Wang, Helen, 225

Wang, Yilin, 236

What Makes Us Human (Santos), 2, 37

Why Translation Matters (Grossman), 49–50, 248

Wilson, A. Leslie, 241

word count

as changing look of translated text, 152–153

charging according to, 220–221

tools for, 201

word lists, 202

WordReference forum, 131

words

connotation and denotation of, 131

focus on context instead of, 25

many meanings of, 155

Words Without Borders (*WWB*) magazine, 249

work, in translation. *See* freelancing; professional translators; staff translators

workspace

overview, 56–57, 173, 197–199

resources and equipment, access to, 200–204

tools of the trade, gathering, 201–204

writing

about translation, 60

additional services involving

closed captioning, 191

copyediting, 189

proofreading, 189–190

subtitling, 191–192

transcribing, 190

capitalization, 54–55

as career beyond translating, 75–76

connotations and denotation of words, 131

cultural knowledge and, 55–56

grammar, 55, 151

language conventions, 150–151

overview, 52–56

polishing and editing texts, 188–190

punctuation, 54–55

as skill needed by translators, 52, 54–56, 67–68

spelling, 55

spreading ideas via, 34–35

tone, 52, 54, 151

vocabulary, developing, 55–56

WWB (*Words Without Borders*) magazine, 249

Z

Zampaulo, Madalena Sanchez, 251

About the Author

Dr. Regina Galasso first started thinking about translation when, as a child, she'd wonder what each of her great grandparents sounded like when they first arrived in New York and New Jersey speaking a language that wasn't English because no one in her family spoke those languages anymore. The absence of their languages — Danish, Hungarian, Italian, and Ukrainian — gave her a space to imagine what family conversations would have been like if they existed in another language. What if all her grandparents kept speaking their parents' languages? Translation does that. It helps things exist in another language. This creative, cerebral space eventually helped her produce tangible results as a translator. Dr. Galasso translates and promotes translation so languages don't get lost, ensuring that what is born in one language can be shared in others. Her first Dummies book she purchased was in Spanish: *Catalán para Dummies* by Ferran Alexandri. She speaks Catalan, English, and Spanish, and she has studied Portuguese and a bit of French.

Dr. Galasso started studying translation and interpreting in the Department of Spanish and Portuguese at Rutgers University, where she earned her BA. As an undergraduate, she studied for a year at the Universitat de València in Spain, where some of the courses she took were in *valencià*, Valencian.

She earned her MA in Spanish from Middlebury College and her PhD from Johns Hopkins University.

In the one year during which she was not studying or teaching at a university, she was a Spanish teacher at the César Chávez Public Charter Schools for Public Policy and an interpreter during the Kennedy Center's AmericArtes Festival in Washington, DC.

Dr. Galasso's first appointment as a professor was in the Modern Languages Department at the Borough of Manhattan Community College of the City University of New York. She is a tenured professor in the Spanish and Portuguese Studies Program of the Department of Languages, Literatures, and Cultures at the University of Massachusetts Amherst, where she teaches translation and literature courses.

Her scholarly work highlights the role of translation in literary histories and contemporary culture. She creates and supports ways to promote translation education to encourage greater understanding of this needed service and intellectual activity. With her students, she curated the 2022 exhibition "Read the World: Picture Books and Translation" for the Reading Library at the Eric Carle Museum of Picture Book Art.

The author of *Translating New York: The City's Languages in Iberian Literatures* (Liverpool UP, 2018), Dr. Galasso is the recipient of the 2017 Northeast Modern Language Association Book Award.

She is the editor of *Translation as Home: A Multilingual Life* by Ilan Stavans (U of Toronto P, 2024) and *This Is a Classic: Translators on Making Writers Global* (Bloomsbury, 2023). She is the co-editor of two edited volumes: *Avenues of Translation: The City in Iberian and Latin American Writing* (Bucknell UP, 2019), recipient of the 2020 South Atlantic Modern Language Association Book Award, with Evelyn Scaramella, and a special Nueva York issue of *Translation Review* 81 (2012) with Carmen Boullosa.

Dr. Galasso is the translator of Alicia Borinsky's *Lost Cities Go to Paradise* (Swan Isle P, 2015) and Miguel Barnet's *A True Story: A Cuban in New York* (Jorge Pinto Books, 2010).

Since 2017, she has been the director of the UMass Translation Center, which provides language services to clients and partners all around the world. She works with public schools to improve and support language access efforts through programming and planning, including an appointment on the Department of Elementary and Secondary Education's School Interpreters Task Force.

Dedication

To future and beginning translators and anyone interested in learning more about and supporting translators. To all the people who are brave enough to move around the world, for whatever reason, and rely on translation for at least some period of time. To all the people who want to further open their minds by reading translated books and supporting translators.

Author's Acknowledgments

I'd like to acknowledge all the people I get to work with and learn from via the UMass Translation Center, including staff, clients, partners, language professionals, workshop leaders, university leadership and administration, fellow faculty members, graduate students, and undergraduates. Every interaction teaches me more about what it means to be a translator and what non-translators need to know about translators for a more equitable and inclusive society. You might see my interpretation of some of our conversations reflected in these pages.

I'd like to thank Jennifer Yee, senior acquisitions editor at Wiley, for approaching me with this project. I'm grateful for her patience, encouragement, and support throughout this process, and most of all for pursuing this project at a time when clicking the Translate icon or typing some words into a box on a screen seems to be the go-to option for getting a translation. Those options hide the knowledge, creativity, and care that go into becoming and being a translator, and they do little to promote a rewarding and beautiful career for people who know more than one language.

The possibility of writing this book presented a challenge for a full-time academic. I'm grateful for the opportunity to take what I teach, research, and write about to audiences beyond the university. I'd like to thank development editor Tracy Brown for her responsiveness and support during the writing process and with other editorial tasks. This project presented the opportunity to work with UMass alum Andrew Schwartz as a technical editor. I thank all the other professionals on the Wiley team who were behind this book. I'd love to find a way to take all the support their model offers and bring it to the world of academic publishing.

Finally, thanks to my friends and family for their support, understanding, encouragement, enthusiasm, patience, and love. Moltes gràcies. I love you. ❤

Publisher's Acknowledgments

Acquisitions Editor: Jennifer Yee

Development Editor: Tracy Brown Hamilton

Copy Editor: Gill Editorial Services

Production editor: Saikarthick Kumarasamy

Managing Editor: Murari Mukundan

Cover Image: © Dean Drobot/Shutterstock

Leverage the power

Dummies is the global leader in the reference category and one of the most trusted and highly regarded brands in the world. No longer just focused on books, customers now have access to the dummies content they need in the format they want. Together we'll craft a solution that engages your customers, stands out from the competition, and helps you meet your goals.

Advertising & Sponsorships

Connect with an engaged audience on a powerful multimedia site, and position your message alongside expert how-to content. Dummies.com is a one-stop shop for free, online information and know-how curated by a team of experts.

- Targeted ads
- Video
- Email Marketing
- Microsites
- Sweepstakes sponsorship

20 MILLION PAGE VIEWS EVERY SINGLE MONTH

15 MILLION UNIQUE VISITORS PER MONTH

43% OF ALL VISITORS ACCESS THE SITE VIA THEIR MOBILE DEVICES

700,000 NEWSLETTER SUBSCRIPTIONS TO THE INBOXES OF *300,000* UNIQUE INDIVIDUALS EVERY WEEK

# of dummies

Custom Publishing

Reach a global audience in any language by creating a solution that will differentiate you from competitors, amplify your message, and encourage customers to make a buying decision.

- Apps
- Books
- eBooks
- Video
- Audio
- Webinars

Brand Licensing & Content

Leverage the strength of the world's most popular reference brand to reach new audiences and channels of distribution.

For more information, visit **dummies.com/biz**

Learning Made Easy

ACADEMIC

9781119293576
USA $19.99
CAN $23.99
UK £15.99

9781119293637
USA $19.99
CAN $23.99
UK £15.99

9781119293491
USA $19.99
CAN $23.99
UK £15.99

9781119293460
USA $19.99
CAN $23.99
UK £15.99

9781119293590
USA $19.99
CAN $23.99
UK £15.99

9781119215844
USA $26.99
CAN $31.99
UK £19.99

9781119293378
USA $22.99
CAN $27.99
UK £16.99

9781119293521
USA $19.99
CAN $23.99
UK £15.99

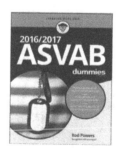

9781119239178
USA $18.99
CAN $22.99
UK £14.99

9781119263883
USA $26.99
CAN $31.99
UK £19.99

Available Everywhere Books Are Sold

nall books for big imaginations

GETTING STARTED WITH Coding
Get Creative with Code!
Camilla McCue, PhD

9781119177173
USA $9.99
CAN $9.99
UK £8.99

MODDING Minecraft
Build Your Own Minecraft Mods!
Sarah Guthals, PhD
Stephen Foster, PhD
Lindsey Handley, PhD

9781119177272
USA $9.99
CAN $9.99
UK £8.99

MAKING YouTube VIDEOS
Star in Your Own Video!
Nick Willoughby

9781119177241
USA $9.99
CAN $9.99
UK £8.99

DESIGNING Digital Games
Create Games with Scratch!
Derek Breen

9781119177210
USA $9.99
CAN $9.99
UK £8.99

GETTING STARTED WITH Raspberry Pi
Program Your Raspberry Pi!
Richard Wentk

9781119262657
USA $9.99
CAN $9.99
UK £6.99

EXPERIMENTING WITH Science
Think, Test, and Learn!

9781119291336
USA $9.99
CAN $9.99
UK £6.99

CREATING Digital Animations
Animate Stories with Scratch!
Derek Breen

9781119233527
USA $9.99
CAN $9.99
UK £6.99

GETTING STARTED WITH Engineering
Think Like an Engineer!
Camille McCue, PhD

9781119291220
USA $9.99
CAN $9.99
UK £6.99

WRITING Computer Code
Learn the Language of Computers!
Chris Minnick and Eva Holland

9781119177302
USA $9.99
CAN $9.99
UK £8.99

Unleash Their Creativity

dummies.com

dummies
A Wiley Brand